WRITERS

ON

DIRECTORS

WRITERS

ON

DIRECTORS

AN ARTISTS' CHOICE BOOK

Conceived and photographed by
SUSAN GRAY
With a foreword by Leonard Maltin

Watson-Guptill Publications/New York

Senior Editor: Robin Simmen
Editor: Victoria Craven
Assistant Editor: Sarah Fass
Designer: Areta Buk
Production Manager: Hector Campbell

Front cover photographs (clockwise from top left): Kenneth Branagh;
Martin Brest; Rob Reiner; Penelope Spheeris; and Ron Howard.

Back cover photographs (from top to bottom): Robert Altman;
Jonathan Demme; Amy Heckerling; Sidney Lumet; and John Woo.

All photographs by Susan Gray (with the exception of Leonard
Maltin's photo, page 10, which was taken by Joe Viles).

Eastman Kodak products used exclusively throughout.

First published in 1999 in the United States by
Watson-Guptill Publications
a division of BPI Communications, Inc.
1515 Broadway, New York, New York 10036

Library of Congress Cataloging-in-Publication Data

Writers on directors / compiled and photographed by Susan Gray ; with
    a foreword by Leonard Maltin.
        p.   cm. — (An artist's choice book)
    Includes index.
    ISBN 0-8230-5971-5
    1. Motion picture producers and directors—Biography.   2. Motion
picture producers and directors—Portraits.   I. Gray, Susan (Susan
Kim)   II. Series.
PN1998.2.W75   1999
791.43'0233'0922—dc21   99-11479
                                                   CIP

Printed in Hong Kong

First printing, 1999

1 2 3 4 5 6 7 8 9 10 / 08 07 06 05 04 03 02 01 00 99

ACKNOWLEDGMENTS

With love and appreciation *Writers on Directors* is dedicated to Charles Evans, Beverly Adler, Lori Andiman, Sue Barton, Bruce Benderson, Stuart Bernstein, Jay Herrmann, Richard Pine, Katharine Sands (my literary agent), Tim Thayer, and, with a special honorary mention, to Tom Robbins of the Union of Mad Scientists. Their belief and encouragement carried me through.

◆

Writers on Directors is not my own and certainly could never have been done without the generosity and amazing talent of my writers. I would also like to acknowledge my deep appreciation to the directors for their time and conviction that *Writers on Directors* was a worthwhile endeavor.

While *Writers on Directors* certainly belongs to the writers and directors, it also belongs to the many people who were behind the scenes—just like in making a movie, I had had a lot of help.

I am very fortunate to be able to say thank you to the many people who made this book possible:

Jonathan Burrows
Diane de la Begassiere
Joan Brunskill
Stephen Doherty
Ray Demoulin
Robert J. Gibbons (The Eastman Kodak Company)
Joel Hecker
Michael Klingher
Alice and Leonard Maltin
Craig Morton
Linda Munson
Ken Regan
Marianne Samenko (The Eastman Kodak Company)
David Weddle

Areta Buk, Hector Campbell, Victoria Craven, Mahesh Dalal, Sarah Fass, Glenn Heffernan, Sharon Kaplan, Martin Murphy, Harriet Pierce, Fatima Ruiz, Robin Simmen, Alison Smith, Joanne Wang, Charles Whang, and Lee Wiggins at Watson-Guptill.

My many sales representatives.

My photo stock agency RETNA (212-255-0622/Julie Graham/Lori Reese).

My mother, Vera Paulsen, for her Californian home-style cooking.

◆

. . . and to the many people who have unfailingly and generously contributed their time and support—remarkably or briefly—all were most important in the making of *Writers on Directors*. I deeply apologize if I have omitted anyone.

Eddie Adams; Addis-Wechsler; Miriam Altshuler; Michael Anselie; Enrica Antonioni; Arista Photo Labs (Robert Cusido, Stephane Kenn); Neda Armian; Arthur Pine Associates (Arthur Pine and Sara Piel); Wren Artnur; Carla Dorea Bartz; Steve Battaglio; Chris Bazzani; Shauna and Jeff Binswanger; Jesse Beaton; Bel Air Hotel (Beverly Hills); Jeff Berg; Jeff Berger; Bill Black; Paul Bloch (Rogers and Cowan); Peter Bloch and Nannette Varian Bloch; Brandt and Brandt (Carl D. Brandt/Gail Hochman/Meg Giles); Dan Brocoli; Christy Brown; Danna Brown; Polly Brown; Donald Bruce; Hal Buehl; Patricia Burke; Amanda Burden; John Burnham; John Callahan; Elizabeth Casparis; Stanley Cohen; Loredana Corti; Frank Darabont; Isabelle Dassonville; Kelly Davis; Monica De Armond; Rylyn Demaris (Toltec Artists); Lisa Dennis; Lisa Diamond; Susan Dicker; Thomas Dickson; Terry D'Ignazio; Jim Donna; Stan Dragoti; Alexandra Drobac; Alexandra Ducocq; Sol and Hendrik Van Ophemert/Roger Williams (Duggal Labs); Katherine Dunn; Mary Dunn; Karen Dusenberry; Lynn Ehrensperger; Morgan Entrekin; Esmeraldo Hotel (Roma/ Walter); The Essex House (NYC); Robert Evans; Kelly Ferguson; Marilyn Field; Melanie Fleishman (SoHo Press); Andy Fox; Gayle Fraser-Baigelman; Sarah Jane Freymann; Priscilla Friedman; Stephen Gaines (Hamptons Film Festival); Josh Gaspero; Geffen Pictures; Fabien Gerard; the late Howard Gilman/Natalie Moody/Cathy Ryan; Julie Gold; Jonathan Goldman; William Goldman; Mills Goodloe; Linda Gordon; Joe Gores; Jill Goularte; Cheryl Gray; Dr. Harry L. Gray; Harry and Pamela Gray; Bob Guccione, Jr.; Guttman Pam (Beverly Magrid); Ken Hansen; Steve Hauser; President Vaclav Havel (Anna Freimanova); Katharina Hembus; Carter Horsley; Emily Jacobs; Lilly Jacobs; Gary Jaffee (Linda Chester Agency/ Joanna Pulcini); David Johnson; Pam Jones; Sara Jordan; Pauline Kael; Elaine Kaufman; David Kebo; Mary Ann Kennedy; Archer King; Lynn King; Douglas Kirkland; Steve Klain; Michael Klingher; Metka Kosak; Gail Kramer; Ray Krell; Doug Kroboth; Grant Lamos; Peter Lampack; Sheri Lansing; Robert Lantz; Lewis Lapham; Wendy Larsen; Owen Laster (William Morris); Margaret Lawless; Les Célébrités (Ciro for the loan of Kenneth Branagh's red cape!); Ellen Levine; Ginny Liagre; Ken Lieberman and Ms. Gail; Lois Lipfield; Celeste Long; Sara Longacre; Gloria and Walter Loomis; Bridget Love & Jude Stewart (Aiken Wylie Stone); Lois Lipfield; Stacy Lumbrezer; Tom Luddy; Bill Malloy (Mysterious Press); Jay Maloney of CAA; Mamiya America Corporation (Henry Froehlich); Rudy Maxa; Sally McCartin Public Relations; Bill McCuddy; Terry McDonell; Judith McNally; Karen Means; Annie Mei-Ling; Naomi Middelmann; Kathy Mintz; Collins Munro; Chappy Morris; Susan Morse; Helen Morris; Rebecca Morton;

Linda Munson; Shawn Maratea; Syms Murray; Cynthia Neber; Augusto
Net; Cable Neuhaus; New York Public Library (Elizabeth Brooks, Frank
Collerius, Michael Diekmann, Paul Martin, Mathew Tallon); David
O'Connor; Mark O'Connor; Donna Ostroff; Brian Palmer; Heidi Parker;
Nancy Peardon; Ken Pearlman; Tine Grew Pfeiffer (Lars Von Tier); Clare
Peploe; Lynn Petrich; Johnny Planco; Michael Plesco; Fiammetta Profili
(Federico Fellini Productions); Louis Quayle; Michael Randall; Peggy
Rajski; The Regency; Ritz Carlton (Marina Del Rey); Barbara Roberts;
J. J. Robertson; Colleen Roome; Marion Rosenberg; Lee Rosenberg; Sami
Rosenstock; Liz Rossi-Sloyan; Yuko Royer; Lew Rudin; St. Regis Hotel
(NYC); Diane Salzburg; Jim Sarnoff; Stephen Schuster; David Schow; Joe
Sciortino; Jan Sharp; Jodi Shields; Candice Shermerhorn; Claire Simoneau;
Chloe Sladder (the Robbins office); Michael Sragow; Anna Kazumi Stahl
(for translating Ricardo Piglia's essay and more); Robert Stein; Laren Stover;
Summers/ Crowley; Sunset Hotel (Los Angeles); Paul and Jenny Sylbert;
Richard Sylbert; Lena Tabori; Abby Terkuhle; Tamar Thomas; Mary Tobler;
Addie Towner; Angela Trento; Karin Trolle; Sandra Tucker; Martin Tully;
Amanda Urban; Mark Urman (Dennis, Davidson Associates); Marika
Vaaranen; Gerard van der Leun; Louisa Velis; Catherine Veyret (Unifrance
Film International); Lisa Vijitchanton; Andrew Wald; Laurence Walsh
and Johanna (John Woo); Sophie Gluck (Wang and Gluck); John Ware;
David Weddle; Melanie Wells; Frolic Weymouth; Dorie Weintraub; Margi
Whitmer; Gavin Wiesen; Vernice Williams; Scott Wilder; Phyllis and Jamie
Wyeth; Nicholas Wyeth; Victoria Wyeth; Bobby Zarem; Robyn Zielan
(Wednesday's House); Suzy Zimmerman. ◆

CONTENTS

FOREWORD BY Leonard Maltin   10

INTRODUCTION   14

Ariel Dorfman ON ROMAN POLANSKI   16

William Goldman ON NORMAN JEWISON   22

Tom Robbins ON ALAN RUDOLPH   26

David Weddle ON RON SHELTON   29

Edwidge Danticat ON JONATHAN DEMME   34

Tobias Wolff ON OLIVER STONE   38

Bruce Wagner ON WES CRAVEN   41

Russell Banks ON CARL FRANKLIN   45

William Goldman ON ROB REINER   49

Wendy Wasserstein ON AMY HECKERLING   53

Katherine Dunn ON GUS VAN SANT   56

Scott Frank ON KENNETH BRANAGH   61

John Ridley ON JOHN WOO   64

Ricardo Piglia ON HECTOR BABENCO   67

Catherine Texier ON JEAN-JACQUES ANNAUD   71

Michael Cristofer ON HERBERT ROSS   76

Bo Goldman ON MARTIN BREST   82

Donald E. Westlake ON STEPHEN FREARS   85

Mike Werb ON PENELOPE SPHEERIS   89

Damian Sharp ON PHILLIP NOYCE   93

Richard Lourie ON AGNIESZKA HOLLAND 97

Seymour Chatman ON MICHELANGELO ANTONIONI 101

Adam Brooks ON LAWRENCE KASDAN 105

Walter Mosley ON RON HOWARD 108

Brian Helgeland ON RICHARD DONNER 111

Jack Womack ON TERRY GILLIAM 114

Darryl Ponicsan ON MARTHA COOLIDGE 118

Joan Juliet Buck ON BERNARDO BERTOLUCCI 121

John Shirley ON JAMES CAMERON 126

Michael Cunningham ON JOHN SCHLESINGER 131

Bruce Benderson ON PAUL VERHOEVEN 135

Michael Weller ON MILOS FORMAN 140

Michael Tolkin ON ROBERT ALTMAN 145

Peter Blauner ON SIDNEY LUMET 149

Patrick McCabe ON NEIL JORDAN 153

Norman Snider ON DAVID CRONENBERG 157

Joe Eszterhas ON WILLIAM FRIEDKIN 161

Thomas Caplan ON SYDNEY POLLACK 164

Steven Gaydos ON ROGER CORMAN 168

Michael Sragow ON MICHAEL MANN 172

CREDITS 177

INDEX 181

FOREWORD

I'm not sure exactly when it happened, but somewhere between my childhood—when I thought movie stars were the be-all and end-all in any film—and my coming of age, film directors not only became a constant subject of conversation among the cognoscenti, they achieved the highest possible level of esteem: being perceived as cool.

You don't hear of film school students who aspire to become art directors or honey-wagon drivers (although I'm sure such people exist). Everyone, it seems, wants to be a director, whether they have the requisite abilities or not. Because, let's face it, it *is* cool.

Don't tell that to screenwriters. Most writers who become directors say the same thing: they've made that transition in order to protect their material. In other words, to gain control. This tacit admission of the fact that the director is the dominant creative force in the shaping of a film, is a fact that many screenwriters are loath to admit in so many words.

Authorship of a film remains the most hotly debated subject in Hollywood (and, for that matter, in the critical community). Ever since directors fought for, and won, the right to take what is known as a possessory credit (A Kyle Crumquist Film), writers have been protesting. Loudly.

How can Kyle Crumquist, or even Norman Jewison, claim authorship or possession when that film is the result of a collaboration, not only with the screenwriter but with producers, studio executives, actors, cinematographers, art directors, and scores of other technicians? (This was as true in Hollywood's golden age as it is now. Douglas Sirk, a darling of auteurist-minded critics, was once heard to say of his most prolific period in the 1950s, "In those days, the studio was the auteur.")

There are studio executives today who think nothing of replacing a neophyte director midway through production of a troubled film; so much for possession of *that* credit! (A successful writer being given his first shot behind the camera was taken off a big-budget western not too many years ago when, according to one eyewitness, he was three days behind schedule after only one day of shooting.)

It's also no secret that some directors are simply hired hands, the last key contributor hired onto a project after a producer has shopped a script around for several years or more. Certainly it's the director who's calling the shots on the set, but if the producer has already "attached" a star to the project (as they say in Hollywood jargon), and the writer has refined his script, how can that film be perceived as a director's work?

This chicken-and-egg argument has been going on for decades. In the 1930s, Frank Capra lobbied long and hard to have his name above the title—a concept (and phrase) that meant so much to him that it became the title of his autobiography. But even as he achieved a level of public recognition above and beyond most of his colleagues, there was resentment in some circles that his partner, screenwriter Robert Riskin, got little or no recognition. An oft-told, and probably apocryphal, anecdote had Riskin dumping a sheaf of blank paper on the director's desk and snapping, "There—give that the 'Capra touch.'"

And yet.

Riskin's attempt to direct his own work didn't pan out as he might have hoped. *Magic Town* is a Capraesque script that's missing something; perhaps it was the director's touch.

Ask anyone who worked for John Ford (who employed a variety of screenwriters during his long career) and they'll tell you that there was a distinctive atmosphere on a Ford set—and a desire to please The Boss, difficult though that might be. Ford inspired people in ways, sometimes intangible or even invisible, that others did not.

Look around today and it's difficult to find towering figures like Capra and Ford, but there are many talented, even gifted, directors. Their challenge is carving out a niche in an increasingly homogenized and box office–oriented movie industry. (Yes, movies were always about making money, but there used to be something called "a prestige picture" that studios would make, just for the hell of it, or perhaps to salve their conscience with a couple of Oscars. You don't hear the term used much any more.)

It's difficult to discern an individual's work amidst all the "product" nowadays, but when a trained eye turns to the output of the really good directors, patterns do emerge. Choice of subject, means of telling a story, matters of integrity: these distinguished the artists and individuals from the journeymen and hacks.

Who better to identify the strengths and qualities of directors than writers? This volume gathers essays by writers of note who happen to be film aficionados, as well as first-hand observations by screenwriters who have great respect and admiration for their visual collaborators.

It's not every day that one can read what a world-class novelist or a Pulitzer Prize–winning playwright has to say about a filmmaker. Russell Banks, to cite just one example, brings a novelist's gift of observation to his assessment of Carl Franklin's career. Franklin hasn't made many films, but since his arresting breakthrough with *One False Move,* he has chosen his projects carefully and well. Banks sees a common thread that an ordinary moviegoer might not. (Banks has also had the experience of seeing his work translated to film; Atom Egoyan adapted and directed *The Sweet Hereafter.)*

It's rare to find a writer who has good things to say about the director who brought his work to the screen. Yet here, in these pages, we find a number of estimable screenwriters who maintain high regard for their partners. No backbiting, no arguing about credit, no carping about changes. How refreshing—and for aspiring screenwriters, how encouraging.

It would be interesting to read anything about the moviemaking process that Michael Tolkin, Scott Frank, Brian Helgeland, Donald E. Westlake, Joe Eszterhas, William Goldman, or Patrick McCabe had to say. That they tell us of fruitful working relationships with directors, and in some cases deep friendships, is especially rewarding.

Whether it's learning how Richard Donner uses practical jokes to communicate with friends and colleagues, or seeing firsthand how Jonathan Demme has earned the title of "humanist," the essays give us a rare, personal view of these filmmakers.

The Butcher Boy, for instance, would have been diminished if it had not found a way to incorporate Patrick McCabe's singular "voice" into the film. Neil Jordan did just that . . . and earned the novelist's gratitude.

Personal accounts, by Goldman, Eszterhas, and others, speak of a camaraderie and a sense of teamwork that I'm sure make many people want to be part of that world. It's the kind of fellowship and creative energy that's emblematic of moviemaking at its best—moviemaking as it ought to be.

Yes, this is a book of praise. For harsh criticism or character assassination, look elsewhere.

As for the marvelous photos that accompany the text, they are as expressive as the essays. We don't know very much about most directors, even the great ones; they remain invisible forces behind the camera, coming out into public only in rarefied venues such as film festivals or appearing on television when there is a new movie to promote.

What do these pictures tell us, then, about these storytellers who affect and influence so many of us?

A playful pose may reveal more than pages of criticism; a serious demeanor may indicate the way the director wants to be seen. (Ron Howard is no longer the child actor we remember from T.V. and movies, but he's still youthful enough in spirit to pose in a baseball cap. Kenneth Branagh may be a "serious" interpreter of Shakespeare, but he can't resist a Cheshire cat smile.)

We can assume that these pictures are the result of a collaboration between the photographer, Susan Gray, and her subjects. Thus, we discover not only what Gray thinks about the filmmaker but what the filmmaker thinks about himself. What a wonderful way to learn more about these people.

A friend of mine contends that the only thing better than watching movies is talking about them. This book feels like a series of spirited conversations—with pictures to match their enthusiasm. I am happy to add my words of praise for both the efforts that went into this enterprise and the happy results.

Leonard Maltin
Los Angeles, California
September 1998 ◆

INTRODUCTION

Let me tell you a secret—there are people in Hollywood who actually *do* read, and not only that, they know a great story when they see one. It's just that certain things get in the way—like verbicide or cinecide or once in awhile something as mundane as a natural disaster. But miraculously when the great machine works and the stories and the people all click into place, we, the audience often get more than we bargained for.

The essays in *Writers on Directors* are stories about the movie business, a collaborative effort between two storytellers. The director tells his or her story with film; the author tells in words the story of his or her personal and critical reactions to the director and his or her work.

These two image makers share the need to create memorable visions—their art. And we steal these bits and pieces of their souls to help us construct a clearer picture of who we are. Thomas Mann said, "No one remains quite what he was when he recognizes himself."

Images are great seducers and we love being seduced. Like Chauncey Gardiner or Chance the gardener in *Being There,* we like to watch. We greedily consume images to nourish ourselves—carefully storing them in archival Internet temples and marble libraries and monogrammed museum wings. Like our memories, images preserve, if not our flesh then certainly our spirit.

Word weavers, byronics, visionaries, moralists, or gossips—storytellers bring us our heritage, living testaments for our personal and sacred dream files. Like old photographs, stories are reminders of our life; they can be powerful catalysts or soothsayers or they can be nothing more than a pleasant way to fill our time card. Superimposing the imaginary on the real, the past on the present, the future on the present—they become our validations, their lifelines extending far beyond the perpetual gas flames in Forest Lawn.

Often, just by remembering a title of a film, a slice of our life whizzes by, a single frame moves into fast forward; an action scene freezes into a single frame.

By remembering, a certain type of parataxis occurs that has the power to remove us from the present and shift us into another skin, another era, another continent, or even into a stranger's arms. Transfixed, spellbound, and captured, we are able to forget who or where we are. Films can date us and yet still propel us forward. We are blasted down the yellow brick road, screeching to a stop against a dingwall, only to realize that it is a movie and not real life.

Yet part of the excitement and challenge comes from not knowing. We do not say but SHOUT, "Don't tell me the ending! I don't want to know." The painter Juan Gris said, "You're lost the instant you know what the results will be."

In some ways *Writers on Directors* is a mutual admiration club— writers stroking directors—but beneath the petting surface there is more. Anyone who has worked in Hollywood knows that Joe Eszterhas's essay on William Friedkin is the prototype of show biz comradeship—similar to the comradeship one finds in war. But such a "basic instinct" can open windows on survival for all to see.

There are many notable writers and directors missing here, but *Writers on Directors* is not about lists or records. The writers chosen for these essays have attempted to create stories that have a life of their own, and some of these living stories, such as Michael Cunningham's or Peter Blauner's, are so intimate and revealing they are excruciatingly painful.

Hollywood, master key holder of our dreams, exists because we make it exist. We give it power, hoping it will deliver us to the Perpetual Gardens of Paradise.

We can laugh at our dreams, but we still want them. Desire always exceeds productivity and "there are always, always icebergs ahead," as John Shirley points out in his essay on James Cameron.

Yet by surmounting icebergs and car crashes and public crucifixions we are never more alive.

We still have a chance. ◆

ON ROMAN
POLANSKI

Something is wrong with the lamp. Roman examines it carefully. We are only a few days away from principal photography, but Roman Polanski acts as if he had all the time in the world. It is an ordinary kerosene lamp, the swinging sort you take on camping trips or you carry around the house when there's a blackout, the sort you would never give a second glance to. But Roman is giving it more than a second glance. He is spending long silent valuable minutes, observing it as if it were about to come alive and pounce on him.

We are on the set of *Death and the Maiden* in the studios of Boulogne just outside Paris. The legendary Pierre Guffroy (a regular on many Polanski films, including *Tess,* for which he received an Academy Award) has painstakingly recreated a Latin American beach house down to the last detail. It is what Roman loves in Guffroy's work, enhanced and fine-tuned during a career at the service of the art design of such masters as Cocteau, Buñuel, Bresson. The set is a character that whispers, shifts, lies in ambush, assists the protagonists, betrays them, comments on their blindness and hopes. And every object in that house—all the props that Roman is now inspecting with an unrelenting gaze—must blend into that atmosphere, must be consistent. Polanski puts the lamp down, then picks it up again, touches it, turns it around. It is almost as if he suspects the lamp of trickery, about to pull a fast one on him, like a fraudulent second-rate actor trying out for a starring role when he doesn't even deserve to be an extra. Roman looks up at the four or five people who surround him, who have been watching him watch the elusive lamp. He does not want help. He intends to figure this one out by himself. Briefly, his eyes fall on me. But they do not ask anything, do not confirm or interrogate. Has he guessed that I happen to know what's wrong with the lamp? Not because I am especially good at visuals. In fact, overly devoted as I am to words and literature, I tend to be extremely, almost stubbornly inept with images. If I understand how this particular lamp should look, it is only because, as a Chilean, I have seen countless replicas of it in my own country. In every beach house like this one, faraway, on that savage Pacific coast, lamps like this one await the night: except they display an added nuance of gray, are more banged up, more tired looking. The lamp that Roman is scrutinizing is a shade too bright, untinged, perhaps clean-cut to a fault.

"The silver tint needs to be darkened," Roman declares finally. "It shouldn't shine like this."

He's right, of course. But how can he know? How can he possibly perceive something that subtle?

Polanski has never been to Chile, never stepped into the beach houses where I have spent months, never seen a photo of the sort of sad and tarnished lamps that occupies my mind. It is not research that gives him the right clues. He can, quite simply, grasp how the lamp should look, because for the last few months—and indeed for several years now—he has been imagining object by object, board by board, the haunted and yet strangely ordinary place where Paulina will encounter and put on trial the man she thinks raped and tortured her fifteen years before. Now that the film is nearing the end of preproduction, he is taking his obsession with making everything coherent, inhabited, perfect, to unlikely extremes. Just to give one crazy example: Paulina's simulacrum of a kitchen is lined with closed cupboards. In them, filled to the brim, are mountains of authentic Chilean food staples in Chilean bags and tins imported specially from Santiago, halfway across the world. There is not one shot that calls for one of those cupboards to ever be opened, to even be remotely glimpsed through the shadows. But Roman needs them to be there, filling the corners of the unseen, lurking beyond the mere surface of perception, beyond what the camera captures, making the house breathe, secretly telling the characters where they are and who they have been and what they have eaten. It is this mania of Polanski's, the extended construction of a reliable imaginary, that warns him that the lamp with its healthy look would stand out, given all these other details, these billowing curtains, this light brown loaf of bread, these threatening knives, this sort of old-fashioned telephone, this Neruda woodcut, this stained table; that the lamp would call excessive attention to itself, would divert attention from what really matters: the madness and dissonance and troubles that are just underneath the surface of that world and that are about to explode. What really matters: human beings are trapped in that house with that lamp and with everything else in their lives, and we are going to watch them during the next few hours trying to escape from the tyranny of that reality, we are going to watch them try and bend that world to their desires, we are going to watch them succeed and we are going to watch them fail.

The ferocious pull of Polanski's best films comes from his ability to implacably place us inside the impossible fantasies of his feverish protagonists and simultaneously force us to acknowledge them coldly, from afar, from the outside, from history they cannot change.

This is what Polanski does, has done in film after stunning film: *Knife in the Water, Repulsion, Rosemary's Baby, Chinatown, Macbeth, Tess, The Tenant, Frantic, Bitter Moon.* Put us inside, deep inside the world he has created, on the frontier where illusion and pain meet, at times separate and at times merge. And this is the paradox: Roman builds each space, each universe, as absolutely, incontrovertibly recognizable, unflinchingly

ROMAN POLANSKI
Born 1933
Paris, France

*Knife in the Water*** 1962
*Repulsion*** 1965
*Cul-de-Sac*** 1966
*The Fearless Vampire Killers*** 1967
*Rosemary's Baby** 1968
*Macbeth*** 1971
*What?*** 1972
*Chinatown**** 1974 Academy Award for Best Original Screenplay
*The Tenant*** 1976
*Tess*** 1979
*Pirates*** 1986
*Frantic*** 1988
*Bitter Moon*** 1992
Death and the Maiden 1994 (based on the play by Ariel Dorfman)
Gli Angeli 1996

  * also screenwriter
 ** also co-screenwriter
*** also uncredited
    co-screenwriter

ARIEL DORFMAN
Born 1942
Buenos Aires, Argentina
(Chilean citizen)

How to Read Donald Duck 1974 (with Armand Mattelart)

Missing 1982

The Empire's Old Clothes 1983

Widows 1984 (play based on novel 1997)

The Last Song of Manuel Sendero 1987

Last Waltz in Santiago 1988

Mascara 1988

My House Is on Fire 1990 (short film based on novel 1997; co-screenwriter; co-director)

Some Write to the Future 1991

Hard Rain 1991

Death and the Maiden 1992 (play; co-screenwriter with Rafael Yglesias; film directed by Roman Polanski)

Prisoners in Time 1995 (co-screenwriter; BBC film)

Reader 1995

Konfidenz 1996

Heading South, Looking North: A Bilingual Journey 1998

The Resistance Theory 1998

The Nanny and the Iceberg 1999

familiar, horribly believable, so as to explore what is hidden, what is bizarre, what is absurd, so that the grid of reality can be tested against the inner demons of his characters, so that we can experience the liquid terror of being that person in that room, in that story, so that we can accompany that protagonist as he, as she, tries to change a destiny that has been imposed from somewhere else. Roman has spent his life mastering and using the techniques of realism in the service of the unspeakable.

So the lamp is there in order to help us understand what the lamp does not know, what cannot be seen immediately through its glow: the almost inaccessible world of the mind and the heart, desperate for love, unable to finally touch the other deeply enough to break out of solitude or delusion. And Polanski, once he has launched us on this voyage, will not relieve us with conclusive answers: his endings are almost invariably ambiguous, his heroes and heroines (if they may even be called by that name) haunted by the bite of uncertainty even as they dash their heads against the mirror of life. At times, as in *Repulsion* or *The Tenant,* they end up lost in insanity. But most of the time, as in *Knife in the Water* or *Tess* or *Death and the Maiden,* they end up lost in the bitter opposite of insanity: they end up lost in awareness, learning how vulnerable they are (they always were), how difficult it is to be moral, to be loved, in a world controlled by more powerful others. Donald Pleasence on his lonely rock in *Cul-de-Sac* and Mia Farrow alone with her devil's child in *Rosemary's Baby* or Jack Nicholson finally understanding who owns Los Angeles in *Chinatown,* all of them face to face with who they are, what the world is. The ferocious pull of Polanski's best films comes from his ability to implacably place us inside the impossible fantasies of his feverish protagonists and simultaneously force us to acknowledge them coldly, from afar, from the outside, from history they cannot change. A vision Polanski rehearsed in his first short, *Two Men and a Wardrobe,* where two Beckett-like fools emerge from the sea with their enormous wardrobe, are rejected by everyone as they wander the cruel city, and unable to fit their oversized burden of the imagination anywhere, return to the waters and are swallowed by them.

Except that Roman was not swallowed. The waters did not close over him. In his art, he found the one possibility not open to his characters: a way of turning his vision away from the abyss of hallucination or the blind alley of frustration and into the shared and joyful realm of communal experience. This he has done at great personal expense, paying the consequences of his independence, aggressively and often rambunctiously rejecting all compromises, refusing to apologize for the mystery of what he was seeing or the tangle of what he was communicating or the transgressions he lived, treading the dangerous line between the commercial and the artistic in a century that has not been kind to visionaries.

That is why Roman Polanski is the ultimate survivor: he has earned the right to inflict this vision on his spectators because he has always been willing to inflict it on himself.

Now, here, on the set of *Death and the Maiden,* he hands the lamp that is too pleasant and cheery to the prop master so that it can be darkened, so that it can help entice millions into his dreams, so that he can close the door shut on those millions and not let them out until they have caught a terrifying glimpse of what Roman's mind and life contain.

He picks up some ropes. He looks at them for a while. He handles them. He ties them into a knot. He unties them. He makes a different knot. In a few more weeks, Sigourney Weaver will be using them to tie Ben Kingsley's hands. Are the ropes the right color? Are they too long? Are the edges too frayed? Would they be the sort a woman would have in her kitchen drawer at a beach house? He looks around at us. His eyes squint at me, at all of us. He is looking at me, but through me, past me, somewhere else. He turns back to the ropes.

"There's something wrong," Roman says. "But you know, I can't figure out yet what it is, what's not right."

He will. He will. ◆

ON NORMAN
JEWISON

Y ou should know this: I am uniquely qualified, as a screenwriter, to talk about what it's like to do a picture with Norman Jewison because not only have I never done a picture with him, I haven't worked with him *three times*. On *Magic, The Princess Bride*, and most woefully, on a musical version of *Grand Hotel*.

The reasons are standard: ego and greed. In one, he ruffled a producer's ego, in another, a studio's ego kept the project moribund. In the third, he could not get the amount of money he knew he needed to make the movie.

> **But Jewison, it must be remembered, is from that generation of directors who stormed Hollywood from television in the late fifties and sixties, and who were brought up in a penny-pinching world.**

The last sounds quaint now: a director actually blowing a project because he knew he would have to lie and come in over budget. But Jewison, it must be remembered, is from that generation of directors who stormed Hollywood from television in the late fifties and sixties, and who were brought up in a penny-pinching world. The only Canadian of the bunch, Jewison is still with us, still on top, still cranky and tough, funny and smart, still plugging away.

Magic story: Norman wants a major star for what became the Anthony Hopkins part. We are in Beverly Hills, a place he feels snarly about. (One of the stories floating around Jewison is that he took *Fiddler on the Roof,* among other reasons, so he could get his kids out of L.A. True or not, he stayed abroad for years.)

Anyway, it is Friday morning and we are happily flying out that afternoon. Phone call. An agent. Telling us a client of his, a Major Star, has read the script, is seriously interested, wants to talk to us about it.

Yesss, as Marv Albert would put it.

Problem: the Major Star is booked up with important meetings and cannot see us until Sunday afternoon. He wants to talk about the script on a nonsuperficial level. Will we wait the forty-eight hours?

There is only one answer to that question.

Sunday afternoon, we drive up to the Major Star's home, park, knock on the door. And wait awhile. We shuffle and squint. I, the more edgy of the duo, trot out to the street to see if we have the right address.

We do.

Eventually the Major Star appears. In a bathing suit. He has been out in the back by the pool and didn't hear.

NORMAN JEWISON
Born in Toronto, Canada

40 Pounds of Trouble
1963

The Thrill of It All 1963

Send Me No Flowers
1964

The Art of Love 1965

The Cincinnati Kid 1965

*The Russians Are
Coming! The Russians
Are Coming!* 1966

In the Heat of the Night
1967 Golden Globe for
Best Motion Picture

The Thomas Crown Affair
1968

Gaily, Gaily 1969

Fiddler on the Roof 1971

Jesus Christ Superstar**
1973

Rollerball 1975

F.I.S.T. 1978

. . . And Justice for All
1979

Best Friends 1982

A Soldier's Story 1984

Agnes of God 1985

Moonstruck 1987

In Country 1989

Other People's Money
1991

Only You 1994

Bogus 1996

*Lazarus and the
Hurricane* 1999

Irving G. Thalberg
Memorial Award 1999

** also co-screenwriter

He is barefoot.

And he is smoking a very large joint.

He ushers us out to the pool. Where a bunch of his friends are frolicking. The Major Star gets in the shallow end and smokes and screws around and pretty soon it's clear he doesn't want to talk to us about the script on any level, superficial or otherwise. Because he hasn't read it. But he says he expects to when he has a chance.

We leave, get back in the car, start to drive.

And Norman is pissed.

"Because he kept us waiting?"
Wrong.
"Because he hadn't read it?"
"Because he didn't offer us the joint."

He drove faster.

"Don't you see—that other stuff is *agent* bullshit. Agent probably said we were desperate just to tell people we said hello, would the guy do us a big favor and nod in our direction. The joint is what's important."

"I didn't want any," I said.

"I didn't want any either—but when he didn't offer it, that's the *star's* behavior. Make it a glass of red wine. If you came to my house and I met you at the door drinking a glass of red wine and didn't offer you any, I'm saying *fuck you.* And that's what he was saying to us. And that's why I'm pissed. *It was not proper behavior.*"

Norman Jewison behaves properly. He is today what he began as: a small-town Canadian Protestant. (His religion is only mentioned because everyone always assumed, because of his name, that he was Jewish and that assumption became writ in stone after *Fiddler.*)

On another flick, he was halfway through shooting with *two* Major Stars. The scene was simple. A street scene. The Boy Star had to open a door for the Girl Star, then follow her inside. They did it. Norman didn't like the take, requested another. They did another. Still not to his liking.

As he quietly requested a third try, the Boy Star, with no warning, threw a roundhouse punch at Norman's face. Norman ducked, the Girl

WILLIAM GOLDMAN
Born 1931
Chicago, Illinois

The Temple of Gold 1956
Soldier in the Rain 1963
Boys and Girls Together
1964
Harper 1966 (screenplay;
based on the novel *The
Moving Target* by Ross
MacDonald)
No Way to Treat a Lady
1968
*Butch Cassidy and the
Sundance Kid* 1969
(screenplay) Academy
Award for Best Writing,
Story, and Screenplay
Based on Material Not
Previously Published or
Produced
The Great Waldo Pepper
1975 (screenplay)
All the President's Men
1976 (screenplay; based
on the book by Bob
Woodward and Carl
Bernstein) Academy
Award for Best Adapted
Screenplay
Marathon Man 1976
(novel and screenplay;
film directed by John
Schlesinger)
A Bridge Too Far 1977
(screenplay)
Magic 1978 (novel and
screenplay)
Tinsel 1979
Control 1982
*The Season: A Candid
Look at Broadway* 1984
The Princess Bride 1987
(novel and screenplay; film
directed by Rob Reiner)
Heat 1987
Wait Till Next Year 1988
(co-author Mike Lupica)
*Adventures in the Screen
Trade* 1989
Misery 1990 (screenplay;
based on the novel by
Stephen King; film
directed by Rob Reiner)
Hype and Glory 1991
Year of the Comet 1992
(screenplay)
Chaplin 1992
(co-screenwriter)
Maverick 1994
(screenplay; film directed
by Richard Donner)
*The Ghost and the
Darkness* 1996
(screenplay)
Absolute Power 1997
(screenplay)

Star burst into tears and fled to her trailer, Norman called a halt to the proceedings, went to his trailer and waited.

The Boy Star, a giant box office attraction at the time (now unemployable—see, there is a God) came to Norman and explained he didn't like doing retakes because he felt they implied criticism of his talent and he was sorry for the interruption but could they get back to work.

Sure, Norman said, after you apologize.

I just apologized to you, the Boy Star said.

You have to apologize to *everybody*. The whole crew. You insulted them. Don't you understand that?

The star said he did. He didn't. But he apologized.

Of the major directors, Jewison tends to be the most ignored. (Seven Oscar nominations, sure, but no awards.) And it seems doubtful to me that there will be any groundswells from the Academy or the media. For mainly two reasons. He has always been, from the start, so commercially successful.

And because he can do anything.

Who else has his versatility? *Moonstruck* and *Rollerball, The Cincinnati Kid* and *Fiddler on the Roof, In the Heat of the Night* and *Agnes of God, A Soldier's Story* and *Jesus Christ Superstar.* And so it goes. Oh yeah, I forgot *The Thomas Crown Affair.* Ooops, should have mentioned *The Russians Are Coming! The Russians Are Coming!*

Trust me on this: There will be no retirement benefits for Norman Jewison. ◆

ON ALAN
RUDOLPH

In the smart and lively movies of Alan Rudolph, nuances are at work like bees in a hive. A busy swarm of subtleties generates a nucleus of narrative honeycomb that has more layers than an archeologist's wedding cake, and the energized reticulum is all the more amazing because its intricacies seem at first ambiguous and offhand.

Horizontal layers of lust and angst crisscross with vertical layers of wit and beauty (despite modest budgets, every Rudolph film is delicious to the eye and ear), but the layer that most delights me (and drives the dullards daft) is the oblique stratum of goofiness that angles through his cinematic matrix like a butter knife that forgot to take its lithium and turned into a corkscrew.

For many people, "goofy" might suggest a kind of good-natured stupidity. With humorous overtones. Practiced observation, however, has led me to define goofiness as "user-friendly weirdness." With humorous overtones. And that is the definition intended here.

In case anybody has failed to notice, our little planet is *très* bizarre. Some of our weirdness is violent and horrific, ranging from fully flowered genocidal warfare to the secret buds of personal evil that David Lynch likes to press in his small-town scrapbooks. Far more prevalent—yet decidedly more difficult for a serious artist to capture—is the non-threatening variety of weirdness; the weirdness of the quirk, the tic, the discrepancy, the idiosyncrasy half-concealed, the passionate impulse that when indulged puts a strange new spin on the heart.

All of our lives are at least a trifle haywire, particularly in the area of romantic relationships. It is Rudolph's special genius to illuminate those haywire tendencies and reveal how they—and not convention or rationality—channel the undermost currents of our being. It is precisely Rudolph's attention to our so-called "off-the-wall" behavior that gives pictures such as *Choose Me, The Moderns,* and *Trouble in Mind* their comic and erotic freshness, their psychological veracity, their ovoid contours.

"Ovoid" is the correct description, although "elliptical" will do. Football-shaped at any rate. Most films or novels or plays bounce like basketballs,

ALAN RUDOLPH
Born 1943
Los Angeles, California

*Welcome to L.A.** 1977
*Remember My Name**
1978
Roadie 1980
*Endangered Species***
1982
Return Engagement
1983
*Choose Me** 1984
Songwriter 1984
*Trouble in Mind** 1985
Made in Heaven 1986
*The Moderns*** 1988
*Love at Large** 1990
Mortal Thoughts 1991
*Equinox** 1992
*Mrs. Parker and the
Vicious Circle*** 1994
*Afterglow** 1997
*Breakfast of Champions**
1999
Trixie 1999 (in
production)

* also screenwriter
** also co-screenwriter

which is to say, up and down, up and down, traveling in a forward direction in a generally straight line. Rudolph's movies, on the other hand, bounce like footballs: end over end, elusively, changing direction, even reversing direction; wobbly, unpredictable, and wild. Goofy, in other words, like so much of life itself. Each of his films produce the aesthetic, emotional, and intellectual equivalents of gridiron kickoffs, followed by bone-cracking tackles or exhilarating returns.

When considering Alan Rudolph, it is crucial not to overlook those jarring hits. As charming and tinged with fantasy as his work can be, it is not fueled by froth. Even a walleyed strut such as *Songwriter* has its dark, serrated edges; and when they cut, they cut deep. The director possesses an urban sensibility, which he focuses sardonically on the sorrows as well as the pleasures of metropolitan romance.

TOM ROBBINS
Born 1936
Blowing Rock,
North Carolina

Another Roadside Attraction 1971
Even Cowgirls Get the Blues 1976 (film directed by Gus Van Sant Jr.)
Still Life with Woodpecker 1980
Jitterbug Perfume 1985
Skinny Legs and All 1990
Half Asleep in Frog Pajamas 1994

The miracle of Rudolph is how he manages to be gritty and dreamy at the same time, even somber and funny at the same time. Not funny in one scene, somber in the next, but funny and somber *simultaneously*. This is a form of profundity that only the nimble-minded can totally appreciate, which eliminates . . . well, you know who it eliminates. I suspect it is the virtuoso manner with which he orchestrates nuances that allows him to ply the tragicomic paradox so successfully.

In any case, those almost surreal interpenetrations of melancholia and gaiety amplify the sense of mystery that haunts Rudolph's every movie if not his every scene (many of which unfold in smoky, neon-lit clubs and bars). What is present here is neither the prosaic mystery of whodunit nor the sentimental mystery of will-boy-get-girl—each a formulaic device calculated to manipulate an audience by means of manufactured suspense— but rather that transcendental mystery that swirls around our innermost longings and that can liberate an audience by connecting it viscerally to the greater mystery of existence.

In the marvelous *Love at Large,* Rudolph (who usually writes his own scripts) has Anne Archer ask Tom Berenger if they will be "glad and dizzy all the time." Ultimately, no matter how moody or bittersweet a Rudolph movie might be, when I walk out of the theater I feel somehow glad and dizzy. If you are aware of a better way to feel, please phone me right now. Collect. ◆

ON RON SHELTON

October 26, 1995, 7:30 p.m. The high desert, sixty miles south of Tucson, Arizona.

Ron Shelton has dragged Kevin Costner, Rene Russo, Don Johnson, Cheech Marin, and a cast and crew of 150 to this remote patch of sand and cactus to make *Tin Cup,* a screwball comedy about an over-the-hill pro golfer who decides to take one last run at greatness by entering the U. S. Open.

"The French can make comedies about someone sleeping with their cousin," says Shelton. "If that happens in an American movie, somebody gets their head blown off."

At the moment, the crew is busy lighting the dilapidated driving range that Costner's character owns and operates. It will be a night-for-night shot, requiring huge Musco and Bee Bee night lights, and forty-five minutes of setup time. Shelton has taken refuge in his trailer, where he kills time by watching the ninety-first World Series between the Atlanta Braves and the Cleveland Indians, listening to tango music that he might use in the movie's final scene, smoking an immense cigar, and reflecting on his formative years. "I had a very healthy, happy, supportive childhood, with all the usual demons that go with growing up in a fairly conservative Baptist family."

"What are those?" the writer asks.

Shelton shifts uncomfortably, smiles, clears his throat. "Well, uh, you just, you didn't get in trouble." He laughs dryly. "You always did the right thing." When he talks about an emotionally charged issue or incident, Ron often begins to refer to himself in the second person.

As a boy, he went to Sunday church services regularly, and Wednesday night prayer meetings often. "I can sit in here and sing two hundred Baptist hymns right now." He found church life "a little boring, a little seductive, very guilt producing, and frightening. Frightening because it painted a very vivid vision of hell and heaven. When you're six years old and they describe eternal damnation, you don't focus on the opportunities for redemption, but the horror of burning in hell forever."

RON SHELTON
Born 1945
Whittier, California

Bull Durham*1988
Blaze** 1989
White Men Can't Jump* 1992
Cobb* 1994
Tin Cup** 1996

* also screenwriter
** also co-screenwriter

The conversation pauses while Shelton watches an instant replay of a phenomenal catch by the Braves' pitcher. Ron takes a long thoughtful drag on his cigar. "You know, there's church music in every one of my movies. The score of *Cobb* is based on 'There Is a Fountain Filled with Blood.'" He begins humming the hymn, and then singing it. "There is a fountain filled with blood, drawn from Emmanuel's veins!" He pounds the thin Formica table with his huge hand as he sings; the whole trailer shakes with the rhythm of the words. "And sinners plunged beneath that flood lose all their guilty stains!"

His singing stops when a batter for Cleveland swats a ball over the right-field fence. Shelton's eyes pop wide open. "Home run!" he cries out. "Five-four! Two-run homer, five-four!"

Shelton lost faith in hell and heaven and most of the other tenets of the Baptist Church during his college years, when he came to realize that the world was "bigger and more complicated" than he'd been led to believe. The first shock came when President Kennedy was assassinated. "It just never occurred to you that the president of the United States could be murdered." Then Martin Luther King fell, and then Bobby Kennedy. "By the end of the sixties everybody was dead." The Vietnam war escalated, and cities across America burst into flames lit by antiwar protests and race riots. Shelton led demonstrations on the campus of Westmont College, in California. "It was this all-white conservative Baptist school. Most of the faculty embraced the war, held it up as a noble cause. The school was trying to stay in this ivory tower, to pretend the world wasn't falling apart, but it was."

Shelton turned his back on the Church and spent "the next twenty years running away from it."

Ron takes a long drag on his cigar, its tip glows yellow-red. A curling gray cloud of smoke obscures the strong jaw and broad forehead, his voice drops to a murmur. "Then one day your mother dies, and you discover that the only thing that calms you down is that old church music."

He was thirty-nine years old when his mother, Margaret Shelton, died of cancer in the winter of 1985. She was a rock-ribbed Baptist, and "one of the most tough-minded people I've ever met, and the most capable of unconditional love of anybody I ever knew. The tired, the poor, the huddled masses, were always sleeping on our couch and coming to dinner. That was her. And yet she was a very tough-minded woman. If you asked her for an opinion she had one. Exceedingly well read, always questioning herself and others. She never got past high school, but she was always reading. At her death she had re-embraced E. B. White. She read great novels, essays, a wide range of books. She was a very bright woman, very capable."

Margaret Shelton died eighty days after her doctor diagnosed her. "The cancer was all over her system when they found it. We had a perfectly good Thanksgiving and six weeks later she was dead. Actually, the chemotherapy killed her. We were *extremely* close. . . . I wish she had had ten more years." Margaret never lived to see her oldest boy direct a movie.

But her death taught Shelton that he was still a Baptist, even if he no longer believed in hell and heaven, and a god who was a bearded man hovering in the sky. "For the first thirty-five years of your life you run from the Church, and somewhere in your thirties or forties you make peace with it and embrace it as part of who you are, and thereby liberate yourself from it. I realized I could take from it those elements that comforted me and helped me to cope, and discard the rest."

Tin Cup is a likeable slice-of-life comedy, similar in tone to Shelton's earlier movies, *Bull Durham, Blaze,* and *White Men Can't Jump.* But the film he finished before this one differed radically from the others. In *Cobb,* Tommy Lee Jones played Ty Cobb, the greatest player in the history of American baseball. It was a shattering portrait. Both on the ball field and

DAVID WEDDLE
Born 1956
Irvington, New York

Memoirs of an Awkward Lover 1980 (play)

Under the Nutcracker 1982 (play)

"If They Move . . . Kill 'em!": The Life and Times of Sam Peckinpah 1994

Star Trek: Deep Space Nine 1997–1999 (executive story editor)

off, Cobb was a certifiable monster: a sadist who aimed the spikes of his shoes at the heads of opponents as he slid into base, who beat his wives and children, and who once killed a man with his bare fists.

Shelton managed to poke at the beast's soft underbelly, exposing the vulnerability beneath the rage. *Cobb* was a quantum leap forward, one of those pivotal moments in a filmmaker's career where the artist can be seen maturing as the movie unreels. For the first time, Shelton dared to plunge beneath the skin of a character and explore his inner realities. But the movie earned polarized reviews in America; critics either praised it as a brilliant exploration of the nation's fetish for myth making, or condemned it as moronic glorification of an appalling human being. At the box office, it failed to earn back its twenty-million-dollar negative cost.

"I'll never understand why the movie wasn't received better, why people didn't go see it," says Shelton. "I thought maybe the festivals in Europe would embrace it, but it didn't get embraced anywhere. I guess it's not an embraceable movie, but it's my best film. I'm sure some people consider it 'Shelton's Folly.' But that's the reason we make movies, is to make a movie like *Cobb*."

When asked what drew him to the subject, Shelton will most often talk of his desire to expose America's pathological obsession with hero worship. The movie does do that, but clearly Shelton's motivations were deeper and more complex than that. Cobb, like Shelton, was brought up in a rock-ribbed Baptist family and, like Shelton, had an extremely close relationship with his mother. But the Georgia boy's love was stained by a traumatic event, from which he never recovered.

Through a series of flashbacks in *Cobb*, that trauma is gradually revealed. When Ty was just sixteen years old, his father, William Cobb, came home unexpectedly one night and burst in upon his wife, Amanda, and her lover. The lover shot William in the chest with Amanda's shotgun. Then, as William Cobb lay on the bedroom porch, looking up at his wife—blood bubbling out of his mouth and eyes pleading for an explanation that would incorporate this reality into his rock-ribbed view of the universe—the lover emptied the other barrel and blew his head off. Amanda was brought to trial for murdering her husband; young Ty stood up in court and swore to the world that his mother was innocent, even though he knew that she was not.

"You're an educated man, Stumpy, tell me what ya think," Cobb inquires of his biographer, Al Stump, near the end of the film. "Either my father was inadequate for my mother, not the man I thought he was, not a great man, not even a good man. Or else my mother was trash, a common whore. It's that simple isn't it? . . . As a boy I stood in court next to that woman, 'cause suddenly I was the man of the house, and as I stood steadfastly at her side and heard the jury say 'not guilty,' I *knew* that woman had been with another man the night of that killing. . . ." Cobb's face knots with torment; his eyes plead with Stump for a definitive answer. "A man must defend his mother at *all* times. Isn't that right, Al? Am I a fool?"

Like all good Baptists, Cobb had done *the right thing.* Yet in his heart, he felt he had committed a terrible betrayal. "That is a staggering inner conflict for a young Georgia boy," says Shelton. The demarcation between right and wrong wavered, the moral foundation of Cobb's world, his entire rock-ribbed vision of the universe, dissolved.

"The Judaeo-Christian mythology has had a tremendous influence over American culture and art," says Shelton. "Americans grow up believing there is a clear-cut right and wrong, a black-and-white moral universe. The most profound American artists are those who discover the world is a great deal more complex than that, and they are thrown into crisis by this discovery. *Things matter* to Americans."

This is precisely why *The Wild Bunch* was such a pivotal movie for Shelton. He went to see it at a little theater in Arkansas in the summer of 1969, while he was still a minor league ballplayer. He walked out of the theater convinced that he would one day become a filmmaker. The picture—made by Sam Peckinpah, another disillusioned fundamentalist who couldn't quite turn his back on his Bible-thumping boyhood—told the story of a band of killers who believe in nothing but gold and self-preservation. They travel to Mexico, get involved with Pancho Villa's revolution, and discover a cause worth laying down their lives for.

"It's such an American movie," Shelton observes. Americans need to believe, need to find the faith they've lost; cling desperately to the Protestant tenet that their actions are of consequence.

"The French can make comedies about someone sleeping with their cousin," says Shelton. "If that happens in an American movie, somebody gets their head blown off. Personally, I prefer that view of the world."

Things matter. ◆

ON JONATHAN
DEMME

I once heard a writer misquoting another writer who had misquoted another writer who had supposedly said that "Compassion is all in the details." If this is so, then Jonathan Demme, the filmmaker, seems to always be on a cinematic quest for compassion.

When I think of Jonathan's films, I always think of his details. Details like the framed sky on the screen behind Spalding Gray in *Swimming to Cambodia,* the careful sip of water Mr. Gray's character so wisely takes before beginning his long and captivating monologue, the pink shadows hinting sunrise (or sunset) at the bottom of the framed sky, the larger and whiter cirrocumulus framing Gray's exuberant head. These details often strike me as the subtle brushstrokes on a piece of art, the final touch, the afterthought—or perhaps even the very first thought—of a highly observant narrator, for whom in the final count the seeming minutiae can make all the difference.

JONATHAN DEMME
Born 1944
Baldwin, New York

*Caged Heat** 1974
Crazy Mama 1975
*Fighting Mad** 1976
Handle with Care 1977
Last Embrace 1979
Melvin and Howard 1980
Stop Making Sense 1984
Swing Shift 1984
Something Wild 1986
Swimming to Cambodia 1987
Married to the Mob 1988
The Silence of the Lambs 1991
Cousin Bobby 1992
Philadelphia 1993
The Complex Sessions 1994
Beloved 1998
Storefront Hitchcock 1998

* also screenwriter

I was lucky enough to spend a few days on the set of Jonathan's film *Beloved,* an Utterly Beloved Production, "Utterly" so in memory of his twenty-five-year Oscar-winning collaboration and partnership with his late friend Kenny Utt. In a steamy and crowded room in July, a group of women sat down to reconstruct a scene from Toni Morrison's Pulitzer Prize–winning novel. The women were deciding whether to exorcise an angry ghost (Beloved) who had returned from the beyond to haunt her mother, the main character Sethe, played by Oprah Winfrey. One of the women in the scene was aggressively fanning herself during a discussion being taped. A cameraman walked over and asked her to surrender the fan because it was blocking the shot. Once the fan was taken away, Jonathan walked over to the woman and said, "They took your fan, eh?"

Later, the woman marvels at this: how did he know that a grown person who had lost a fan on a big-time movie set could feel as though she was a little girl who had just unwillingly surrendered a lollipop in a schoolyard fight.

Jonathan Demme, the man, knows compassion too.

On trips to Haiti, in markets vivacious with vendors and artists wanting as much to chat and hear compliments about their stock as to sell their wares, Jonathan often lingers longest to examine the slightly unusual pieces of art, the ones where a rooster is just as likely to have a man's head as he is to have a fiery crimson jagged wattle.

Walking besides him at an antiquarian market in a predawn pink clouded morning in Maine, you watch him handle old hook rugs, 1950 diner chairs, and Mason jars so carefully you would think that he knew every detail of the life experience each item had seen. And you realize that perhaps nothing is wasted on this man, the way he has acknowledged to trying very hard to make it so that no frame is wasted in his films, each face, each point of light coming together to tell the larger story, whether it be Hannibal Lecter's cannibalism in *The Silence of the Lambs* or Andy

Beckett's battle with AIDS and discrimination in *Philadelphia,* or the social activism of his cousin, the Reverend Robert Castle, in *Cousin Bobby.*

I once spent three consecutive months going to a student-run television studio at Ramapo College in New Jersey to meet Jonathan and an exiled Haitian journalist, Jean Dominique. Each week the three of us would sit down before the cameras at the college media center discussing the history of Haitian cinema. Week after week, we'd call out the titles of films we had trouble finding even from their creators, many of whom in fleeing a dictatorship had not had time to collect family photos, much less their chef d'oeuvres. Most mornings Jean Dominique would narrate for us the plots of films which even after months and months of searching we were never able to find. Together we would all grieve the details of those films, with Jonathan lingering to ask, "What color dress was that character wearing? How did she hold the broom when she swept?" desperately seeking an imaginary reconstruction of these missing frames.

One of my favorite early Jonathan Demme films is *Who Am I This Time?,* based on a short story by Kurt Vonnegut Jr. In *Who Am I This Time?,* film critics Michael Bliss and Christina Banks confer that Jonathan is "in his most pure form: all of his major themes—disguise and ultimate realization of identity, the redemptive power of love, the importance of community—are to the forefront, and are fully developed." In this film, Harry, a timid man and seemingly unlikely thespian, takes on the more aggressive personality traits of his characters when he hits the community theater stage. The contrast between Harry's stage personas and his real-life bashful demeanor reminds me of the transformative power of film, which at its best can introduce us to the height of experiences which everyday life does not offer. And for that we count on the director's eye to guide us with his or her ability to make the experience so palpable that we can feel it throbbing beneath the screen in the actor's performances, the staging, and especially the music, which often operates as just another propelling and spirited character in most Jonathan Demme films.

In *Swimming to Cambodia,* the Spalding Gray character recounts telling his girlfriend that he could not leave Cambodia because he was waiting to experience a perfect moment, a beautiful sunset, a revelatory epiphany through nature. As he describes his perfect moment, one can't help but think that he is looking for a discovery which can only take place in man's mind between him and his shadows, or which could only be created for him by the film director behind the camera to which he's speaking. A filmmaker like Jonathan Demme who grants the human voice as much space as the lights and its gracious movements and who

EDWIDGE DANTICAT
Born 1969
Port-au-Prince, Haiti

Breath, Eyes, Memory 1995

Krik? Krak! 1996

Island on Fire 1997 (with Jonathan Demme)

The Farming of Bones 1998

Odilon Pierre: Artist of Haiti 1999 (with Jonathan Demme)

in *Stop Making Sense,* for example, allows David Byrne's songs to be as unobstructively heard as his big suit is to be vibrantly seen.

One of the most admirable and personally endearing traits of Jonathan's growing oeuvre is its long list of strong female leads—from Clarice in *The Silence of the Lambs* to Angela in *Married to the Mob* and now Sethe in *Beloved*—his women are resilient and powerful, struggling with inner and outer forces to keep their challenging pasts from intruding on their future. However, in the end, whether with male or female leads, there is no doubt that Jonathan's movies—like his documentaries and music videos against such social ills as apartheid and gang violence—are all mirrors which hold within our view the best as well as the worst in ourselves, to gaze upon with both passion and compassion. ◆

ON OLIVER
STONE

OLIVER STONE
Born 1946
New York, New York

*Seizure*** 1974
*The Hand*** 1981
Salvador 1986
*Platoon** 1986 Academy
Award for Best Director;
Golden Globe Awards for
Best Director and Best
Motion Picture (Drama)
*Wall Street*** 1987
*Talk Radio*** 1988
*Born on the Fourth of
July*** 1989 Academy
Award for Best Director;
Golden Globe Awards for
Best Director and Best
Screenplay
*The Doors*** 1991
*JFK*** 1991 Golden
Globe Award for Best
Director
*Heaven and Earth***
1993
*Natural Born Killers***
1994
*Nixon*** 1995
U Turn 1997
The League 1999
(in production)

* also screenwriter
** also co-screenwriter

There's that indelible moment in *Natural Born Killers* when the domestic life of the abused, murderous girl suddenly appears as a fifties sitcom, complete with laugh track and antique, telescoping fades. The more foul and cruel and menacing the girl's father becomes, the louder the laughter gets. It is weird and disturbing, less for the content than for the way Oliver Stone presents it. His problem here was to break through the detachment that constant exposure to the subject of the "dysfunctional family" has formed in us. By putting this grotesque household portrait in the nostalgic frame of *Ozzie and Harriet,* Stone produces a sense of shock and disgust, and at the same time uses the conventional notion of the perfect American family against itself. He both exposes and exploits the crude artifice by which the nostalgic vision was sustained, even as he creates another vision: that of the family as the perfect finishing school for killers.

Stone's delight in subverting pleasant or consoling myths with troubling counter-myths goes to the heart of his power as a director, and also explains the fury that his movies have called down upon him. The cries of indignation that inevitably follow the completion of a Stone flick have become, like the stories of wild times on the set, part of the release package; we'd miss them if they weren't there.

The fact is, no other filmmaker in this country takes on so much, so ferociously; therefore no one else commands the interest Stone commands. Whether you hate it or love it, his work demands a response. He is faulted for his violence and "excess," but every American director of stature has heard that tune; the truth is, our history and culture don't point in the direction of *Claire's Knee.* As Flannery O'Connor said in answer to the same criticism: For the blind, you draw big pictures—for the deaf, you shout. Stone is not a crafter of polite, well-mannered movies, but for all his passion and relentlessness he is memorable as much for the private, restrained moments of his work as for the operatic: Charlie Sheen's letters to his grandmother in *Platoon,* softly read over images of exhaustion, suffering, and death; James Woods in a confessional in *Salvador,* making a doomed yet comically touching attempt to renounce his dissolute ways; Nixon with his dying brother in a desert sanitorium. I didn't think it was possible for anyone to make me feel compassion for Richard Nixon, but Stone's movie awakens

a sense of his humanity, however blighted; none of Nixon's apologists (nor, for that matter, Nixon himself) ever quite managed to do that.

The most serious argument against Stone's work has to do with its deficiency as history. Henry Kissinger's complaint about *Nixon* in the *Los Angeles Times* is the perfect example. He finds fault with certain elements of the plot and with the way Richard Nixon is represented. How much more responsible and interesting a movie it would have been, he says, if Stone

TOBIAS WOLFF
Born 1945
Birmingham, Alabama

In the Garden of the North American Martyrs
1981
The Barracks Thief 1984
Back in the World 1985
This Boy's Life: A Memoir
1989
In Pharaoh's Army: Memories of the Lost War 1994
The Night in Question
1996

had told the *real* story! And whose story would that be? Henry Kissinger's, naturally. Here is his version of Nixon's record on Vietnam: "In the end, Nixon did achieve what he had promised: a settlement that preserved our allies and ended our participation in the war." He forgets to mention that Nixon spent five long years reaching that settlement (remember his "secret plan"?); that more of our men—and our allies—were killed during that time than during both of the preceding administrations; that our allies were not in fact preserved; that Nixon—at Kissinger's urging—extended the war to Cambodia, thus giving the previously marginal Khmer Rouge a new rallying cry, and setting off the slaughter that continues there to this day. Mr. Kissinger doesn't really like history; he likes his version of history. And his version of history is a self-serving myth. Stone's is a skeptical counter-myth. I know which one I trust more.

But let's not quibble, Henry. The real lesson here is that only a moron gets his history from the movies, and Stone, intentionally or not, has made us aware of the extent to which we were doing exactly that, with the encouragement of the politicians and sages who are now squealing in outrage. Where were they when *PT 109* was unleashed on us? It was widely known in their circles that the story of young Jack Kennedy's exemplary courage and competence was a concoction, but it was allowed to stand unchallenged. Why? Because it was a soothing concoction, that served those in power; propaganda, in other words. The movies have been suborned for propaganda of one kind or another ever since they became popular enough to be useful. Stone's and my generation was brought up on films designed to teach us that our leaders were brave and incorruptible, our national past a series of humane victories over barbarism, our people pure-hearted, our wars crusades. Stone has had the gall to use this powerful myth-making machinery to question the authorized version of the past, and those who profit by it. Of course they cry foul.

Movies are persuasive. More than any other medium, they suggest that real life is happening before our very eyes. This is especially true when the stories concern actual people, as in *Nixon* and *PT 109*. We have to learn to see movies for what they are—concoctions, myths. Their truth, if they have any, is the truth of art, not of science. (As to the truth of "history"—whose version? But that's a subject for another day.)

In the end, Oliver Stone's movies will endure as works of art, or not at all. I have no doubt they will endure. Beyond their technical mastery and nervy power, their sheer visual daring, they have humanity and the indispensable virtue of being necessary. We would not know ourselves and our situation quite so well without them. Stone is a singular and visionary witness, whose moving pictures of the American soul do not shrink from portraying its violence and greed, nor its stubborn dream of transcendence. ◆

ON WES
CRAVEN

INFERNALLY YOURS

WES CRAVEN
Born 1939
Cleveland, Ohio

*Last House on the Left** 1972

*The Hills Have Eyes** 1978

*Deadly Blessing*** 1981

*Swamp Thing** 1982

*A Nightmare on Elm Street** 1984

*The Hills Have Eyes Part II** 1985

Deadly Friend 1986

The Serpent and the Rainbow 1988

*Shocker** 1989

*The People under the Stairs** 1991

*Wes Craven's New Nightmare** 1994

Vampire in Brooklyn 1995

Scream 1996

Scream 2 1997

50 Violins 1999

Scream 3 1999

* also screenwriter
** also co-screenwriter

Back in the Stone Ages, long before Internet child porn, *A Nightmare on Elm Street* was a phenomenon only beginning its slow leak to the national press—a movie rattling the hotbed cages of gothic Midwest drive-ins, gusting through with the rank breeze of (who could have thought it possible?) a bona fide *Texas Chainsaw* equivalent—well, way back then, I decided to have a look. Right on Hollywood Boulevard there, east end, foreboding in itself. A friend and I cruised a matinee next to the XXX theater and that already aroused the bloodlust (the best Yuppie-in-the-woods slaughterfests had an X-ey, slapdash feel). By the time Heather Langenkamp went outside, took a look at Freddie Krueger with his twenty-foot wingspan, and muttered, "Oh my God!"— the scarified demon replied by pointing to the razored hand (fingers not yet Toys "R" Us'd) and declaimed, "*This* is God"—well, my friend and I thought that was pretty far out, as Arlo Guthrie might have said. We liked that there weren't too many people in the theater, either—that Midwest teens still owned the thing, all the small towns with scary American psychic winds howling through: Ichabod Crane winds of incest, football-hero rape, and the first wave of high school satanists stabbing sibs and sodomizing forest-ambushed toddlers, cultural footnotes to heavy metal, warlocks and wiccas, Stephen King, and so on.

We liked that *Nightmare* was still creeping them out in the prairieland and hadn't really virus'd into the big city, because when it did, it would surely teach the urbanites a thing or two about nightsweats.

Nightmare would be the last movie that friend saw. He was a doctor and never got time to see movies anyhow. He overdosed not too much later. We cleaned out his dorm room at the hospital (half-eaten burgers, blood on discarded sheets from where he'd variously stuck himself over the past months) and it looked like the four walls had done a bit of the old Cravenesque rotation-splatter. There you have it.

Of course, I told Paul Bartel how much I dug the movie and Paul asked Wes to dinner, and Wes read a script I wrote called *They Sleep by Night* and wanted to know if I would work on *Beetlejuice*, but that fell apart because the powers-that-be thought Wes too fucking creepy for the fantasia they had in mind. So we wound up having dinner with Bob Shaye at the old West Beach and writing *Nightmare 3: Dream Warriors* instead. (Chuck Russell and Frank Darabont came onboard, but by then Wes and I were done.) Along the way I learned that Mr. Craven flew planes and played classical guitar, his foot propped up on one of those portable gas-pedal scaffolding things the way those classical guitar-playing people do. In short, he was supercivilized and debonair, and mischievous-looking too, in the manner of, say, a professor of medieval languages in Turin or Prague. I became very fond of Wes. I enjoyed the insect winglike whir of his mind sorting and cataloging; the sober intake of breath as he delicately regurgitated something random and vile for those in proximity to be appalled by. Like the time after a night of gambling in Quito. We flew in a small plane to the Galapagos Islands and Wes stared through the fogged, blistery window toward the prop and said, "Something's wrong. I'm a pilot: I know."

A friend was recently hospitalized with a brain tumor. They went in through the sinus and got seventy-five percent before drilling through the skull for the rest. During recovery, he had a dream. "I dreamed," he said, "that they wanted to know if I would be Chairman of the Disembodied." I asked, "What did you tell them?" "That I would," he said—and here came the gorgeous reason—"because I have some time on my hands."

When Wes was a callow nineteen-year-old college boy, he got the measles. He was in the infirmary with a fever. In the middle of the night, getting up to pee, he couldn't feel his legs. Within a few hours, the kid was in ICU with paralysis of unknown etiology creeping up waist to belly, belly to nipple, nipple to sternum—a quicksand of flesh. In the morning, when the fever decamped, the paralysis remained. They called it some kind of myelitis, then revised that to a rarer thing: Guillain-Barré syndrome. Wes lay in hospital six months. He could move everything from the armpits up; no movement or feeling any place else. One day he saw something move across the bottom of the bed and was startled to discover—Oliver Sacksian epiphany—that it was a foot, and the foot was his own. It took years getting back to normal and I wonder: can it be this weird, dreamy time (time on his hands), body in revolt, dead to impulse and command, massaged and turned each day by bored vocational nurses so bedsores wouldn't bloom—could this be the root of the shockmeister's obsession with body-death and escape through dream portals?

BRUCE WAGNER
Born 1954
Madison, Wisconsin

*Scenes from the Class
Struggle in Beverly Hills*
1989 (screenplay)
Force Majeure 1991
Tensegrity 1993
(director of volumes
one, two, three; video
series based on Carlos
Castaneda's works)
Wild Palms 1993
(creator)
I'm Losing You 1996
(film based on novel
1998; screenwriter and
director)
*A Nightmare on Elm
Street 3: Dream Warriors*
1998 (co-screenwriter
with Chuck Russell,
Wes Craven, and Frank
Darabont)

With apologies to my de-tumored friend, I would like to install Mr. Craven—at least for the duration of this essay and the warmth of feeling it has elicited—as Honorable Chairperson Pro Tem of the Disembodied; I furthermore wish to assure said friend his duties will not be usurped in any way, for the man who penned the following (*The Hills Have Eyes*) is a true gentleman, and gentle soul:

"I'll see the wind blow your dried up seed away! I'll eat the heart of your stinking memory! I'll eat the brains of your kid's kids! I'm *in*—you're *out!*"

Salud! ◆

ON CARL
FRANKLIN

Carl Franklin, because he is African American, is expected to use his films to tell us about race in America. We expect his films, like those of most other African American directors, to be about race. But they aren't. When you find yourself swimming in the sea out of sight of land, unless you're learning navigation or locked into some kind of weird, aquaphobic denial, you don't discuss water much. You just keep on stroking. In America, the sea we all swim in is race, and we've been out of sight of land for centuries. It's a defining fact of our shared existence. Most of us understand that and, therefore, racists and perhaps intellectuals aside, we tend to just keep stroking. The others discuss the water and, mouths open, risk drowning.

Carl Franklin knows this in his bones, and consequently the characters in his films know it, too. It's what makes them, on the subject of race, utterly believable. They, like the rest of us Americans, like the whole long painful history of the country itself, are contextualized by race, and therefore his films are not, on the one hand, about race, nor do they, on the other, pretend that, unlike the sea, it won't kill us. It's just there, friend, like it or not, and regardless of how it shapes our story, which it surely does, as the sea shapes the swimmer's, it's not the story itself.

I can think of no other director whose films present the fact of race in American life as an inescapable matter of fact, showing it to us straight, without apology or defense, not sentimentalized, not sensationalized, but merely and inescapably there, a ground-level reality in all Americans' lives, whether they like it or not. This is not news, of course, especially to black Americans, but it remains news to most whites, which may account for some of the popular resistance to his films. White and black audiences alike are used to black film directors functioning as message-boys or -girls who bring us news that we already know—that racism is bad, for instance, and that it's a habit of mind possessed mainly by bad white people, people who we ourselves, whatever our skin color, most assuredly are not. And the further, equally familiar news, that black people, if they are bad, are so because of racial oppression. This simplistic morality is what informs practically every movie in the history of American cinema that has allowed onto the screen the mere fact of race. And it's why so few of the black

CARL FRANKLIN
Born 1949
Richmond, California

Nowhere to Run 1989
Full Fathom Five 1990
One False Move 1992
*Devil in a Blue Dress** 1995
One True Thing 1998
Rule of the Bone (based on the novel by Russell Banks) 1999

* also screenwriter

> **In rejecting that tired, simplistic morality, Franklin has made it possible for actors (Denzel Washington and Don Cheadle in *Devil in a Blue Dress,* for example, and Michael Beach and Cynda Williams in *One False Move,* and the entire ensemble cast of *Laurel Avenue)* to become characters, not abstractions, people, not black people, so that they are loved and hated, admired and feared, for their own sake, not ours, and remembered for the role they play in the *film's* story, not the role they play in ours.**

characters in films, even those played by great actors like Poitier and Belafonte and Robeson, are remembered as actual characters; instead, they're usually remembered as abstract ideas or principles in one of our culture's favorite morality plays.

In rejecting that tired, simplistic morality, Franklin has made it possible for actors (Denzel Washington and Don Cheadle in *Devil in a Blue Dress,* for example, and Michael Beach and Cynda Williams in *One False Move,* and the entire ensemble cast of *Laurel Avenue)* to become characters, not abstractions, people, not black people, so that they are loved and hated, admired and feared, for their own sake, not ours, and remembered for the role they play in the *film's* story, not the role they play in ours. Actors, especially black actors, must love working with Franklin. They're allowed to play real human beings for once, freed by the director to become characters who are unique and memorable and moving for their own sake, for each man's or woman's own private, home-grown brand of humanity. That Franklin, before he was a director, worked for years as an actor is surely not incidental to his understanding of character in film. When you meet him, you recognize his broad, handsome face from having seen it so often on television in the eighties, Captain Crane in *The A-Team* and roles in *McClain's Law, Fantastic Journey,* and *Caribe.* He also worked widely and successfully in theater, Shakespeare at Lincoln Center in New York and at the Arena Stage in Washington, D.C.

So, no, Carl Franklin is nobody's message-boy. He's more like the great jazz musicians of the 1950s, as politically incorrect as a Miles Davis or a Charles Mingus—truth tellers and, before all else, artists. Thus he's not at all didactic, nor is he locked into any weird kind of denial about the harder facts of life. He's a storyteller, one of the purest storytellers we have in film, and in terms of how his films go about providing his modern American audience with catharsis, he's downright Aristotelian. His characters and the situations they get into and the tough, slowly closing resolutions he provides to those situations evoke in us a wave of fear and pity, not for ourselves, not even for someone necessarily like us, but for all us poor, forked creatures alike. His films, by concentrating on the individual, make the particular universal.

Easy Rawlins in *Devil in a Blue Dress* has a quotidian life like no other film noir hero—a modest house, a mortgage, a job on the line that he's just lost. He's home from the War, and all he wants is what every American wants, a little piece of the pie to call his own and maybe somebody to share it with. He's no Chandleresque Galahad, no principal of stoical, existential virtue operating in a fallen world. He's just a guy trying to get by, like the rest of us.

RUSSELL BANKS
Born 1940
Newton, Massachusetts
(raised in New
Hampshire)

Continental Drift 1985
Success Stories 1987
Affliction 1989
The Sweet Hereafter
1991
Rule of the Bone 1995
(film directed by Carl
Franklin)
Cloudsplitter 1998

The young woman, Fantasia, in *One False Move,* after a ragged start in rural Arkansas, like so many pretty young Americans, has changed her name and lit out for the Great White Way. But she's fallen in with bad company, a couple of coke-stealing killers, and now all she wants is to get back home, home to her Mama and her baby, there to deal properly with the man who done her wrong. Just as *Devil in a Blue Dress* borrows the genre conventions of film noir and fills them with real human beings instead of stereotypes, *One False Move,* in form and structure, is a B-thriller that happens to be about recognizable people, folks who might well be living next door, making too much noise at a party.

This may be Carl Franklin's essential genius, the ability to take old and seemingly used-up genres and exploit their narrative efficiency without resorting to stereotypes or clichéd abstractions for his characters. It makes his films at once instantly familiar (they go down easy) and marvelously surprising, just like real people. His brilliant three-hour HBO film, *Laurel Avenue,* works a similar magic, this time with the multigenerational family soap opera. It wholly reinvents the genre that it springs from and at the same time lets us see why and how it worked so long so effectively and for so many people.

The best artists, whether they're novelists, painters, musicians, or filmmakers, all do it—they begin with the tried-and-true popular forms, recognizing and exploiting the swift effect that a popular form derives from simplicity, directness, and power of archetype and myth, and they bend that form around content that is as believable to us as our daily lives. Cervantes worked from medieval romance, Dickens from the serialized potboiler, Armstrong and Ellington from the blues. All the best artists take the forms of popular fantasy and utilize them instead to imagine our lives freshly, to reveal rather than conceal the truth of the world we live in daily and die of every night. ◆

ON ROB
REINER

WILLIAM GOLDMAN

"I don't think you want to meet with Rob Reiner," my late and very great agent, Evarts Ziegler said to me. "I do not believe it wise for you to do so."

Because?

"I don't think he can make it happen. Period."

The "it" was *The Princess Bride,* my favorite of all the things I've written. The year was 1985 and the project was already a dozen years old. It had almost gone into production so many times before. Once, a powerful studio head who genuinely wanted to make the movie met with me in New York on a Friday, we pledged our undying love, and he was fired that weekend. Once, a small studio that was going to make the movie went into bankruptcy before we even got into production.

What's so special about Rob is this: he can out-stubborn anybody.

Somehow the project had become jinxed—I despaired of its ever getting made. And Reiner, at this point, did not seem like anybody's lucky charm. He was still known primarily as "Meathead," that being the character he played in the famous T.V. success of the seventies, *All in the Family.* He'd directed but one flick, *This Is Spinal Tap*—which was thought of by the Powers Out There as being a not-untalented flop. Today, of course, it's an acclaimed cult film and is generally considered one of the two or three major debut films of the eighties. But in 1985, few foresaw that. Reiner had just finished his second feature, *The Sure Thing,* which he had come east to sneak preview, when we met.

He arrived at my New York apartment with his friend and producer, Andy Scheinman, and we talked. My first memory of Rob was that he was big. (Most movie people—not just action stars, are waaaaaay smaller than you think.) And passionate about many things, among them sports. So am I, and as I remember, that's mainly what we talked about. (Before all script meetings we still discuss the combat of the preceding night for as long as we can, then regretfully bleed into talk of the screenplay.) It was all very pleasant, the meeting, but I remembered Zig's admonition.

ROB REINER
Born 1945
Bronx, New York

*This Is Spinal Tap***
1984
The Sure Thing 1985
Stand by Me 1986
The Princess Bride 1987
(based on the novel by
William Goldman, who
also wrote the screenplay)
When Harry Met Sally . . .
1989
Misery 1990
A Few Good Men 1992
North 1994
The American President
1995
Ghosts of Mississippi
1996

** also co-screenwriter

Plus, I had not seen Reiner's work yet. When I saw *The Sure Thing* I thought it was nice enough. I then saw *This Is Spinal Tap* and knew, before it was over, Rob was a man I would happily follow into battle.

What's so special about Rob is this: he can out-stubborn anybody.

When we did *Misery*, he was convinced that what became the Kathy Bates part should be played by an unknown, because the character she plays, Annie Wilkes, is herself an unknown—this whacko murdering nurse who hibernates by herself in a house in a sparsely populated part of Colorado. And he was just as convinced that the Jimmy Caan part should be played by a star, because that character, Paul Sheldon, was a famous novelist.

When Kathy Bates was first mentioned to him, Rob said this: "Oh good. She's great. We'll use her." That was it. Done. He met with other stars and could have had almost any actress in Hollywood—it was clearly not a terrible role—but all out of politeness.

When he finally met with Kathy, what happened was this: he brought her in and they talked—*for less than a minute*—before he offered her the part. She was somewhat taken aback because not only had she never played the lead in a Hollywood film, this was the lead in essentially a two-character story based on Stephen King's number-one best-selling novel.

> Anyway, he offers it to her.
> And, now a pause.
> Rob just sits there.
> "I've got the part?"
> Rob nods.
> "The Annie part? I'm playing Annie?"
> "Yup."
> "And it's all set and everything?"
> "Definitely set," Rob tells her.
> There is a silence before Kathy said it: "Can I tell my mother?"

◆

Casting the male lead was where the stubbornness kicked in. When the rejections began.

What rejections? How about these? (Billing alphabetical, of course.) Beatty and the three Ds: De Niro, Douglas, and Dreyfuss; and let's not forget the three Hs: Hackman, Hoffman, and Hurt; as well as Harrison

Ford, Kevin Kline, and Robert Redford. We are talking six months of ego-rattling turndowns. And, amazingly, not once did he waiver, ask for changes, or lose confidence. Sooner or later I knew it was all going to be the script's fault.

Never happened. Not to me certainly. In thirty years of movie work, I've never experienced anything like it.

WILLIAM GOLDMAN
Born 1931
Chicago, Illinois

The Temple of Gold 1956
Soldier in the Rain 1963
Boys and Girls Together 1964
Harper 1966 (screenplay; based on the novel *The Moving Target* by Ross MacDonald)
No Way to Treat a Lady 1968
Butch Cassidy and the Sundance Kid 1969 (screenplay) Academy Award for Best Writing, Story, and Screenplay Based on Material Not Previously Published or Produced
The Great Waldo Pepper 1975 (screenplay)
All the President's Men 1976 (screenplay; based on the book by Bob Woodward and Carl Bernstein) Academy Award for Best Adapted Screenplay
Marathon Man 1976 (novel and screenplay; film directed by John Schlesinger)
A Bridge Too Far 1977 (screenplay)
Magic 1978 (novel and screenplay)
Tinsel 1979
Control 1982
The Season: A Candid Look at Broadway 1984
The Princess Bride 1987 (novel and screenplay; film directed by Rob Reiner)
Heat 1987
Wait Till Next Year 1988 (co-author Mike Lupica)
Adventures in the Screen Trade 1989
Misery 1990 (screenplay; based on the novel by Stephen King; film directed by Rob Reiner)
Hype and Glory 1991
Year of the Comet 1992 (screenplay)
Chaplin 1992 (co-screenwriter)
Maverick 1994 (screenplay; film directed by Richard Donner)
The Ghost and the Darkness 1996 (screenplay)
Absolute Power 1997 (screenplay)

But he had been stubborn on *The Princess Bride,* too. Casting Fezzik, the strongest man of the world, was not that easy. We met with all kinds of big people. Most of them weren't big enough. Of course, some guys were *huge,* but not giants. Some guys were giants, but skinny. "I don't want to put my giant in a costume to make him look big," Rob said. "I want someone, when you meet him, you say, 'Oh yeah, right, of course, he's the strongest man in the world.'"

Rob finally flew to Paris to meet André the Giant. He auditioned André in a hotel room. Could not understand one *syllable*—André's voice was very deep, his French accent very thick. Mattered not. Rob had his giant. He offered him the part, taped André's role for him, accent and all, and sent it off to him so he could learn to say it in English while he was on the road battling the Hulk Hogans of the world.

◆

It is now over fifteen years since *This Is Spinal Tap* and Rob is presently preparing his eleventh film. More and more, he is coming to remind me of the directors of my growing-up years, guys who started, some of them, even before there was sound and they were still hanging tough in the fifties. They were not dainty, my early heroes, and sure, they made some stinkers.

But they had more than their share of glories, too. Between 1945 and 1955, Ford, Hawks, Hitchcock, Huston, Kazan, Stevens, Wilder, and Wyler directed *sixty-six* movies. Not many directors today have that kind of record. Together with the firm knowledge that what matters is not this week's wonder, but your body of work.

Rob's like that. He can make it happen.

Period. ◆

ON AMY HECKERLING

I am waiting for Amy Heckerling at Hugo's restaurant on Sunset Strip. Frankly, I have no idea who I am waiting for, or rather exactly who is going to be walking in. I'm a little bit frightened that some Hollywood babe, roughly forty or late thirtysomething, wearing blue jeans and a two-thousand-dollar T-shirt will be joining me for lunch. I know whoever it is I'm waiting for has had three "Boffo at the B.O." genuine Hollywood hits. Obviously she must know how to play the game.

Into Hugo's comes a petite women in a jumper and clogs. It's your basic outfit I wore to high school thirty years ago and would still wear if only my feet weren't flat and my arms weren't quite so undefined. My lunch date has brown curly hair, no makeup, and could much more be mistaken for a student than most Hollywood babes who make thirty times the effort.

Amy Heckerling is one of those women you meet and think, I already know this person. She was my best friend who I called after the horrible date with the guy who kept turning around during dinner to look at other women and took me home early. She was also the first person I called after reading *Anna Karenina,* and she was the one who made me feel better about screaming at my mother. And the friendship wasn't just about her being smart, sympathetic, all that good girl stuff. Friends like Amy Heckerling not only can see the humor in the situation but, more important, how it fits into the bigger picture. These kind of girlfriends make first-class filmmakers.

AMY HECKERLING
Born 1954
Bronx, New York

Fast Times at Ridgemont High 1982

Johnny Dangerously 1984

National Lampoon's European Vacation 1985

Look Who's Talking* 1989

Look Who's Talking Too** 1990

Clueless* 1995

* also screenwriter
** also co-screenwriter

The films of Amy Heckerling have a musical energy. The opening sequence of *Look Who's Talking,* a sperm swimming upstream to the ovaries while the Beach Boys sing "I Get Around" is the *Hello, Dolly!* of reproductive musical numbers. Unlike films crammed with the greatest hits of all times with a clear eye toward platinum soundtrack sales, music is integral to a Heckerling film. The characters at *Ridgemont High,* and later the Beverly Hills High School of *Clueless,* define their lives by their music. They each have their own inner underscoring.

Are Amy Heckerling's films clearly those of a woman director? Is there a difference between the films of a male and female director? That's a question pretty much answered by that *Look Who's Talking* title sequence.

But it would be wonderful to hear the discussion the senior English class in *Clueless* has on the topic. I'm sure Alicia Silverstone as well as Cher could deliver an exegesis on the virtues of a Heckerling production of *Gunga Din*. Maybe it's gender, but it could also be magic that an Amy Heckerling film seems to be peopled with female characters who seem familiar. Just like meeting the director, we recognize them, and genuinely like them right away. Kirstie Alley, the single mother accountant in *Look Who's Talking*, Alicia Silverstone, the spoiled rich girl who is secretly sensitive—neither are victims, nor role models of the week. They're just smart, stupid, generous, narcissistic, funny, lonely, simple, and complicated just like the rest of us.

WENDY WASSERSTEIN
Born 1950
Brooklyn, New York

Uncommon Women and Others 1978 (play)

The Sorrows of Gin 1979 (play based on a short story by John Cheever)

Isn't It Romantic 1985 (play)

The Heidi Chronicles 1989 (play)

Bachelor Girls 1990

The Sisters Rosensweig 1993 (play)

Pamela's First Musical 1996

An American Daughter 1997

The Object of My Affection 1998 (screenplay; based on the novel by Stephen MacCauley)

The enormously successful *Clueless* is roughly based on Jane Austen's *Emma*. Ms. Austen is the hottest Hollywood source material since Edith Wharton. Of course, the Bröntes are making a comeback, and Dickens and Tolstoy can't be far behind. But there's more in common between Heckerling and her adaptee than just plotline. The Misses Austen and Heckerling are both keen social observers. They know absolutely cold the language and the mores of their societies, from fashion to marital eligibility. Their wit is sharp, not bloody, pointed, or wildly farcical but always on target, bull's-eyes. Every detail is exact and without brittle malice. Almost impossible to do.

Amy asks me at lunch if I mind if she orders "girl food." In Hollywood that translates into spinach, hard-boiled eggs, mushrooms, no oil, no butter, no salt. We chat about her ten-year-old daughter, her current boyfriend, the insanity of the movie business, and how Alicia Silverstone is getting calls to wear, as a great favor, every sample designer suit in the world, and Amy is yet to be offered a free perfume.

Immediately I want to say that the truly great thing about meeting her, and seeing an Amy Heckerling film, is that designers don't ask her to show up in their suits. Neither the director nor her films are self-serving. Quite the opposite, instead of "An Amy Heckerling film," we focus on Bruce Willis as that ubiquitous chatty baby, and now the Valentino *Clueless* collection of clothing with the *Clueless* girl in mind. Amy Heckerling is one of those truly rare filmmakers, who calls attention to the work and not to herself. Her films are beautifully structured, impeccable in characterization, funny, bright, true, and immensely popular—just like Jane Austen. I wonder what "girl food" meant to Jane. I wonder what "as if" would mean to her. ◆

ON GUS
VAN SANT

G us Van Sant is an independent filmmaker in a world where "independent" means more script than special effect, more story than star.

Van Sant is a fine storyteller, but in public he's quiet. A watcher. A listener. At home in the river town of Portland, Oregon, he's unassuming, politely eccentric, disinclined to wilderness hikes. He prefers sidewalks. His fine house on the hill is well kept, the grounds groomed, but the rooms inside are hectic with lights, cameras, props, screens, musical instruments, souvenirs, electronic mazes—whatever he's working on at the moment, and he is always working. One visitor roamed the entire house without being able to figure out where he sleeps. The neighbors have been heard to mutter about odd comings and goings, an occasional horse on the lawn or punk band in the garage, and trashy vehicles parked out front. The last car I saw Van Sant driving was a rumbling old Detroit monster with a dragging muffler—maybe the sixties Cadillac the gang drove in *Drugstore Cowboy*.

The waiters and bartenders here know him even when he's disguised by ragged sweaters, a battered flasher's raincoat and a three-day beard as scruffy as any of his characters. He trails around like that for weeks sometimes. The locals say, "Gus has gone native." The idlers debate whether he's submersing himself in the lives of his characters or trying for invisibility among the roving detritus of the pavements. But he doesn't explain and nobody asks.

He's a hometown hero, of course. The tuxedo set shows him off to visiting dignitaries as a municipal asset, like a scenic view or a winning NBA team. If the civic boosters wish he'd stop depicting their town as a sleaze-pit, they won't mention it to him. He's a nice guy, after all, a ready supporter for good causes. His film openings are AIDS benefits. He never forgets a friend, they say, and his friends range from chic to seedy. He leans in the shadows at gritty club concerts, tavern readings, and alley art shows. He sips counter coffee at the greasy spoon.

He spent his adolescence here as a child of privilege—expensive if unconventional private schools, discreet money, the luxury of choice and

Van Sant's work is as recognizable by the stories he chooses as by the way he tells them. They are tales of the people Mama warned us about. They are love stories in which love is a power source and a dangerous vulnerability. They are dissections of familial units in which the family is a temporary construct—a gang, maybe, or a work crew—but the dynamics of shifting and unequal power reflect all such relationships, blooded and otherwise.

wide horizons. As a kid he was fascinated by Andy Warhol and even now interviewers claim to note a resemblance—enhanced, probably, by his laconic tendencies during interviews. And he experiments constantly.

His paintings hang in hill mansions, four-star hotels, and the occasional taco house up and down the West Coast. Shows of his photographic portraits draw crowds to see the local bouncers, gutter poets, winos, and other hipsters made mythic. He plays his own songs on piano and guitar. For a while he led a local rock band called "Destroy All Blondes." Every year for his birthday he makes a short film in a kind of ongoing cinematic diary. He makes music videos and writes fiction as well as most of his own movie scripts.

Most writers, like painters, are accustomed to complete control over their own work. And Van Sant started life as a painter—in sole command of the image. He studied painting at the Rhode Island School of Design, and afterward, turning to the necessarily cooperative art of film, he still wanted to control everything.

During his brief Hollywood apprenticeship, and a stint on Madison Avenue producing commercials, he made his own short films with five-hundred-dollar budgets. His black-and-white adaptation of William Burrough's story, *The Discipline of D.E.*, is delivered in the trademark deadpan of Van Sant's humor. He wrote, directed, and paid for an unshown comedy titled *Alice in Hollywood* before he turned thirty.

With twenty thousand dollars he'd saved, and his script from a novella by poet Walt Curtis, Van Sant returned to Portland. He put together a crew of three, and a cast consisting of one stage actor, two local teens, and a clutch of friends and street dwellers, to make his second feature, the dark and emotionally complex *Mala Noche*. Every shot was predesigned in a huge Hitchcockian storyboard, a miracle of efficiency. Still, shooting in alleys and flophouses with the tiny crew, he had the flexibility to snatch the luck of the moment—a colorful citizen stopped on the street for a ten-second interview, a real cop car parked long enough for the stars to stroll past as the camera rolled.

Mala Noche won the Los Angeles Film Critics Association Award for Independent/Experimental Film or Video in 1987, and launched Van Sant at a time when the innovative thrift of independent filmmakers was attracting attention from a Hollywood industry gagging on big-budget machinery. As his own budgets and crews grew, Van Sant's calm determination to retain control of the image and the story must have required endless guerrilla warfare. The proof of his success is in his unmistakeable signature in every frame of his work.

GUS VAN SANT JR.
Born 1952
Louisville, Kentucky

*Mala Noche** 1985
*Drugstore Cowboy*** 1989
*My Own Private Idaho** 1991
*Even Cowgirls Get the Blues** 1993 (based on the novel by Tom Robbins)
To Die For 1995
Good Will Hunting 1997
Psycho 1998

* also screenwriter
** also co-screenwriter

The eighties were also a decade in which major strides in homosexual rights swept the nation, and as far as I know, Gus Van Sant was the first American film director to be openly acknowledged as gay. There were no explosions. It was no big deal, he told me, "It was simply understood." But growing up as an outsider in the straight world may go far to explain this rich kid's fascination with society's rejects.

Van Sant's work is as recognizable by the stories he chooses as by the way he tells them. They are tales of the people Mama warned us about. They are love stories in which love is a power source and a dangerous vulnerability. They are dissections of familial units in which the family is a temporary construct—a gang, maybe, or a work crew—but the dynamics of shifting and unequal power reflect all such relationships, blooded and otherwise.

His best work deals with the intense lives of the despised denizens at the grubby end of the social food chain. These are private stories driven by the passions of small people who are generally considered barely tolerable, much less likeable. The junkie drug thief, the seducer of desperate illegal immigrants, the homeless boy hookers, the losers, the lost, the madly dreaming mediocrities, all take on fleshly dimensions under Van Sant's tenderly relentless eye.

These low-life worlds are both exotic and normal, existing below the surface in every city. Their emanations bubble up in minor headlines, or in statistics as suggestive and faceless as a whiff of clogged drains. The sustained shock of Van Sant's depictions is his nonjudgmental observation of what is usually labeled as criminal, immoral, exploitative, and pathetic. The politics are distinct but unobtrusive. The point of view is the hustler's of the hustle, the techniques of the scam and the rip-off are meticulously defined. Tools, wardrobes, and mannerisms are lovingly observed.

The inevitable cultural clash of predator and prey, exploiter and victim, inspired and inspirer, is seldom simple in a Van Sant film. These relations are as complicated as life.

Van Sant has the gift of the bifurcated eye that sees his primary characters from the inside and the story from the outside. The characters speak directly to the camera in classic asides, or their jerky home movies let us see through their eyes. At other times we are high above them, seeing them small. This combination of dispassionate distance and empathic recognition produces an inextricable tangling of tragedy and comedy. His films are funny and scary at the same time. No miserable moment is untinged by the ridiculous. Every hilarity has its shadow.

And Van Sant lures us to sympathy and even affection for his unlikely characters, not despite their failings but because of them. Their identity is defined by passion amounting to obsession. They are revealed by their yearnings, by what they love, and how their love destroys them.

The scripts Van Sant writes or chooses combine with his supportive direction to give actors a chance to be reborn—to create their own dimensions.

Matt Dillon in *Drugstore Cowboy,* River Phoenix in *My Own Private Idaho,* Joaquin Phoenix in *To Die For,* and Matt Damon and Robin Williams in *Good Will Hunting* all plunge into the dark and emerge beautiful in the light of their own emotions. They are knowing victims, unsurprised by a fate they always expected.

Good Will Hunting was nominated for nine Academy Awards including Best Picture and Best Director. The 1997 film won Oscars for Best Original Screenplay and Best Supporting Actor. When Robin Williams accepted his Oscar he thanked Gus Van Sant, "For being so subtle you were almost subliminal."

These roles in these stories are subtle and irresistibly complex, as intricate and chaotic as reality, or the art of a fine storyteller. ◆

ON KENNETH
BRANAGH

The first time I met Kenneth Branagh was backstage at the Dorothy Chandler Pavilion in Los Angeles. He was in town with his Renaissance Theater Company starring in and directing productions of *A Midsummer Night's Dream* and *King Lear*. After catching a performance of the former, my wife and I went backstage to meet Branagh. The reason: a week earlier, he had signed on to direct and star in a script I had written called *Dead Again,* and I was curious to find out, well, why?

His only other film credit at that point was *Henry V* and I couldn't help but wonder why the guy would want to direct a loopy, film noir thriller like mine after doing, of all things, *Shakespeare*. Upon meeting him, however, the answer became abundantly clear: Kenneth Branagh wants to do *everything*.

Having already performed in a dozen plays for the RSC; written and starred in his own play, *Public Enemy;* started his own theater company (which counted, among others, the Prince of Wales as a patron); he had just published his autobiography.

And the guy wasn't yet thirty years old.

KENNETH BRANAGH
Born 1960
Belfast, Northern Ireland

*Henry V** 1989
Dead Again 1991
(screenplay by Scott Frank)
Peter's Friends 1992
*Much Ado About Nothing** 1992
Mary Shelley's Frankenstein 1994
*A Midwinter's Tale** 1995
*Hamlet** 1996

* also screenwriter

Interestingly enough, the thing that surprises most people when they meet Ken is how funny he is. Given his pedigree and his work in the *Theatuh,* I think people expect this dour stiff. Yet, instead, what they get is this tremendously self-effacing guy with a knife-edge wit as well as a brilliant mimic who can instantly do *anybody,* including you.

When you think about it, this playfulness comes through on film as well. As a director, Branagh always brings a winking, "Let's-have-fun" sensibility to his work. It's as if he imbues all that he does with a filmic smile, a shit-eating grin that makes us wonder, he's kidding, right?

After all, this is the man who remade *Henry V* into a rollicking party of a film that made The Bard a lot more fun than my tenth-grade English lit teacher ever did. And without the *Cliffs Notes.* In that film, it seemed

everyone's having fun being serious. When Branagh, as the young king, implores his troops with, "Once more unto the breach," he could just as easily be saying, "Let's boogie!" Well, all right, to me anyway. The point is, he's having a good time.

Working with Branagh, I found that he knows exactly what he wants without being such a perfectionist (read: overly cautious) that he takes all

SCOTT FRANK
Born 1960
Fort Walton Beach, Florida

Little Man Tate 1991
(screenplay)
Dead Again 1991
(screenplay; film directed by Kenneth Branagh)
Malice 1993
(co-screenwriter)
Get Shorty 1995
(screenplay; based on the novel by Elmore Leonard)
Heaven's Prisoners 1996
(co-screenwriter; based on the novel by James Lee Burke)
Out of Sight 1998
(screenplay; based on the novel by Elmore Leonard)

of the edge and energy out of his work. Yes, things have to make sense, but in many of our script discussions, the phrase "Movie Magic" became the solution to a lot of problems. In other words, to Branagh's thinking—it's just a movie. God bless him.

While he does like to carefully, and in great detail, plan ahead, he also thrives on the spontaneity and verve that come from working quickly and making decisions on the fly. *Go go go.* That's his mantra. He's a whirling dervish who likes to blow through each of his beloved projects with his arms out, spinning, grabbing hold of all that he can, while he can. For Branagh, spending too much time in one place is just too damn depressing. As with a shark, standing still is death for him. His body may have been ensconced in the editing room doing last-minute cutting on *Dead Again,* but his head was already into *Peter's Friends* and *Much Ado About Nothing* as well as the dozens of other offers that were coming his way daily.

But by far, for me, the most astonishing thing about our working relationship was that Ken actually cared about what I had to say. On the set of *Dead Again,* it was not unusual for him to come up to me after five or six takes and ask if there was anything else that I thought he might try.

Needless to say, the first time this happened, I looked at him like he had an ear growing out of his forehead. I was baffled. After all, in the best of situations, the writer has a voice but no say in Hollywood. In other words, they'll listen to you, but they certainly are under no obligation to take you seriously. Ken was different. Ken didn't know any better. Coming from the theater, he was trained to make the words on the page work as they were; as opposed to the way it works in Hollywood, where the words are mere suggestions for actors and directors and anyone else to take and run with as they wish.

In today's climate, where so many of our once great filmmakers are paralyzed by fear of failure to try new things, to stretch, it's refreshing to watch someone work without a net, unafraid to evolve and figure it all out right in front of us. And we don't mind watching Ken Branagh take risks, because he's having such a jolly good time doing it, that we are, too.

So here's to a lot more "Movie Magic" from the man who can't stop moving; the *whirling dervish* who knows what he wants, and knows too that sooner or later he's going to get it. ◆

ON JOHN WOO

Woo.

JOHN WOO
Born 1946
Guangzhou, Canton,
South China

The Young Dragons 1973
The Dragon Tamers 1974
Countdown in Kung Fu 1975
Princess Chang Ping 1975
Money Crazy 1977
Follow the Star 1977
Hello, Late Homecomers 1978
*Last Hurrah for Chivalry** 1978
From Riches to Rags 1979
To Hell with the Devil 1980
Laughing Times 1981
Plain Jane to the Rescue 1982
The Time You Need a Friend 1984
Run Tiger Run 1985
*A Better Tomorrow** 1986
The Sunset Warrior
(Heroes Shed No Tears) 1986
*A Better Tomorrow II*** 1987
Just Heroes 1987
*The Killer** 1989
*A Bullet in the Head*** 1990
*Once a Thief*** 1991
*Hard-Boiled*** 1992
Hard Target 1993
Broken Arrow 1996
Face/Off 1997

* also screenwriter
** also co-screenwriter

Go on. Get it out of your system. Think everything you're going to think when you hear the name John Woo; everything you're going to conjure up about his movies: action, violence, stunt men bloodied up like they got their squibs at a discount. All that is what's likely to pop into your brain box, but if all that is what you think when you think Woo, then you literally don't know what you're missing. The action, the violence—that's the superficial. The stunts are Woo 101.

The thing about him—the thing about this guy who rapid-fired *The Killer*, *Hard-Boiled*, and *A Bullet in the Head* over from HK and fed the Hollywood machine with *Broken Arrow* and *Face/Off*—is that dealing in the superficial gets you nowhere when you're trying to understand the man and his films. Both the man and his films are way too incongruous for instant assessment—puzzle boxes held together by odd, but somehow interlocking pieces. Woo's films are vicious, but profound. Inhumanly bloody, but richly humane stories of hope and redemption. Woo and his films are heavy on the deep.

At first off it seems kinda weird that a guy who was raised a devout Lutheran, to the point he was *this* close to becoming minister, would end up turning out hyperfierce pix like *A Better Tomorrow* parts I and II and *Heroes Shed No Tears*.

At first it seems that way, but more than likely it's this upbringing, this spiritual side of Woo, that separates him from the rest of the Hollywood action pack who turn out workmanlike films on a workmanlike basis. Woo's films are violent, yeah, but violent to a point of metaviolence.

Sounds crazy, but what you have to dig is that there are two sides of the jigger used to make a Woo film. One is the Woo that Woo is known

for—the running gun battles and the micromanaged set pieces. And it's both as easy as it is tempting to junkie-riff on his beautifully choreographed ballets of flying bodies with the thousand flesh-tearing, bone-cracking bullets that are their unseen partners. But beyond all that, the stunts and the shooting, Woo's other gift, his greater gift, is his ability to express the subtler, yet harsher emotional violence that accompanies a soul corrupted, a life in turmoil.

JOHN RIDLEY
Born 1965
Milwaukee, Wisconsin

Cold Around the Heart
1996 (screenwriter and
director)

U Turn 1997 (screenplay
based on his novel *Stray
Dogs;* film directed by
Oliver Stone)

Love Is a Racket 1998

*Everybody Smokes in
Hell* 1999

Three Kings 1999
(screenplay; film directed
by David Russell)

Dead Game 1999
(screenwriter and
director)

The films themselves are fairly simple in plot. In *The Killer*, a hit man wants the money he's owed for a job. In *Hard-Boiled* a cop wants to take down an arms dealer. *Heroes Shed No Tears* is the story of a mercenary who just wants to get back home.

One-liners all.

Rather, it is the people Woo chooses to populate his films with who are complex. With "fuck-that" regard to standard notions of iconography, he has the audacity to give his audiences conflicted characters who are snared in an intricate web of crisscrossed loyalties, loves, and allegiances, crafted with the same tender lovin' care he gives his action sequences. His good guys aren't necessarily good guys, just the least amoral guys in the show. His bad guys are just as often caught up in a cat's cradle of inner turmoil and confused feelings. It's with this cocktail of tumultuous personalities and naked passion that Woo's special brand of violence can most effectively be served. Not as a fusillade, but typically as one shot fired or one bullet taken in anger, absolution, or heartbreak. An undercover cop forced to kill the crime lord who has become his surrogate father. A mercenary who lives only for money, but who sacrifices his own life for others. A munitions dealer who loses the woman he loves to the war he profits from. At their best, Woo's films are ships of raw emotion driven by a fuel of love, honor, betrayal, and redemption.

This is Woo's metaviolence—operatic moments of high human drama that ultimately resonate at a deeper, more personal level and with greater impact than could ever be delivered from just the barrel of a gun. They are sermons wrapped in eye candy; parables delivered from a pulpit of the visual.

Amen, and preach on.

It's unfortunate that with the texture and tone, the subtleties and richness, some moviegoers are still blissfully okay with the shoal—the shooting and the blood. The action—where Woo is concerned. They'll take what they get, and not look for much else. It's unfortunate that some don't see that beyond what merely flashes across the screen at the speed of a bullet there is so much more substance. It's unfortunate because all that "so much more" is what you need to think when you think John Woo. ◆

RICARDO PIGLIA

ON HECTOR
BABENCO

translation by Anna Stahl

FAR FROM HOME

When I met Hector Babenco, he was finishing *At Play in the Fields of the Lord*. He had spent nearly six months filming in the Amazon and had already been locked up in an editing room for several weeks in San Francisco. There, he was giving form to a film that had the breadth of a *roman fleuve* like those of the nineteenth century.

Babenco always tells the story of an individual at the margins, divided between two worlds, at the outer limits of the law, on the border of society.

The tension and strife surrounding the production of an independent film costing over twenty million dollars, of course, means one experiences being constantly on the edge. Cinema has gotten us used to these battles; there are already various mythical stories of mythical (and extraordinary) films like *At Play in the Fields of the Lord* or like *Apocalypse Now* that are always on the edge of disaster and are accomplished under the kind of conditions that bring their creators to the brink of collapse.

In the midst of a veritable storm of versions, counter-versions, and new renderings of the material, Babenco made a phone call to me, trying first in Princeton, New Jersey, where I had been living at one point, and later in Buenos Aires, where he finally found me.

As also happens with novelists, the best thing one can do when a work is about to be released is to start thinking about what's next. Babenco thought he'd go into the premiere of *At Play in the Fields of the Lord* already involved in another project, and he sought me out to work with him on the screenplay.

He did this, basically, because he had read *Prisión Perpetua (Life in Prison),* a novella I had written that had come out in translation that year in Brazil. The story made reference to the legendary bar, Ambos Mundos ("Both Worlds"), in Mar del Plata (a city on the Atlantic coast of Argentina that in its years of splendor had been a remote replica of Biarritz). Babenco wanted to meet me because he himself had frequented that bar in the early sixties, and he considered it the place where he had begun his apprenticeship.

HECTOR BABENCO
Born 1946
Buenos Aires, Argentina

King of the Night**
1975
*Lúcio Flávio, o Passageiro
da Agonia*** 1977
Pixote** 1981
*Kiss of the Spider
Woman* 1985 Cannes
Film Festival Official
Selection
Ironweed 1987
*At Play in the Fields of
the Lord*** 1991
Foolish Heart** 1998
(co-screenwriter Ricardo
Piglia) Cannes Film
Festival Official Selection

** also co-screenwriter

In "Both Worlds," bohemians and aspiring young artists came together and stayed up nights debating and imagining extraordinary projects and fantastical plans that would allow them to escape the provinces and get to the capital city, and from the capital make the leap to Paris or New York. At the same time, those were the years when a strange transformation was beginning to take place on the intellectual horizon: cinema was no longer merely a magical place where people went to see their hopes and fantasies brought to life; now young people started to dream, directly, of making films themselves.

Those were the years of the explosive theory of "auteur cinema," the years of *Cahiers du Cinema*, of the British *Free Cinema*, the years of Cassavetes' first films, and of the Polish filmmakers of the Lodz School. Becoming a film director became an ambition and a possibility, as in other times it had been the ambition of young creatives to become a painter or a writer. It signified a personal artistic project, difficult but not impossible, one that required talent, determination, a spirit of sacrifice, and, of course, a lot of luck. Babenco (who embodies all of these qualities) is one of the first who was capable of making that dream a reality.

There is something very contemporary about the story of an eighteen-year-old youth who leaves a provincial city on the Argentine coast for Europe, lives a series of vicissitudes until he lands in São Paulo, Brazil, shooting Polaroids by night, and a few years later comes to win international recognition as a cinema director. It seems to me there is an intimate relation between Babenco's work in film and those dark years of searching and uncertainty. There are artists whose work bears no similarity to what we know of their destinies; this is not the case with Hector Babenco, who has made of his personal experience the invisible raw material for his films.

Babenco always tells the story of an individual at the margins, divided between two worlds, at the outer limits of the law, on the border of society. Pixote, Lúcio Flávio, Luis Molina, Francis Phelan, Lewis Moon—these characters are reincarnations of the same person who appears again and again and persists, with variations, in all of his films. The hero has no home; he is a shipwrecked loner who has lost everything, a persecuted soul trying to escape. (In a certain sense all of his films tell the story of a frustrated escape.)

The story takes its point of departure from a tough, testimonial core (the death squads, the street kids, sexual discrimination and political terror, the destruction of nature, barbarism and civilization, the world of the homeless), but the conflict is situated in the hero's own consciousness. Fundamentally, Babenco has a penchant for documentary. That type of

distanced narrative (the invisible camera, the classic frame) defines the
style of all his films, yet that form always meets up with a plot, centered
on a strange character and on his most secret hopes.

It has been said that from its origin, the cinema has defined its two
principal paths as follows: either one makes a documentary (and one is
Lumière) or one makes dreams (and one is Méliès). Babenco, of course,
films dreams as if they were documentaries. Or better put, he films his
personal dreams, his deepest fantasies, as if they were part of the removed,
objective universe of another.

RICARDO PIGLIA
Born 1940
Buenos Aires, Argentina

Nombre Falso (Assumed Name) 1975

Respiración Artificial (Artificial Respiration) 1980

Crítica y Ficción (Criticism and Fiction) 1986

Prisión Perpetua (Life in Prison) 1988

La Ciudad Ausente (The Absent City) 1992

Foolish Heart 1995 (co-screenwriter with director Hector Babenco)

La Sonámbula (Sleepwalker) 1996 (screenplay)

Plata Quemado (Burnt Money) 1997

Babenco's position is defined in the opening of *Pixote:* dressed in white, speaking in uncertain Portuguese, he appears in person and announces the veracity of what we are about to see. The story is a true one, and will be filmed right there, where it happened, and with those very street kids who are its protagonists. That immediacy makes me think about the times during which Babenco made his living taking instant nighttime snapshots with a Polaroid camera in São Paulo. Grasping the immediate, documenting whatever is seen, and being there. Cinema always pursues that extraordinary, fragile instant when time and memory seem to condense into an image.

The scene of "La Pietà" in *Pixote* or Molina's fantasies in *Kiss of the Spider Woman* or the panoramic finale in the jungle in *At Play in the Fields of the Lord* all have something of the familiarity, the nearness, and the fixed quality of dreams.

Babenco tries to distance himself from mere representation and to construct a direct and personal vision. In this sense, his cinema is very near in spirit to certain modern novelists: Camus, Knut Hamsun, Henry Miller, Kerouac, these were his true influences (those very authors and books that were read and discussed around the tables of Ambos Mundos). These heirs to Kafka and Dostoyevsky speak in the first person and tell of their lives. But not their lives as writers, not even their real lives, but their lives as abandoned children, as homosexuals, as delinquents—their lives as vagabonds and expatriates.

Babenco's personal experience reproduces this break from the world of the family. Born in Argentina, he has lived in Europe, resides in Brazil, and films in the United States. He has crossed various borders and various languages. His filmmaking is a line of escape (not all related to Argentine cinema, nor to Brazilian or North American cinema). Babenco is a part of the tradition of the exiles and nomads who so abound in the history of cinema. The artist defines himself as a foreigner: his patria is the furthest one; lost and remote, it only abides in childhood. That is why one of the most intense and most secretly personal moments of Babenco's cinema is the image of the empty room illuminated by the morning light in *Ironweed*. In the world we live in (in the stories we tell) it seems there are only ebbs and flows without borders, only blank spaces. Babenco's work in film captures that emptiness, yet at the same time says that, for all of us, always, there is a place waiting for us, in our memory, a place full of sunlight in our childhood home. Possibly, rather than coming from there, we are going toward it. ◆

CATHERINE TEXIER

ON JEAN-JACQUES ANNAUD

When I think of Jean-Jacques Annaud's films, these are the first images that come to my mind: the bear cub taking swipes at a butterfly in the opening sequence of *The Bear*; the relentless buzzing of insects in the West African village of *Black and White in Color;* the white mosquito nets surrounding the beds set up in the boarding-school courtyard in *The Lover;* the rough mountains bearing down on the medieval monastery in *The Name of the Rose.*

In Annaud's work nature is more than background, it is character. It doesn't just stand there looking beautiful or majestic, it breathes, it sings, it buzzes, it erupts, it growls, it provides the soundtrack.

> **His images are so powerful that sometimes it seems they would rather do without words. They come straight at you, unmediated by what has become typical Hollywood verbiage.**

Most of Annaud's films share these distinctive trademarks: (1) a minimal score (often replaced by sounds of insects, footsteps, leaves rustling, overheard voices); (2) voice-overs, a device that many directors avoid at all costs for fear of appearing too literary and that Annaud employs almost as a musical soundtrack to free his images; and (3) a slow, sometimes solemn pacing that becomes hypnotic and forces you to slow down and sink into the images.

The combination of these three elements—the silence, the slow pace, the occasional voice-over—infuses Annaud's films with an almost Oriental sense of mystery. Annaud is an intensely visual filmmaker. His images are so powerful that sometimes it seems they would rather do without words. They come straight at you, unmediated by what has become typical Hollywood verbiage. It is not that his films are not active. They are. Some of them are action movies in the purest sense of the word. In *Quest for Fire* tribes of Neanderthal men, whose grunts and growls (created by Anthony Burgess) are just barely human, are pitted against each other in a desperate attempt to get hold of the magic fire until they are able to figure out how to kindle a spark from rubbing a stick against a rock. *The Bear* is the story of a bear cub adopted by a grizzly and chased by a band of stupid hunters in the wilds of British Columbia.

But even in Annaud's literary adaptations, *The Lover* (based on Marguerite Duras's autobiographical novel) and *The Name of the Rose* (from Umberto

JEAN-JACQUES ANNAUD
Born 1943
Draveil, France

*Black and White in Color*** 1976 Academy Award for Best Foreign Film
Hothead 1978
Quest for Fire 1981
The Name of the Rose 1986
The Bear 1988
*The Lover*** 1991
*Wings of Courage*** 1994
Seven Years in Tibet 1997

** also co-screenwriter

Eco's best-seller), the words tend to be spare and low-key. The voice-overs are haunting, like that of Jeanne Moreau reading passages of Duras's novel in *The Lover.* Jeanne Moreau's voice, telling the story of the author's first love affair fifty years ago, gives the film a depth of knowledge and nostalgia that it wouldn't have had without it.

But ultimately, the words fade before the power of the images: the pressure of the Chinese man's hand on the girl's hand in the car taking them back to Saigon (*The Lover*) sparking the beginning of their sexual passion; the simian face of the Quasimodo-like monk in *The Name of the Rose* (the same actor, Ron Perlman, plays a Neanderthal man in *Quest for Fire),* which conveys, in one arresting glimpse, how backward and superstitious the world of the medieval church truly is, for all the sophisticated theosophical exchanges between the monks.

Annaud's world is a world of terror and passion, desire and joy, and the most basic and powerful emotions silently emerge from the actors' faces and bodies as if Annaud didn't completely trust words.

At first glance, Jean-Jacques Annaud's later films seem quite disparate from his early French movies. *Black and White in Color* and *Hothead,* for example, are tight, hilarious comedies embedded in the French and French colonial social realities. His later American productions bear the mark of what one would call Hollywood "international style," from the 1982 superproduction of *Quest for Fire* to *Wings of Courage,* a three-dimensional Imax extravaganza about a 1930s French aviator who is stranded on a frozen lake in the Andes after his mail plane crashes. Still, there are striking connections, and if you watch Annaud's films back to back, you begin to find a common thread that unites all of his films in spite of the wide range they cover.

Like all young Frenchmen, Jean-Jacques Annaud had to do military service, but he chose to do it as a *coopérant* (a French military version of the Peace Corps), and went to work for the French Ministry of Information in Cameroon. In interviews, he says he fell in love with Africa, that he was surprised not to find savages there, but educated people who spoke perfect French.

Annaud's first film, *Black and White in Color,* was shot in Africa. And although his later films were shot in other continents, Africa, or maybe what it represents as a metaphor—a primitive land where innocents struggle against the brute stupidity of those in power—is still the stage for Annaud's films. And he seems to have a predilection for filming in the wild. *Quest for Fire* was shot in Alberta and northern Ontario; *Wings of Courage,* which takes place in the Andes, was shot in British Columbia; *The Name of the*

Rose is set in a weather-beaten and remote Italian landscape of rugged mountains; *The Lover* takes place in the pounding and humid heat of Southeast Asia.

Against that background of primitive culture and foreboding nature, Annaud's heroes often appear to be characters on the edge of knowledge, naïfs who understand the world just a little better than the fools who surround them. *Black and White in Color* is the story of a group of French

CATHERINE TEXIER
Born in France

Chloe L'Atlantique 1983
Love Me Tender 1987
Panic Blood 1990
Love Is Strange 1993
(co-editor with Joel Rose)
Breakup: The End of a Love Story 1998

settlers in Africa during World War I who find out six months after the fact that France has declared war on Germany, and decide to send a battalion of natives to attack the neighboring German outpost. In their arrogant stupidity and appalling ineptitude, the French would sacrifice all the natives to the more adept Germans, and risk the destruction of the French outpost, if a young geographer from Paris—smarter, and a little more sophisticated and progressive—didn't come up with a plan to save the situation.

The group shots in all Annaud's films are composed like Renaissance tableaux—camera tight on the faces, at first almost static, then slowly panning from head to head to reveal the brute stupidity and/or the sly cunningness of the characters. Good examples of this technique come back again and again: the French colons gathered in the general store, plotting to attack the Germans in *Black and White in Color;* the monks listening to the Sean Connery character in *The Name of the Rose;* the Neanderthal men watching their precious fire die, their primitive faces reflecting horror and incomprehension in *Quest for Fire.*

Annaud's films are more about the characters than they are about politics. And it is the character of the smarter naïf versus the fools' stupidity that constitutes the motor of all his stories.

In *The Name of the Rose,* the young novice monk plays the role of innocent witness to the strange murders committed in the monastery, while the Sean Connery character investigates the mysteries. Sean Connery is the hero, but the novice is the one who is seduced by the peasant girl and introduced to the power of sexuality. The scenes of lovemaking between the girl and the novice are almost entirely without words and are extremely erotic in the way the girl flaunts her breasts and buttocks.

That raw, in-your-face sexuality is also a key to Annaud's films. It is a greedy, animal sexuality. Some scenes or fragments of scenes tug at your memory, like the Neanderthal man passing by the naked buttocks of a female bathing in a river, and rushing to take her from behind like a dog humping a bitch on the run (*Quest for Fire).*

The Lover, Annaud's 1992 adaption of Marguerite Duras's novel, is the story of a love affair between a fifteen-year-old French girl and a twenty-five-year-old wealthy Chinese man. Every day the lovers meet in the man's bachelor pad in a seedy section of Saigon to live an intensely erotic passion, but to her mother and brothers, the girl pretends she sleeps with the Chinese man for the money he gives her, because that's the only thing she believes her poor and struggling family can understand.

The Lover has been criticized for its very graphic sex scenes, and some viewers have wondered if the actors were actually making love in front of the camera. The sex scenes are long, slow, steamy, and often wordless, going on and on almost in real time, the bodies sweating in the tropical heat, the fans whirring, the midafternoon sun coming in slanted through the drawn blinds. They make you feel palpably the sticky, pungent sensuality of sex in the tropics.

There is an element of grotesque violence in Annaud's movies, too, but his bloody images are not about violence per se—as mindless, gun-toting, shoot 'em up violence—and not about evil either, but rather metaphors for the primitive side of mankind: the body found head first in a vat of pig's blood in the slaughterhouse (*The Name of the Rose*) and the mother bear bleeding to death (*The Bear).*

The bloody images, the raw sexuality, the wild landscapes, the wordless passions: they all connect us with the deep forces that command nature and men, against which civilization, in Annaud's vision, is but a foolish, thin, and arrogant veneer. ◆

ON HERBERT
ROSS

Never trust a musical comedy man. That's what my mother always said. Well, easier said than done. You know? Because, in the first place, you have to know one to avoid one. You have to identify the person whom you are not going to trust. And identification in this case ain't easy. A musical comedy man is a very slippery character. That's the nature of the beast. Otherwise the question of trust would not be an issue. Would it?

You take this fellow Herb Ross, for instance. Now, we all know he was born in Brooklyn. But, see, almost before you can say that for sure, he's gone. And, all of a sudden, he's in Miami. This of course is already a symptom, this restlessness, this movement at an early age from place to place. And, needless to say, Brooklyn itself is a clue if you're searching for something disreputable. At least that's what we always thought growing up in Jersey.

So, Miami. Yes. But not going to school like a normal ten-year-old. No, no, no. Not at all. Which fact is, to say the least, a surprise to his father who finds the kid one fine day flying off the diving boards at the Coral Gables swim show. Now, there are clues and clues—but this one just about closes the case. Not so much the show, which in and of itself is pretty conclusive. But the lies he tells. See? The lies are the best evidence. Because a good lie is the musical comedy man's stock in trade. And a *very* good lie—the kind that is so good it actually tells you the truth—that kind of lie could turn you into a bona fide artiste.

And this is a fact that little Herbert seemed to pick up like flypaper, which in those days they still had. So he lied, telling his old man he was going back to New York to spend the summer with some relative or other. (The facts, you have to understand, are all pretty unreliable, as is the case in most reconstructions of the musical comedy personality.) The truth of the situation was that he had signed up with some traveling group of similarly afflicted theatrical amateurs, all of them perfecting one way or another this mysterious art of the lie. Well, what can you say? They're born, these guys. Not made. And what we have here is pretty much the perfect example. Possessed, see? Out of control. Right from the beginning. Dropping out of school completely, living in a four-dollar-a-week room, calling himself an actor but not satisfied with that. Looking for something else, more, better. So he noses around. He reads plays, novels, poetry . . . he eats them up like candy. Studies painting from the inside out. Models nude for a few extra bucks. That I would have liked to see. Well, never mind. Move on. Move on. Looking for something. But what?

And then it happens. One night in a dark theater, a human body flies through the air—no kidding. A human being sucks up a musical phrase and turns reality into magic. Dancers. Oh, boy. Dancers. It must have hit him like a ton of bricks. Too tall, he knew that. Bones, too big. Feet not good. Still, he knew. He had to be one of these whatever they were. He had to be one. Which was a mistake. But it didn't matter.

Never trust a musical comedy man. Because that's all he needs. And when the timing is right and the rhythm is true, that smallest move will make a dent in your heart like a sledgehammer. And then, it's over. See? And you never even saw it coming.

They have an instinct, these guys. Because even when they're going in the wrong direction, they're right. You know what I'm saying? They have a rhythm that's always true. A style that just feels right. A kind of rock and roll heartbeat that never goes away. No matter how complicated, how sophisticated the highway gets, you never feel you traveled too far from your basic four-four time. That's the trick. See? The heartbeat. That's the magic of the musical comedy man. And the danger. The heartbeat and the lie.

So he dances. Yeah. Broadway. When they used to pronounce it with the accent on the <u>second</u> syllable. Broad<u>way</u>! When the shows had names like *Bloomer Girl* and *Beggar's Holiday* and *Look, Ma, I'm Dancing*. And he was. In all of them. And it feels almost right. To him and to everybody else, too. Almost. But not quite. Not yet. So when he falls down in Chicago and busts an ankle, he calls it a lucky break. See? They know, these guys. Even when it's going wrong, they know it's right. So he moves on. He starts calling the shots himself. Choreography, they call it. Where you control the dance. You shape the movement. You translate the music into some kind of human form. Or, to put it simply, you tell everybody else what to do. For which task you need to have an idea or two. Which he did. Ideas he picked up long ago from the plays and the poetry and the art. Steal from the best—Goya, Genet, Ovid. What are they saying? Figure that out and then figure how you can say that without the words, in time and space, on a stage, in a body.

Theater, yes. That's one way. And drama. And a few laughs. Television. Cabaret. Moving fast. Words and music and movement. Putting them all together. And, in the process, making a few bucks, yes. This is beginning to look like a career. But maybe moving <u>too</u> fast. And going where? There's a question he didn't have an answer for. Going where? So, stop. Just stop. Take a breather. Take a look around. Take a minute. Stop. Wait.

HERBERT ROSS
Born 1927
Brooklyn, New York

Goodbye, Mr. Chips 1969

The Owl and the Pussycat 1970

T. R. Baskin 1971

Play It Again, Sam 1972

The Last of Sheila 1973

Funny Lady 1975

The Sunshine Boys 1975
Golden Globe Award for Best Motion Picture (Musical/Comedy)

The Seven-Per-Cent Solution 1976

The Goodbye Girl 1977
Golden Globe Award for Best Motion Picture (Musical/Comedy)

The Turning Point 1977
Golden Globe Awards for Best Motion Picture (Drama) and Best Director

California Suite 1978

Nijinsky 1980

Pennies from Heaven 1981

I Ought to Be in Pictures 1982

Max Dugan Returns 1983

Footloose 1984

Protocol 1984

Dancers 1987

The Secret of My Success 1987

Steel Magnolias 1989

My Blue Heaven 1990

True Colors 1991

Undercover Blues 1993

Boys on the Side 1995

Sometimes the world knows who you are before you do. Sometimes when you flounder, the world sends you a messenger who says, "Hey, this way." In this case, the messenger was a dame—in the best sense of that word. And her name was Nora Kaye.

Herb and Nora. Even when you didn't know them, you knew them that way. Working. Living. And loving—if the rumors are true. And a born and bred musical comedy man begins to understand who he is and where he's going. He looks in his trunk and sees everything he's collected—the books, the poetry, the painting, the people from Imogene Coca to Marlene Dietrich, the music from Richard Rodgers to Richard Wagner, the sacred and the profane, the base and the pure, the soft shoe and the grande jettée. The heartbeat and the lie. Well, this is beginning to make sense.

And it does. A little more time on Broadway. Just long enough to give us some gold, you know? Gold in the shape of four broads—four ladies in four of the most unique performances in the history of musical comedy. Barbara Cook in *The Gay Life,* Vivian Leigh in *Tovarich,* Barbara Harris in *The Apple Tree,* and the stage debut of that great broad from Brooklyn, Miss Marmelstein, a.k.a. Streisand in *I Can Get It for You Wholesale.* Not just a choreographer now. A director. When the New York theater really meant something. When the American musical comedy was still an art form and not the endangered species it has become. When a musical comedy man could have aspirations beyond his bank account. There was even the off chance of his becoming a genuine artiste. In his own sly way, of course. Hitting all the notes, following all the rules, banging out the rhythm in a familiar sort of way. But doing all that in order to disguise the invention, conceal the boldness so that you never see the magic coming. It's only as you leave the theater that you feel your heart beating too fast and you know that something has happened. But you're not quite sure what. Something true has been revealed. But you're not sure how. I mean, it's only a show. Sure. But these guys, they do a show and, behind your back, when you're not looking, they turn it into a work of art. And just when you figure it out, they move on. Move on.

Legend has it that Miss Marmelstein needed a screen test. Some studio probably needed convincing that the broad from Brooklyn really had the makings of a movie star. Well, it's a joke now. But then . . . So Herb Ross steps into the land of the silver screen. He directs the test. He stays around to direct the musical numbers. (Why do they call them "numbers"?) And before he leaves town—which he still hasn't done—he knocks off twenty-five films in less than twenty years. Those were the days, of course—not so long ago really—when the studios were actually in the business of making movies, when they actually wanted to make movies and did. Unlike today, when all they really want to do is cut their losses and build theme parks.

MICHAEL CRISTOFER
Born 1945
Trenton, New Jersey

The Shadow Box 1975
(play and screenplay)
Ice 1976 (play)
Black Angel 1978 (play)
Falling in Love 1984
(screenplay)
The Lady and the Clarinet 1985 (play)
Witches of Eastwick 1987 (screenplay; based on the novel by John Updike)
The Bonfire of the Vanities 1990
(screenplay; based on the novel by Tom Wolfe)
The Blues Are Running 1994 (play)
Amazing Grace 1995
(play)
Breaking Up 1995
(play and screenplay)
Gia 1998 (director and screenwriter)
Jello Shots 1998 (director and screenwriter)

In those days, a guy could work hard and come up with a batting average that today looks pretty miraculous. Hell, I take that back. When you count up the Academy Awards and the nominations and the stars, including Streisand, Peter O'Toole, Woody Allen, Tony Perkins, Stephen Sondheim, George Burns, Walter Matthau, Richard Dreyfuss, Marsha Mason, Laurence Olivier, Robert Duvall, Anne Bancroft, Shirley MacLaine, (this is a long list, I know), Baryshnikov, Maggie Smith, Alan Bates, Michael Caine, Goldie Hawn, Michael J. Fox, Whoopi Goldberg, Sally Field, Dolly Parton, Julia Roberts, and more. Or if you just take 1977. Two films in one year. *The Turning Point* and *The Goodbye Girl.* Now get this—together these two films earned a total of sixteen Oscar nominations. In the same year. This is a batting average that is a miracle no matter what condition the business is in.

And we are still talking musical comedy? Oh, yes, we are. Because even the ones without music still sing. And if you look real close, you can even find the eleven o'clock spot. In fact, you can find just about every element that defines the form. When Michael J. Fox is tripping over sofas to escape the hot hands of Maggie Whitton in *The Secret of My Success*—that is dancing. Same for Dennis Quaid fending off the muggers with a baby carriage. Or Shirley MacLaine and Anne Bancroft going at it, mano a mano. Dancing. Or Sally Field, digging out the pain and the grief and anger over the loss of her child—that is singing. And when have you heard a better "duet" than Maggie Smith and Michael Caine trading insults that are a testament to their affection? Bitter sweet music. And sometimes they really do dance. Christopher Walken and Steve Martin in *Pennies from Heaven*—the film that reinvented the musical and married it to film noir. (You really can't trust those guys, I'm telling you.) And sometimes they really do sing. Yeah, Miss Marmelstein, sure. And on the bow of a tugboat. Who could forget that? But also Whoopi singing goodbye to her lost, lost love at the end of *Boys on the Side.* And how about the stories themselves? Like the best of the great musicals, every one of these films tells the same one. The same tale of the human spirit, rising triumphant over the loneliness and the despair of simple living. Told by the guy with the not-so-simple life. The life he shares with the princess now. Lee Radziwill. A different muse. A different kind of music. But a dame in her own right. And underneath the elegance, always the simplicity of the old soft shoe.

Sometimes the lyrics are just the spoken lines. And the dancing is only a reach of the hand or even the turn of a head or the crack of a smile. Never trust a musical comedy man. Because that's all he needs. And when the timing is right and the rhythm is true, that smallest move will make a dent in your heart like a sledgehammer. And then, it's over. See? And you never even saw it coming. You can fret and fuss and call foul if you want to.

But you might as well give in. There ain't no escaping that rhythm. Because that's the rhythm of your own heartbeat. And there's no escaping that perfect timing. Even if you wanted to. Which you don't. And there's for certain no escaping that perfect lie, the lie that can't help telling the truth. But never mind. Your feet are already moving to the beat. You can tell yourself that you know where you're going. But you'd be wrong. You can say it's okay, you're in control. But you're not. It's Herb Ross who's in charge. And you? You are dancing—just like the rest of us. Like the best of us. Whether you want to or not. You are shuffling off to Buffalo with the genuine article, the bona fide artiste—that never, ever to be trusted musical comedy man. ◆

ON MARTIN
BREST

Martin Brest is a bomb thrower with a heart of gold. He is unrecognized as most bomb throwers like to be, and he also keeps the golden heart under wraps. But it is there in Colonel Slade's (Al Pacino) last-reel epiphany to The Baird School in *Scent of a Woman* and it pervades the pivotal scene in *Midnight Run* when Jack Walsh (Robert De Niro) visits his ex-wife in Chicago and lays eyes on his baby daughter for the first time. Walsh does not know what to say, he is overcome, but he will not feign emotions he cannot articulate, and Marty is the same; he lets his work do it for him.

Marty was a mistake, the surprise son of a middle-aged mother and a father who morphed from Bronx iron welder into Talmudic scholar; his siblings are old enough to be his parents. Perhaps that explains Marty's interest in the aged, his empathy for and pain to understand them. *Going in Style*, his first feature, is Three Musketeers off a park bench in Queens (George Burns, Art Carney, Lee Strasberg), a celebration of seniors before they were popular or, more exactly, politically correct. It is a tale reflecting his empathy for the infirm and losers of this world who have fallen on hard times through no fault of their own; only age, or in Robert De Niro's case, an obstinate incorruptibility; or again in Slade's outcastness that stumbles on its own redemption through the purity and, once more, incorruptibility of Charlie (Chris O'Donnell), a boy who cannot inform on classmates whom he unconsciously loathes. Charlie cannot act on his own earned opinion because he has to answer to a higher authority within himself: honor. He is the youthful apotheosis of antisnitch, a tortured noncanary.

MARTIN BREST
Born 1951
Bronx, New York

Going in Style* 1979
Beverly Hills Cop 1984
Midnight Run 1988
Scent of a Woman 1992
(screenplay by Bo
Goldman) Golden Globe
Awards for Best Motion
Picture (Drama) and Best
Screenplay
Meet Joe Black 1998
(screenplay by Bo
Goldman and others)

* also screenwriter

Lest all of the above seem like characters from John Bunyan's *Pilgrim's Progress*, they are exactly the opposite, icons of morality, parables of life's imperfections, but turned on their heads through humor. The cackle that Eddie Murphy suppresses as Detective Axel Foley in *Beverly Hills Cop* is the echo of Marty's empathetic laughter with the human condition; yet he rarely laughs *at* (except to puncture pomposity or empty authority), what he does is bravely inhabit his characters. George Burns as an octogenarian bank robber in a fright wig and dime store nose is an alter ego of Marty,

who spent the summer of his senior year at N.Y.U. in the basement of a tenement in Williamsburgh, exploding models of the Statue of Liberty, emptying the powder from cartridges locked in a shop-school vice. He almost blew himself up, but that is where the obsession with detail was planted, and paid off in *Hot Dogs for Gauguin,* what is widely considered the *Birth of a Nation* of student films, featuring Danny DeVito as a Groucho Marx terrorist.

BO GOLDMAN
Born 1932
New York, New York

*One Flew Over the
Cuckoo's Nest* 1975
(co-screenwriter; based
on the novel by Ken
Kesey; film directed by
Milos Forman) Academy
Awards for Best Director
and Best Adapted
Screenplay; Golden
Globe Awards for Best
Director and Best
Screenplay

The Rose 1979
(co-screenwriter)

Melvin and Howard 1980
(screenplay; film directed
by Jonathan Demme)
Academy Award for Best
Original Screenplay;
Writers Guild Award for
Best Screenplay

Shoot the Moon
(screenplay) 1982

Scent of a Woman
1992 (screenplay; film
directed by Martin Brest)
Golden Globe Awards
for Best Drama and
Best Screenplay

City Hall 1996
(co-screenwriter)

Meet Joe Black 1998
(co-screenwriter; film
directed by Martin Brest)

Marty Brest is not known well enough, maybe that is why he is so good. He can't be shoehorned into some critic's stereotype of "action-comedy director" or "director of commercial comedy-dramas," on the other hand the above terms hint at the truth because they seem self-contradictory: and that is what Marty is. A hypochondriac in catalog clothes and undergraduate tennis shoes, and, should the temperature fall below sixty-five, he is into a merino wool overshirt and earmuffs, an understated yet late-blooming Kilroy who has carved out a corner of the cinematic jungle that is uniquely his own. He loves his audience and, like any genius, he is impatient with anybody who comes between him and them. The man is a joy and a scoundrel, fighting for every penny he can steal to put on the screen, boomeranging the ticket buyers from laughter to tears and then, himself, collapsing for years between work from the exhaustion of being so true to himself. ◆

ON STEPHEN
FREARS

DONALD E. WESTLAKE

Here are two things Stephen Frears said to me. The first was several months before *The Grifters* was made and, in fact, before either of us had signed on to do the project. We had just recently met, brought together by the production company that had sent us to California to look at the place. Driving back from La Jolla toward L.A., me at the wheel of the rented car, Stephen in the seat beside me musing on life, he broke a longish silence to say, "You know, there's nothing more loathsome than actually making a film, and it's beginning to look as though I'll have to make this one." The second was the night of the same film's New York premiere, at the postopening party, when he leaned close to me in the noisy room and murmured, "Well we got away with it."

I think what attracted me to Stephen in the first place is that, in a world of manic enthusiasm, here at last I'd met a fellow pessimist. Someone who would surely agree with Damon Runyon's assessment: "All of life is six to five against."

If we aren't going to enjoy ourselves, why do it?

Not that he's a defeatist, far from it. For instance, he refused to let me turn down the job of writing *The Grifters,* a thing that never happens. The normal sequence is, a writer is offered a job, thinks it over, says yea or nay, and that's that. Having been offered this job, I read Jim Thompson's novel—or reread, from years before—decided it was too grim, and said nay. That should have been the end of it, but the next thing I knew, Frears was on the phone from France, some Englishman I'd never met in my life, plaintively saying, "Why don't you want to make my film?" I told him my reasons. He told me I was wrong, and proceeded to prove it—"It's Lilly's story, not Roy's," was his insight, not mine—and I finally agreed to a meeting in New York, which was the beginning of the most thoroughly enjoyable experience I've ever had in the world of movies.

Here's another thing Stephen said to me: "I like the writer on the set." This is not common among directors, and I wasn't at all sure what it meant. Did he want a whipping boy? Someone to hide behind? Someone to blame? (You can see that I too am not a manic enthusiast.)

STEPHEN FREARS
Born 1941
Leicester, England

Gumshoe 1972
Bloody Kids 1983
The Hit 1984
My Beautiful Laundrette 1985
Walter and June 1986
Prick Up Your Ears 1987
Sammy and Rosie Get Laid 1987
Dangerous Liaisons 1988
The Grifters 1990 (screenplay by Donald Westlake)
Hero 1992
The Snapper 1993
Mary Reilly 1996
The Van 1996
The Hi-Lo Country 1999
High Fidelity 1999

DONALD E. WESTLAKE
Born 1933
Brooklyn, New York

The Mercenaries 1960
The Fugitive Pigeon 1965
God Save the Mark 1967
The Hot Rock 1970
Cops and Robbers 1973
(novel and screenplay)
Jimmy the Kid 1974
Dancing Aztecs 1976
Hot Stuff 1976
(screenplay)
Nobody's Perfect 1977
Kahawa 1981
Why Me 1983/1990
(novel and screenplay)
A Likely Story 1984
The Stepfather 1987
(screenplay)
Sacred Monster 1989
The Grifters 1990
(screenplay; based on the
novel by Jim Thompson;
film directed by Stephen
Frears)
Drowned Hopes 1991
Humans 1992
Don't Ask 1993
*What's the Worst that
Could Happen?* 1996
The Ax 1997
Backflash 1998

Anyway, no. As it turned out, what he wanted was a collaborator, and what we did was a collaboration. I didn't direct and he didn't write, and between us both we licked the platter clean.

I am not a proponent of the auteur theory. I think it comes out of a basic misunderstanding of the functions of creative versus interpretive arts. But I do believe that on the set and in the postproduction process the director is the captain of the ship. Authority has to reside in one person, and that should most sensibly be the director. So my rare disagreements with Stephen were in private, and we discussed them as off-set equals, and whichever of us prevailed—it was pretty even—the other one shrugged and got on with it.

The result has much of Jim Thompson in it, of course. It has much in it of the talents of its wonderful cast and designer. It has some of me in it. But the look of it, the feel of it, the smell of it, the three-inches-off-the-ground quality of it; that's Stephen.

If we aren't going to enjoy ourselves, why do it? Stephen's right, much of the filmmaking *is* loathsome. Pleasure and satisfaction have to come from the work itself and from one's companions on the journey. *The Grifters* was for me that rarity; everyone in the boat rowing in the same direction. I hadn't had that much fun on the job since I was nineteen, in college, and had a part-time job on a beer truck with a guy named Luke. ◆

MIKE WERB

ON PENELOPE
SPHEERIS

ANTS IN HER PLANTS

In Preston Sturges's 1941 classic *Sullivan's Travels*, fictional director John Sullivan desperately wants to make "Oh Brother, Where Art Thou?," a realistic drama about the human condition. The studio hands him a comedy sequel "Ants in Your Plants." He goes AWOL and travels the country as a penniless hobo. Landing in prison, Sully learns all about the human condition—and changes his mind. "Ants in Your Plants," is just the tonic. He now understands the healing power of comedy and simply wants to make people laugh.

Arriving late on the Paramount lot, I wobbled in (early meeting) to find Penelope commanding her troops with the authority, and often dry wit, of a Winston Churchill. Eighty people at attention, not soldiers or circus folks to be sure, but perhaps not all that different.

Fifty years later, in 1991, a nonfictional director faced a similar dilemma. Penelope Spheeris's filmography had pigeonholed her as an urban celluloid guerilla. She made edgy documentaries like *The Decline of Western Civilization*, aggressively bleak dramas like *The Boys Next Door.* Her films searingly reflected the human condition and she became a cult moviegoer's favorite.

Penelope was at a psychological, spiritual, and creative crossroads. There had been so much violence and angst and pain and death—not only in her work as a filmmaker, but also in her life. Staring her in the face was an HBO documentary on Patton State Hospital for the criminally insane. She didn't want to do it.

Looking down that dust-choked road, she saw a feral pack of hospitalized fruitcakes. Looking the other way, she saw . . . more drooling fruitcakes. Except these nuts weren't in a hospital. They were on television and they had names. Like Wayne and Garth.

Inspired by the prayer session Madonna (!) led in *Truth or Dare,* Penelope prayed and asked God to grant her the other assignment she was up for: directing *Wayne's World.*

The rest is cinema history. Spheeris is one of the most commercially bankable comedy directors in Hollywood. To say she came from humble beginnings is to have her set the standard for that cliché.

PENELOPE SPHEERIS
Born 1946
Algiers, Louisiana

*The Decline of Western Civilization** 1981
*The Wild Side (Suburbia)** 1984
The Boys Next Door 1985
Hollywood Vice Squad 1986
Dudes 1987
The Decline of Western Civilization II: The Metal Years 1988
Wayne's World 1992
*The Little Rascals*** 1993
The Beverly Hillbillies 1994
Black Sheep 1996
Senseless 1997
The Decline of Western Civilization III 1998

* also screenwriter
** also co-screenwriter

As a Jew suckled in the middle-class bosom of the San Fernando Valley, I find Spheeris's background astounding. That she didn't end up dead or in jail, as she herself puts it, is even more astounding. And she is every bit as fascinating as the circumstances under which she was raised.

Born in Algiers, Louisiana, her father, Andrew Spheeris, owned and operated a forty-truck carnival called the "Magic Empire Shows." On the road, he met and fell in love with Gypsy Redd. Already married to a pig farmer, Gypsy ran off with Andrew anyway. "I left with him like a wild goose, 'cause I was in love with him," Gypsy recently recalled. After a stint in jail, they were finally allowed to marry. They had four kids together— Penelope being the first. She grew up in trailers and tents and trucks, sharing space with midgets and clowns and Siamese twins. Freaks to outsiders, the Spheerises never taught their children to look at the performers that way. They were all just family. The kids got into the act, too, and there exists a stunning newspaper clipping of a six-month-old Penelope performing a balancing act, cupped in her father's palm.

Unfortunately, the show did not go on. When Penelope was only seven, her father was shot through the heart defending a black employee against a racist white patron. Three hundred people witnessed the murder.

Gypsy married seven more times, and the kids were moved from state to state. Refusing to go on welfare, she worked two, sometimes three jobs to put food on the table. That left most of the childrearing duties to Penelope. Her only fun was taking her younger siblings to the movies on Saturdays. There, she escaped into the madness of Abbott and Costello, Martin and Lewis. For two hours a week she could forget about babysitting, sewing, cleaning—and the abuse, both physical and psychological, sometimes inflicted by her mother's occasionally ill-chosen companions.

And yet Penelope is extremely close to her mother and considers her a great role model. Gypsy's independent, free-spirited, "I'll do whatever the hell I want" attitude set a strong example for young Penelope, at a time when most girls were trying to emulate Donna Reed, Patty Duke, or Gidget.

While working on the Chris Farley/David Spade comedy *Black Sheep,* Penelope asked my partner, Michael Colleary, and me to attend the first full production meeting. Arriving late on the Paramount lot, I wobbled in (early meeting) to find Penelope commanding her troops with the authority, and often dry wit, of a Winston Churchill. Eighty people at attention, not soldiers or circus folks to be sure, but perhaps not all that different. She handled everything so skillfully, so seamlessly—a legacy left to her, no doubt, by both her father and mother. From her mom Penelope acquired the skills needed for babysitting, organizing, and juggling a dozen things at once. From her dad she inherited an innate instinct for entertaining the masses.

Penelope also got her looks from her father's gene pool. As you can see from her picture, she is the epitome of hippie beautiful—mane of thick, jet-black hair cascading over high, classic Greek cheekbones. Andrew Spheeris was an Olympic champion wrestler, the circus strong man—and came in second to Charles Atlas in the World's Most Perfect Body contest.

MIKE WERB
Born 1960
Hollywood, California

The Mask 1994
(screenplay; based on
the Dark Horse comic
book series)
Face/Off 1997
(co-producer;
co-screenwriter with
Michael Colleary)

Similarly, Penelope is long, lean, and athletic, and moves like a prowling panther. I know this sounds moronic, sexist, and utterly inappropriate, but the first time I met Penelope I went a little brain dead. All I saw was her body.

I walked in (late again) to a story meeting, hardly noticing the dozen executives sitting around Lorne Michael's office, for there it was, blinding me like I was some dumb-ass deer on a mountain road. She caught me staring and her bemused smile brought me back to the work at hand. Although I fretted about getting off on the wrong foot, so to speak, she graciously never mentioned the incident and we quickly became friends.

At the press junket for Black Sheep, Penelope told me that the media (yet again) were hounding her about selling out to Hollywood. When was the celluloid urban guerilla going to stop taking the fat paychecks and get back to making gritty films about the human condition? Not soon, I hope. She's doing far too good a job making people laugh. And while her career will undoubtedly take many, many more radical left turns, I expect she will never completely lose those damn ants in her plants. ◆

ON PHILLIP
NOYCE

hillip Noyce, a very big man, grabbed the writer, a significantly smaller man when compared to the stentorian director, and ushered him out of the room like a ventriloquist's dummy and onto the sidewalk. It was at a Thanksgiving party in Beverly Hills and the writer had just been asked, in very polite and formal terms, to join a famous actor, to whom he had just been introduced, at his table, where he was entertaining a coterie of producers and agents. The director had interceded on the writer's behalf, telling the messenger to thank the famous actor, but that both he and the writer already had a prior engagement and had to leave.

Noyce searches for, and manages to find, an emotional connection in these big and brawny pictures.

"What engagement?" asked the writer, bewildered.

"It doesn't matter," said Noyce with gravel-voiced authority. "He's asked us to join him, so now we have to leave. We're new in town, and it's important that we preserve our mystique."

"What mystique?" asked the writer, once again confounded.

"Trust me. I've got your best interests at heart. If you didn't have a mystique before, you're well on the way to having one now."

"So, in terms of preserving one's mystique, when do you get to sit down and simply meet someone and chat with them over a bottle of wine?" asked the writer, still struggling to overcome his innocence and comprehend it all.

"You don't," said Noyce matter-of-factly. "Not in this town. You have to be very careful. You can do that only with family."

"Then I guess mystique gets so preserved around here that's it's practically pickled," said the writer forlornly.

"Weren't some of those women in there deliciously tall?" said Noyce.

This was, of course, relatively early on, after his maritime thriller *Dead Calm* had aroused some very real interest in the Australian director, along with Nicole Kidman, in Hollywood, and had brought him to Southern

PHILLIP NOYCE
Born 1950
Griffith, New South
Wales, Australia

*Backroads*** 1977
*Newsfront** 1978
*Heatwave** 1982
Echoes of Paradise 1987
Dead Calm 1989
Blind Fury 1989
Patriot Games 1992
Sliver 1993
Clear and Present Danger
1994
The Saint 1997
The Bone Collector 1999
*Blast Off** 1999

* also screenwriter
** also co-screenwriter

California, the labyrinthine pathways of which he was then navigating in search of the Big Picture, the one he was not able to make within the vast confines of his native shores. This was his period of adjustment, in which, like in the Tennessee Williams play of that name, it was necessary for all problems, personal, financial, and otherwise, to be "obfuscated" and the paramount vision of success maintained with unwavering clarity and determination. He said, at the time, that he felt like Cortés when he burned his ships.

With the success of *Patriot Games* and *Clear and Present Danger,* his mystique is as preserved and as wondrous as a well-rigged sailing ship in a bottle. Of course, everyone in Hollywood lives in fear of sudden shipwreck, material, social, and spiritual (in that order—there are some cases where one may venture to say artistic); it is often a Faustian bargain in which the stakes are high and the personal costs great. Everyone knows this. Part of Noyce's mystique is that of the dedicated family man who makes efficient high-action money-making thrillers. He prides himself on, and has established a reputation for being, a "Mr. Fixit" of the genre, a hard-working director who can make lean and intelligent and humane sense out of what Terrence Rafferty in *The New Yorker* calls "the huge, rippling expanses of verbal flab," like "watching Rush Limbaugh run a marathon," that are the novels of Tom Clancy. This naturally has not made him popular with the author—Noyce's view that the machinations and technological hardware of power are more inherently suspect and evil than good, even when employed in the name of a just cause, are directly opposed to Clancy's simple-minded right-wing sense of patriotic awe—but it has greatly enhanced his status both at Paramount and with the nation's film critics at large. *The New Yorker*'s review of *Patriot Games,* entitled, with obvious double entendre, "To the Rescue," cut swiftly to the core by stating that "Phillip Noyce's *Patriot Games*, adapted from one of Tom Clancy's jillion-selling suspense novels, is a much more effective thriller than it has any right to be. . . . What's surprising about the movie is that Noyce and the screenwriters . . . have eliminated much of the novel's hot air without entirely knocking the wind out of the material."

Noyce searches for, and manages to find, an emotional connection in these big and brawny pictures. In *Patriot Games,* he humanizes the villain (Sean Bean) by making his motive one of obsessive blood revenge for the death of his younger brother, and also inferring that the hero Jack Ryan (Harrison Ford) has a darker side, a violent, angry shadow, and that he harbors secret moral doubts about the very forces he sets in motion, giving what might otherwise be an all-boy's action-adventure an earnest and plausible and complex edge.

His success, though, has received mixed reaction at home. Many Australians still foster a kind of parochial resentment toward their expatriates, especially those who achieve a modicum of fame overseas, and especially in the United States, that behemoth of cultural imperialism. But Noyce, although one of Paramount's heroes, and unabashedly enjoying that fact, remains adamantly true to and proud of his roots, to which he returns regularly for rest and recuperation, and even creative rejuvenation. To demonstrate his strong autochthonous sense, Noyce once returned to Los Angeles from Sydney accompanied by a notorious Australian black activist, a professional Aborigine whom he'd met years before while making *Backroads*, his Australian road movie about wayward whites and blacks aimlessly driving through the Outback, and during which the Aborigines named him "The Hawk." The Hawk had paid for the activist's ticket, and maintained him for several weeks as a sidekick and factotum while the two of them went around the town entertaining and bamboozling the locals with arcane Australianisms both white and black. *Newsfront,* also written

DAMIAN SHARP

*When a Monkey Speaks:
And Other Stories from
Australia* 1994

by Noyce from an original screenplay by Bob Ellis and produced by Palm Beach Pictures, was a highly textured and often humorous—in terms of laconic Australian humor—lament for the passing of the era of the newsreel cameraman to television and the takeover of the Australian industry by what the film presents as garrulous and brash American multinationals.

"Hollywood," says Noyce, "is not necessarily the best place to make a picture. But it is the best place to make a big picture and get it distributed."

At another Thanksgiving celebration, this one a dinner in his newly acquired home in the Hollywood Hills, the wine was flowing freely and the guests were milling around the long banquet table, waiting to be assigned to their chairs and curious as to their formal positioning and whom they would be seated next to. The ritual had only just commenced when the director appeared, having gone to fetch even more wine.

"All right," he boomed above the polite but raucous chatter. "Dinner's served. Now everyone sit down and make a new friend."

And they did. ◆

RICHARD LOURIE

ON AGNIESZKA HOLLAND

It was love at first preview. Living abroad and desperate to hear the yack of pure American, I attended a showing of *Goodfellas* in the one theater in Marseilles that ran what the dubbing-mad French call VO, *version originale.* The movie proved a disappointment—the fine art of swearing, so brilliantly rendered in *Raging Bull,* here seemed stylized, a parody, fake. As often happens, by the time I'd stood up and put on my coat, I'd forgotten the entire film. It was the afterglow of a preview that left the theater with me. One image in particular—teenage boys swimming across an Olympic-sized pool whose white-tiled bottom was inlaid with a gigantic black swastika. The contrast between that lethal abstraction and the vitality of their youthful bodies said more about the price of war than any scenes of battlefield carnage, which are, as a rule, oddly unmoving. And I had also liked the title, *Europa, Europa,* which sounded like a bitter but indulgent sigh.

That preview did exactly what previews are supposed to do—it made me die to see the movie. And I caught it the first chance I got back in the States. It was a great tale, terrifically told, story and sensibility in perfect synch. I had never seen anything quite like it, the feeling you always get when encountering a real talent, a *version originale.*

Europa, Europa is the true account of Solomon Perel, a handsome Polish Jewish youth separated from his family at the outbreak of World War II. His adventures are picaresque—a plaything of ideologies, he's tossed back and forth from the Young Communists to the Hitler Youth. But he leads a charmed life, protected by a silky aura of erotic charisma that attracts both men and women of every nationality. Despite genuine moments of anguish, loss, and danger, the hero eludes death till the end when he is saved by the last of many miracles. So many that we have already long since accepted his fate as real precisely because it is so marvelous.

Not only could no one have concocted a character like Solomon Perel, if anyone had, that person would have been vilified on moral grounds for creating a picaresque Holocaust. And in fact *Europa, Europa* was criticized, not for being made up but for being made at all. Though emotionally understandable, that argument doesn't hold if you believe that art is suppose

AGNIESZKA
HOLLAND
Born 1948
Warsaw, Poland

*An Evening with Abdon**
1975

*Screen Tests*** 1977
(co-director)

Sunday Children 1977

*Provincial Actors*** 1979
Cannes Film Festival
FIPRESCI Award

Fever 1980

*Woman On Her Own***
1981

*Angry Harvest** 1985

*To Kill a Priest*** 1988

*Europa, Europa** 1991
Golden Globe Award for
Best Foreign Film

*Olivier, Olivier***1992

The Secret Garden 1993

Total Eclipse 1995

Washington Square 1997

The Third Miracle 1999
(in production)

The Falconer 1999
(in production)

* also screenwriter
** also co-screenwriter

to add to our experience of reality. Besides, the hero does lose his family—*Europa, Europa* is a darker picaresque than anything the eighteenth century could ever have conceived.

Perel's fate illustrates the utter perversity of war, whose chaos can create combinations unthinkable in peacetime. A connoisseurship of the perverse is in fact central to the Polish sensibility. That a civilization that passed through all Europe's phrases—Medieval, Renaissance, Enlightenment—and whose kings were elected by the nobility should be crushed by the barbarians of Russia was a violation of everything just, reasonable, and good. Fate w as defied by taking delight in the baroque shapes suffering could assume. But, at its best, in *Europa, Europa,* there's more to that sensibility than that. There's wit, a real feel for history, genuine compassion.

On what had to have been a small budget, Holland managed to convey the epic upheaval of war better than any mega-million-dollar blockbuster, where every button has been researched and actual vintage planes are flown in the aerial combat scenes. In *Europa, Europa,* history has none of the stiffness of a "subject" but is just another name for life at a certain time, in a certain place, under the sway of definite forces.

And one of the real details of that time and place was that the simplest way for a Nazi to determine whether a given male was a Jew was to check whether he was circumcised. (I once asked an Armenian friend whose wife had just given birth to a boy whether his son would be circumcised. "Oh no," he said. "During the Armenian holocaust, the Turks would check—if someone *wasn't* circumcised, that meant he was an Armenian. The Moslem Turks were all circumcised." It's a possible subject for a serious monograph—*The Penis in History.*) In one of the most distressing scenes in the movie, Perel, whose charms and odd luck have landed him in an elite SS youth academy, uses a needle and thread in an attempt to conceal the fact of his own circumcision. Though still operating within the confines of her very Polish sensibility, Holland suffused this scene with a sisterly sexual compassion, a beautiful achievement, both artistically and humanly.

After that, I made it a point to see Agnieszka Holland's movies and came to know her as a person, in the best possible way, over bottles of good red.

The party after the premier of her latest, *Total Eclipse,* was packed and frenetically festive but there was an undertone, an undertow of gloom. And it took a cruelly short time for those forebodings to be realized—the film was a flop in the only two places that count—reviews and receipts. But *Total Eclipse* was a very rich failure and deserves better than oblivion. At times, Holland's Rimbaud comes to life—snotty and incandescent.

The homosexual love scenes between Rimbaud and Verlaine are shocking in their beauty and their cruelty. Verlaine's tormenting of his virtuous and voluptuous wife jolt you with their bitter knowledge of men and women. And Holland caught the Paris of the times, which French artists detested—as Gauguin writes in *Noa Noa*, he was not only fleeing his frigid wife, the Bourse, and the bourgeoisie, but grim, parsimonious Paris.

RICHARD LOURIE
Born 1940
Cambridge,
Massachussets

Sagittarius in Warsaw
1973
Dreamland 1980
(feature-length
documentary; producer
and writer)
Everything Is Lovely
1980 (documentary;
producer and writer)
First Loyalty 1985
Zero Gravity 1987
*Predicting Russia's
Future* 1991
*Russia Speaks: An
Oral History from
the Revolution to the
Present* 1991
Bread and Salt 1992
(feature-length
documentary; producer
and writer)
Hunting the Devil 1993
*Andrei Sakharov:
A Biography* 1999
*The Autobiography of
Joseph Stalin* 1999

Total Eclipse went straight to video, the paperback of film. Like all other such technology, video passed from marvelous to the banal without missing a beat. Yet, recently I had a moment of happy wonder at being able to see one of Holland's first films so easily—three bucks, five days—and to play with it using my remote, which can do freeze-frames and slo-mo. *Angry Harvest* (a bad title that sounds like every anthology of Eastern European dissident writing published during the cold war) is an almost claustrophobically close-up depiction of the relationship between a Jewish woman and the Polish man who hides her from the Nazis. Here the usual sexual drama of power is played out in circumstances so extreme that people are compelled to react only from instinct and essence. It can't end well.

Though that terrible collusion of lives leaves a lasting resonance, it was something else about the movie that remains most vivid for me. The sequence was short, almost casual. A Jew and the Pole who had hidden him are in the back of an open truck guarded by a single German soldier. They are going along an ordinary country road at normal speed. There is zero overt drama. Each of the three men is submerged in the separateness of his fate. The Pole will die because he hid the Jew. The Jew will die because he is a Jew. The German soldier will shoot them because those are his orders. And that is that. The truck disappears over a rise in the road. It all couldn't have been more ordinary or more awful. And maybe that's precisely why that image is still lodged in my mind, a Technicolor splinter. ◆

SEYMOUR CHATMAN

ON MICHELANGELO ANTONIONI

I saw my first Antonioni film in 1965. Like some critics, I didn't understand it—I had to watch *Red Desert* five times before I caught a glimmer of what it was about. Then I started looking for screenings of the earlier films; fortunately, living in the San Francisco Bay Area, I was able to see most of them. I awaited each subsequent film with keen anticipation. I met Michelangelo Antonioni briefly in 1975 when *The Passenger* had its American premier at Wheeler Hall, University of California, Berkeley. A huge audience of students gathered to see the man whose *Zabriskie Point* had captured the revolutionary spirit of their generation, a spirit which, a few years before, had had its most visible demonstration in Sproul Plaza and on Telegraph Avenue.

> **Whatever pessimism informed his films, there was none marking his craggy features. The man was—and remains—brimming with life and creative energy. I saw how wrong critics had been for accusing him of obsessing about the dark side of life—suicide, depression, personal failure.**

But I only came to know him in 1980, while working in Rome on my book, *Antonioni, or the Surface of the World*. Antonioni had had a rough time in America while making *Zabriskie Point*. The studio was difficult and intrusive, critics (not to speak of politicians) disliked it, and some interviewers described the director as "standoffish" and "difficult." I was a bit apprehensive about approaching him but was gracefully helped by Carlo di Carlo, himself a gifted director, and a man devoted to archiving Antonioni's long and productive career. Carlo arranged a meeting. My inhibition was quickly dissipated by the warmth, the generosity, and, above all, the unpretentiousness of the handsome man who welcomed me to his apartment. Spacious, comfortable, unostentatious, but *elegantissimo*. The walls were covered with art—a still life by Morandi, a pen sketch by Saul Steinberg, some of Antonioni's own drawings. Art books by new artists lay spread on the huge coffee table. Clearly, Antonioni's brilliant mise-en-scène, his sense of design, did not come out of the blue. He told me how he had commissioned Mark Rothko to do a painting, and how death had cheated him of his purchase. The telephone rang: it was his wife, Enrica, in India studying yoga and shooting a documentary. Waiting to resume our conversation, I sat by the window of this art-laden room, overlooking the Tiber (itself a work of art). The ambiance reminded me of the images I had stop-framed on the flatbed editing machine at the Centro Sperimentale di Cinematografia: the De Chirico–like scene in *L'Avventura* set in the silent piazza of the dead mezzogiorno town in Sicily; the rooftop of Gaudi's

MICHELANGELO ANTONIONI

Born 1912
Ferrara, Italy

*Cronaca di un Amore (Story of a Love Affair)*** 1950

*La Signora Senza Camelie (The Lady Without Camellias)*** 1953

*L'Amore in Città (Love in the City)*** 1953 (the episode entitled *Tentato Suicidio* "Suicide Attempt")

*I Vinti (The Vanquished)*** 1953

*Le Amiche (The Girl Friends)*** 1955

*Il Grido (The Outcry)*** 1957

*L'Avventura*** 1960 Cannes Film Festival Jury Prize

*La Notte (The Night)*** 1961

*L'Eclisse (The Eclipse)*** 1962 Jury Special Prize, Cannes Film Festival

*Red Desert*** 1964

*I Tre Volti (The Three Faces)*** 1965 (the episode entitled "Il provino" [The Screentest])

*Blow-Up*** 1966

*Zabriskie Point*** 1970

*Chung Kuo*** 1972

*The Passenger*** 1975

*The Mystery of Oberwald*** 1980

*Identification of a Woman*** 1982

Notto, Mandorli, Vulcano, Stromboli, Carnevale 1992 (co-director Enrica Antonioni)

*Beyond the Clouds*** 1995 (co-director Wim Wenders)

Academy Award for Lifetime Achievement 1995

** also co-screenwriter

Barcelona apartment building in *The Passenger,* where Jack Nicholson meets Maria Schneider; the cold interior of Monica Vitti's flat in the Ravenna of *Red Desert.*

It was 1980, Antonioni was sixty-eight but he looked fifty: tennis had kept him youthful. Clearly, he was serious, but not grave, and certainly not melancholy. Whatever pessimism informed his films, there was none marking his craggy features. The man was—and remains—brimming with life and creative energy. I saw how wrong critics had been for accusing him of obsessing about the dark side of life—suicide, depression, personal failure. He was less interested in talking about themes and meanings than about techniques. He spoke of beautiful shots left on the cutting-room floor as a father speaks of abandoning his daughter's music lessons for lack of money. He expressed admiration for *Blade Runner,* and a desire to make a science fiction film. His voice was husky; quiet, yes, reticent, no. He was totally engaged, a good listener and a thoughtful respondent. He quickly sensed that I was uninterested in gossip (his love affairs; the silly marijuana business at the London airport). I cared about his films, not his biography. He warmed to me as he would to anyone serious about his art.

Even more than critics, other artists hold Antonioni in highest esteem. Not only filmmakers, like Martin Scorsese (whose eloquent encomium

at a Lincoln Center retrospective was so memorable), but painters and writers and architects have told me how much his art has influenced them. There was an exhibition in Venice and Madrid a few years ago—called *Architecture in Vision*—that documented the impact of Antonioni's films on photography, on city planning, on fashion, on advertising—indeed, on the whole look of our era.

Antonioni refused to give up after the devastating stroke that hit him in 1985, paralyzing one side of his body and leaving him virtually speechless. He got tired of sitting at home, and accompanied a traveling retrospective of his films, new prints of which had been struck by Cinecittà, the Italian distribution company. In 1995 he finished a feature film, *Beyond the Clouds,* based on four stories from his book *That Bowling Alley on the Tiber.* The film was made with the help of Wim Wenders (to satisfy the insurance company), but Wenders did more watching than directing. In the spring of 1995 Antonioni came to Hollywood to receive the Lifetime Achievement Oscar from the hands of Jack Nicholson. And in the autumn, he was back again for the American premiere of *Beyond the Clouds.*

He was staying at one of those little bungalows on the grounds of the Sunset Marquis Hotel. *The New York Times* reporter didn't quite know how to interview a speechless man. Enrica, his producer Stephane Tchal-Gadjeff,

SEYMOUR CHATMAN
Born 1928
Detroit, Michigan

A Theory of Meter 1965
Essays on the Language of Literature 1967 (co-editor Samuel R. Levin)
Literary Style: A Symposium 1971
The Later Style of Henry James 1972
Approaches to Poetics: Selected English Institute Essays 1973
Story and Discourse 1978
Proceedings of the First International Congress on Semiotics 1979 (co-editor Umberto Eco)
Antonioni, or the Surface of the World 1985
Michelangelo Antonioni: Identificazione di un Autore 1985
Michelangelo Antonioni's L'Avventura: A Screenplay 1989 (co-editor Guido Fink)
Coming to Terms: The Rhetoric of Narrative in Fiction and Film 1990
Reading Narrative Fiction 1992
"2 ½ Film Versions of Heart of Darkness" in *Conrad on Film* 1998 (edited by Gene Moore)

and I interpreted the questions for him. (His English, excellent in 1980, had vanished with the stroke.) But the vigor of his nods and handshakes, his gestures and, supremely, his pencil sketches, were eloquent enough. Only once was he at a loss: he couldn't remember the name of a film that he had recently seen and liked. To help him became an exercise not unlike charades: we'd guess, and he'd shake his head and urge us on. And that's just how he communicated with his actors on the set of *Beyond the Clouds;* you can see him at work in Enrica's fine hour-long documentary about the making of the film and in Wim and Donata Wenders's splendid photographs in their book documenting the shoot, *Die Zeit mit Antonioni (The Time with Antonioni). Beyond the Clouds* has had great success in France and Italy and has recently been picked up by an American distributor.

The next day, Antonioni was honored by a tribute at the graduation ceremonies of the American Film Institute. The audience of budding filmmakers sat hushed in reverence. I was asked to say a few words on his behalf, and after finishing, he squeezed my hand with his one good hand. Its strength was astonishing. ◆

ON LAWRENCE
KASDAN

LAWRENCE KASDAN

Born 1949
Miami, Florida

*Body Heat** 1981
*The Big Chill*** 1983
*Silverado*** 1985
*The Accidental Tourist***
1988
I Love You to Death
1990
*Grand Canyon*** 1991
*Wyatt Earp*** 1994
French Kiss 1995
(screenplay by Adam
Brooks)
*Mumford** 1999

 * also screenwriter
** also co-screenwriter

The phone rang at nine in the morning. "Let me be first to congratulate you," said the agent's voice. "*French Kiss* will be Lawrence Kasdan's next film." So began a day-long flurry of phone calls from producers, agents, lawyers, and friends. There was a hysterical energy to all of it, the breathless Hollywood buzz you get when there's a glimpse of the green light that might make your movie a reality.

When we met for dinner that evening, Kasdan asked the questions. Personal, professional, philosophical, his appetite for information is voracious. When he starts up the question mill, the novice is slightly put off, but he is also invariably flattered. "*Mr. Kasdan wants to know . . .*" There is something rabbinical in the process, the delving deeper, the eyes dancing in delight at your discomfort. Larry teases, he comments, then he asks you another question.

But he can talk. He did talk. After I had satisfied him about my career, wife, children, oedipal conflicts, and guilty pleasures, we discussed the script. He told me what he thought, what he liked, what he was concerned about. His voice is distinctive. At one time or another you will feel inclined to try an imitation. I don't think Kasdan likes his voice but I do; it makes demands, it implies high expectations. Before dinner I had been sent three pages of irritatingly banal notes by one of the producers; by dessert Kasdan had discarded them with practiced nonchalance. I liked him more and more. Which was fortunate, because we spent much of the next eight months in each other's company.

A work session with Kasdan is delayed as long as possible. Coffee, snacks, gossip. Movie talk. Endless chatter about every movie except the one that we're working on. His director heroes are not who I would have guessed. Many of them are epic filmmakers—David Lean, Akira Kurosawa, John Sturges. Their films have a sweeping narrative momentum, the characters and their conflicts are clear-cut, the images are heroic and masculine. Kasdan's affinity to these filmmakers is evident in his westerns, but most obviously in the screenplays for *Raiders of the Lost Ark, The Empire Strikes Back,* and *Return of the Jedi,* blockbuster movies all helmed by other directors.

Larry's own films (including the westerns) are more concerned with contradictions and ambiguity; the stories occupy a moral gray zone where characters struggle between their need for control and a desire to explore, transgress, reach out. Their struggles can have dire consequences (*Body Heat*) or they can lead to personal epiphanies, a liberation of soul and character (*The Accidental Tourist, Grand Canyon*). So it's no surprise that Howard Hawks is another of his favorites.

A work session with Kasdan is delayed as long as possible. Coffee, snacks, gossip. Movie talk. Endless chatter about every movie except the one that we're working on.

ADAM BROOKS
Born 1956
Toronto, Canada

Almost You 1985
(director)

Red Riding Hood 1987
(director)

Heads 1993 (screenplay)

French Kiss 1995
(screenplay; film directed
by Lawrence Kasdan)

Duke of Groove 1995
(screenwriter)

Beloved 1998
(co-screenwriter; based
on the novel by Toni
Morrison; film directed
by Jonathan Demme)

Practical Magic 1998
(co-screenwriter; based
on the novel by Alice
Hoffman)

It is on the set that Kasdan seems to be able to achieve the zen balance that he aspires to in the rest of his life. He doesn't waste energy, he doesn't talk a lot. He reads, he does his correspondence. The filmmaking process swirls around him with its attendant crises, hissy fits, dollar disasters. He finds the eye of the storm and sits there calmly in his director's chair. He takes a nap at lunch. He doesn't waste time coddling his department heads: when he doesn't like something he tells them directly, without rancor, and expects them to quickly come up with three more good ideas. He is surprised to hear that some of the people who work on his movies are intimidated by him; but he's not entirely unhappy about it. He isn't afraid to admit it when he has no idea what to do next. He's happy to take a good idea from anyone on the crew, he knows the credit will be his in the end. He only shoots with wide-screen anamorphic lenses. And in each scene he strives to find an elegance in the mise-en-scène, and a flourish, a gesture (with the camera, the acting, or the writing) that will ultimately define the scene and bring it to life. He usually knows exactly how it will all come together in the cutting room. He tells me that in all these things he used to be a control freak, but he is learning to let go and explore what happens in the moment, to take whatever he can from the talent and possibilities around him.

Kasdan sits at the center of concentric circles of family and friends who surround him with fortresslike strength. The same actors and technicians appear over and over again in the credits of his films. Kevin Kline, Bill Hurt, Danny Glover, Owen Roizman, Charles Okun, Carol Littleton. Kasdan is rigorous in his loyalties and still has many friends from his college days. His wife, Meg, wrote *Grand Canyon* with him. It is an intensely personal film and I think my favorite of his movies. At the story's center is a happy and successful middle-class Los Angeles family. Their lives and the lives of their friends suddenly spin out of control with the unexpected onslaught of a chain of violent acts. Some of these are natural (an earthquake, a kitchen accident, a heart attack), others are not (a mugging, a baby abandoned). A moral and philosophical reordering becomes necessary, the time has come to confront unfulfilled promises, longings that will no longer be repressed, communal ties that can't be ignored. New friends are made, family is extended; by the end a bittersweet balance has been attained. Life goes on. ◆

ON RON HOWARD

Actor, filmmaker, director, and man—Ron Howard is a perfect example of the quality of American genius. Not like the physicist who divines an order in the universe that only a select few can comprehend, but the everyman who embodies and crystallizes the heart of the nation. Not Hollywood, not M.I.T.—America.

At a time when pyrotechnics, sex, and animation form the driving core of popular filmmaking, Mr. Howard searches out the heroism and drama in everyday life. He doesn't shrink from scientific innovation but at the same time he remembers that his audience is made up of women and men who care most about love and God and the future of their children.

Many so-called serious films often seek out the extreme spy, killer, thief, or victim. Detailed character development shows us the tortured individual and his or her odyssey in a depraved and nihilistic landscape. But Mr. Howard sees that it is our working life that informs us, that makes who we are and, more importantly, who we can be.

The firefighter, the reporter, the nighttime janitor. Everyone in Ron Howard's best films has a job. Either they're working hard or they've worked a hard life and are now facing an end.

We learn from these films, but Ron Howard is not a teacher. He merely shows us a world that we know or remember. We learn from that moment of recognition when we see ourselves and, hopefully, smile.

Throughout his acting career Howard brought that generous spirit to his roles. He created characters who believed in something beyond themselves. That something is you and me. As his artistic convictions grew he realized that he had to go beyond the narrow confines of film portrayals.

Hollywood didn't want another actor who thought he could direct. Luckily Ron Howard didn't care what they wanted. He wanted something and, like any true director, he got it.

RON HOWARD
Born 1954
Duncan, Oklahoma

*Grand Theft Auto*** 1977
Night Shift 1982
Splash 1984
Cocoon 1985
Gung Ho 1985
Willow 1988
Parenthood 1989
Backdraft 1991
*Far and Away*** 1992
The Paper 1994
Apollo 13 1995
Ransom 1996
EDtv 1999
How the Grinch Stole Christmas 1999
(in production)

* also screenwriter
** also co-screenwriter

I said that everyone in Howard's best films has a job. Everyone on the set of his films has a job, too. Grips, best boys, caterers, and special consultants all equally feel that they have the director's ear. His assistant has been with him for sixteen years. The film being made is the product of the whole crew and cast. No one is denigrated or insulted. Past writers aren't blamed for current problems.

It sounds like a worker's dream. But what about the product? The crew can be dancing on the set but if the movie doesn't make it, then the party was ill-conceived. But it is because of the movie that will be made that the crew works so hard and long. They know that they will be doing their best work under his guidance, and so they buck up when he flashes that boyish grin and directs them to redo a job already done a dozen times.

WALTER MOSLEY
Born in Los Angeles,
California

Devil in a Blue Dress
1990 (film directed by
Carl Franklin)
A Red Death 1992
White Butterfly 1993
Black Betty 1994
"The Watts Lion" 1994
(short story)
RL's Dream 1995
A Little Yellow Dog 1996
"The Thief" 1996
(short story)
Gone Fishin' 1997
Always Outnumbered,
Always Outgunned
1997 (co-screenwriter
for HBO movie, *Always*
Outnumbered, 1998)
Blue Light 1998

The best actors in Hollywood flock to Howard. Award winners, bread winners, and stars come to make his films. People who love acting and who know that their legacies will be sealed forever in the films they make. Pyrotechnics, they know, will not be remembered because the future will outdo them. Blood and guts, sex and violence, are ends in themselves and rarely help to show off the actor's abilities.

These actors know that a strong role anchored in a true moment of cinema, and cultural history, is the best work they can do. They know Ron Howard will make them look good in a film that will still be looking good in fifty years.

Mr. Howard is one of the most important directorial voices of our age. He speaks to the heart and the future of film in America. He speaks to our dreams and dramas. And if you look closely at the powerful and unique ego in his films you will see something of yourself—because Ron takes our possibilities and imbues them with light. ◆

ON RICHARD
DONNER

Somebody once said that a director's body of work reflects their personality. That's certainly true of Dick Donner. Like his movies, Donner is an event: entertaining, full of surprises, and above all—larger than life. When Krypton explodes in *Superman,* that's Donner losing his temper. When Mel Gibson leaps from the roof in *Lethal Weapon,* that's Dick throwing himself headlong into another project. When Donner made the love story *Ladyhawke,* he met and fell in love with his future wife, producer Lauren Shuler. Which came first, the chicken or the egg? I don't know the answer. The man and his movies are impossible to separate.

Donner loves hijinks. On film and in life. When you try to leave a room and the door won't open, odds are Dick Donner's on the other side holding it shut. Witness the Rube Goldberg devices in *The Goonies.* Bowling balls which roll into blow torches which burn through ropes which hold up . . . well, you get the idea. What you don't know is that, in the best possible way, that's how Donner's mind works. But it isn't all fun and games. The man's ego is prodigious. With his leonine head and booming voice, he seems more like a movie star than the stars he's directing. When Donner shouts "Action!" on a set, it's the voice of God coming down from on high.

To his credit, it's never just about Donner. Dick loves people—their problems and foibles as well as their triumphs and strengths. If he finds out it's your birthday, run for cover. His people skills are amazing but never manipulative. They show up in the end product. He empowers his crew. Each person he talks to tries a little harder because Dick has made them feel that their job is the most important job on the set. And anyone who he's ever called "Kid" has seen how wonderfully the man can turn the fact that he's forgotten your name from an embarrassment to an honor.

Ultimately, Donner is the kind of man whom you speak of anecdotally. Like remembering scenes from a film. When someone asks you, "How's Dick?" You don't say he's fine or he's got the flu or he's away in Hawaii. You tell stories about him. Don't ask how Dick is unless you have twenty minutes to hear the answer. For me, the story will always be—William Goldman's Banana.

RICHARD DONNER
Born 1930
New York, New York

X-15 1961
Salt and Pepper 1968
Lola 1969
The Omen 1976
Superman 1978
Inside Moves 1980
The Toy 1982
Ladyhawke 1985
The Goonies 1985
Lethal Weapon 1987
Scrooged 1988
Lethal Weapon 2 1989
Radio Flyer 1992
Lethal Weapon 3 1992
Maverick 1994
(screenplay by William Goldman)
Assassins 1995
Conspiracy Theory 1997
Lethal Weapon 4 1998

111

I was working on the final polish of a screenplay that Donner was a few weeks away from shooting. Warner Brothers had sent me up to Seattle to rendezvous with him. We were going to scout locations in Puerto Rico for a few days and then return to Donner's home in the San Juan Islands to finish up work on the script.

Donner flew in that afternoon by seaplane and I went to the dock to meet him. The door opens and William Goldman steps off. Now I don't know him, but I recognize him. The man practically does rewrites for God. Thinking I'm an assistant of sorts, he sets his bags down in front of me. Next off the plane is Donner. He spots me, turns to Goldman and says, "Bill, this is Brian Helgeland." Goldman gives me a wry smile. "So you're the genius Dick's been telling me about." Dick Donner—never faint with praise. Overwhelmed by modesty, I carry one of Goldman's bags.

Five days later Donner and I have returned from our scout (there are a dozen anecdotes there alone) and arrived in the San Juan Islands. Donner's house there is big, vaulting, but never ostentatious. It reminds me of a Viking hall. And there's Donner enjoying every inch of it. When he dies, I swear I will personally set him on fire and float him out into Puget Sound in a longship. His house is full of great stuff which I'll load in the boat with him.

To his credit, it's never just about Donner. Dick loves people—their problems and foibles as well as their triumphs and strengths. If he finds out it's your birthday, run for cover.

BRIAN HELGELAND
Born 1961
Providence, Rhode Island

Assassins 1995
(co-screenwriter; film directed by Richard Donner)

Conspiracy Theory 1997
(screenplay; film directed by Richard Donner)

L. A. Confidential 1997
(co-screenwriter)
Academy Award for Best Adapted Screenplay

A sentimental man, he has a passion for antiques and bric-a-brac. They have become the way he marks his life and career. There's furniture bought on film locations. Art purchased during scouts. A revolving hotel door picked up while in exile in London. A tablet taken off the side of the old bath house at Coney Island is mortared into the center of the fireplace. Donner went there as a kid and now that memory has become part of his home.

Anyhow, we're unpacking groceries and Dick points out a bowl of fruit. A few apples, oranges, and a banana. All of it's been sitting here at least a week. The banana is completely brown. Donner makes sure I see it. "You should eat that banana," he says to me. It's on the ragged edge of being rotten. I tell him I'm not interested. Dick shrugs and that's the end of it, I think. Two hours later he's making coffee. "You should really have that banana." I want to know why. Dick doesn't answer. Now the question is cream or sugar.

That evening we're getting ready to go out to dinner. I'm finishing a soda and out of the corner of my eye I see Donner considering the banana and then considering me. I see him visibly decide not to bring up the subject of the banana again. I don't ask any questions, but the hook is in. My destiny and the banana's are somehow intertwined.

The next morning at breakfast, Donner gets right to the point. "I'd seriously think about eating that banana if I were you." I can't take it anymore and I ask him why. "Because," Donner smiles knowingly, "That's William Goldman's banana." He goes on to explain that Goldman loves bananas and that the week before he'd bought a bunch and this one was the only one he didn't eat. I look at the banana. It's worse than the day before. I tell Donner it's rotten and I can't eat it. "You don't have to," he answers, "I just thought it might bring you some luck."

Luck. I fight it for an hour or two, but I already know I'm going to eat the banana. It's William Goldman's banana. Richard Donner told me it would bring me luck. Hollywood luck. I couldn't not eat that banana now if I wanted to. A little before lunch I step into the kitchen. It peels real easy. Half of it has turned to mush. I slice it into the trash. But the other half? I deem it edible. Three quick bites and like he can see through walls, Donner steps into the kitchen.

I give him a sheepish grin, but he smiles big, then starts to laugh. "That's not William Goldman's banana!" I've been reeled in like a big, fat fish. The difference is, I'm a fish that thoroughly enjoyed the experience. That's what the man does to you. That's what his movies do to you. Of course, he later swears up and down it really was Goldman's banana, but I know it wasn't. All the same, I feel pretty lucky for having eaten it, and blessed for knowing Mr. Richard Donner. ◈

ON TERRY
GILLIAM

Gilliam has through the years developed his own view of existence so clearly, and so deftly, that to a degree greater than any other director he is now able to create any kind of world, historical or imaginary, and make it absolutely believable and understandable to the audience.

Monty Python and the Holy Grail was the first movie I ever saw where people were literally falling out of their seats laughing. As marvelous as the television show had been (and at that point the programs had not yet become the *I Love Lucy* of the public networks, their scripts memorized and quoted ad infinitum), fans who went to see the film had no idea how inexplicably perfect, and hilarious, the combination of African sparrows, Trojan rabbits, silly English kiniggets and holy hand grenades would prove to be. One of the biggest laughs came when hapless King Arthur and his imbecile knights, set upon by a particularly ludicrous animated critter, are miraculously rescued when "suddenly the animator suffered a fatal heart attack."

The animator, of course, was Terry Gilliam, sole American member of the troupe. His comedic style was expectedly different from that of his British co-performers, but his animation style was and remains like nothing else seen in film. There wasn't anything particularly complicated about his techniques, quite the contrary; essentially, he assembled various images from books and then filmed them in stop-action photography in order to cause them to move. It was the images he selected and the unexpected ways he made them move that turned what were essentially transitional bits between sketches into unforgettably bizarre (and hilarious) cinematic classics. Sometimes they were like the scenes from Warner Brothers shorts that early on hit the cutting-room floor (the unseen baby who seizes and eats a succession of sweet old ladies who lean over its carriage to cluck and coo over it), but as often they were like Ernst collages come to life (in *Grail,* the monk attempting to shoo off the heavy-legged sun as it leaps up and down at the horizon). And, at the time, there was no way of knowing that when Gilliam turned his attention to directing, the vision that informed his movies would be as unique as the vision that sustained his animation.

Confronted with the art of one who seems—and is—so utterly original, it's good to remember that no art is created in a vacuum. A director's work is as infused, consciously or unconsciously, with the artistic influences he or she has experienced as the work of any writer, musician, painter, or sculptor, and the work can be best understood by the audience if the influences are understood as well. To understand Gilliam (and not everyone does—those who do understand need no theory or justification, and those who don't, never will), it's good to be aware of two of his predecessors, one of whom is an admitted influence: Hieronymus Bosch and Harvey Kurtzman. The former is high art, according to critics, the latter, low; in their case as in Gilliam's, critics too often miss the point. All three are of a piece: inimitable, marvelous, magical in its truest sense.

If in every great director's movies there are sequences in which you perceive the influence of an equally great painter, it's impossible to see almost any scene from any film of Terry Gilliam's without thinking of the sixteenth-century Dutch artist Bosch, who without evident effort looked at this world and saw the one underlying, a world no one else would have *wanted* to see until he made them look. Bosch is the funniest of all the old masters. Unable to depict heaven without reminding the viewer of hell, he was plainly unable to think about hell without laughing— morbid laughter, granted. It's one thing to imagine tiny, bird-headed demons snacking on sinners as if they were strips of beef jerky, and something else entirely to make it clear to the viewer how much the tiny demons are enjoying themselves doing it. This kind of sense of humor that, in Gilliam's greatest film, *Brazil,* manifests itself when the state charges Mrs. Buttle for the cost of having (by mistake) arrested, interrogated, and killed Mr. Buttle; this admitting to an awareness of the world as it is, in all its horror, and realizing at base how ludicrous that horror is. A person possessed of such awareness won't forgive his or her torturers, but will instead laugh at them, thereby denying them the satisfaction they figured on enjoying.

TERRY GILLIAM
Born 1940
Minneapolis, Minnesota

*Monty Python and
the Holy Grail*** 1974
(co-director)
*Jabberwocky*** 1977
*Time Bandits*** 1981
*Brazil*** 1985
*The Adventures of Baron
Munchausen*** 1989
The Fisher King 1991
12 Monkeys 1995
*Fear and Loathing in Las
Vegas*** 1998

** also co-screenwriter

JACK WOMACK
Born 1956
Lexington, Kentucky

Ambient 1987
Terraplane 1988
Heathern 1990
Elvissey 1993
*Random Acts of
Senseless Violence* 1994
*Let's Put the Future
Behind Us* 1996
Going, Going Gone 1999

Gilliam has said that his tendency to load his scenes with background detail was inspired by his love of studying the crammed panels of *Mad* magazine in his childhood. Harvey Kurtzman, who created *Mad* in 1952, became his mentor in the early sixties, after Gilliam moved from Southern California to New York. Kurtzman hired him to work on the humor magazine *Help!*, where Gilliam practiced the comic techniques he would later perfect, as well as meet others who worked with the magazine, notably John Cleese. Although even today Kurtzman is not nearly as well known as he should be to the general public, there is no one working in comic art—whether written, spoken, or visual—in the second half of the twentieth century who does not owe a tremendous debt to Kurtzman (who died in 1992) for having created the framework upon which contemporary humor has grown. From Kurtzman's example Gilliam learned and developed, I think, the ability to not merely sense and elaborate upon the grotesqueries of everyday life, but to never lose sight of the fact that the world and its people, even at their most malign, almost always remain hopelessly, unavoidably human, and therefore are best looked upon with humor, rather than despair.

Gilliam has through the years developed his own view of existence so clearly, and so deftly, that to a degree greater than any other director he is now able to create any kind of world, historical or imaginary, and make it absolutely believable and understandable to the audience. *Grail,* which he co-directed with fellow Python member Terry Jones, and *Jabberwocky,* the first film he directed by himself, recreate the medieval European world so exactly that they almost seem to have been filmed on location, at the time (the knights of Ni and Jabberwock itself notwithstanding). I now find it impossible to watch any other movie whose action is set in this period without being aware of how fraudulent they are—what do the characters do about heating those castles?—let's not even talk about plumbing. In *The Adventures of Baron Munchausen,* the interior of a ship-swallowing fish, or the surface of the moon, is as precisely portrayed as the besieged city of Vienna; since *12 Monkeys* came out it's been impossible to look at Philadelphia's city hall without picturing it buried in snow drifts and sheeted ice; and every time I descend the stairs that lead into Grand Central Terminal in New York City, I hope that for once the commuters will for a few minutes forget about catching the 5:45 to Stamford and, as in *The Fisher King,* pair up and start waltzing.

But as unforgettable as the visual elements are in Gilliam's films, as equally memorable are his characters. Most are deeply flawed in one way or the other, but this only—especially—emphasizes their humanity; even the most outlandish remain real people. Think, for example, of the assorted little men, of Sean Connery's King of Mycenae, and of Sir Ralph Richardson's God in *Time Bandits;* think of the Baron and his assistants in *Munchausen.* And where, in his earlier films, normal—relatively normal—characters tended to be but sketchily drawn (Jill, for example in *Brazil*), by the time Gilliam made *12 Monkeys* in 1995, his skill in depicting such characters was such that through them he could evoke the most profound emotional responses from the audience. In the scene of that movie which never fails to affect me, however often I see it, Bruce Willis and Madeline Stowe sit in her car, both crying. Stowe cries because Willis, a former patient of hers during one of his wild swings back and forth through time, has kidnapped her, and she's terrified that it's only a matter of minutes before he kills her; but Willis is crying because as he listens to "Blueberry Hill," he is overcome by its beauty: "I love the music of the twentieth century." Neither Stowe nor Willis has any idea why the other is so upset; the viewer, understanding both the tragedy as well as the humor of the situation, finds that both emotions are equally heightened through their proximity. I can't think of any director other than Gilliam willing to try pulling off such a scene and succeeding.

For better or worse, writers must deal with publishers, painters must deal with galleries, filmmakers must deal with producers. The process of filmmaking, like all acts of artistic creation, contains within itself the danger that through the effort necessary to produce the work, the art itself will be forgotten, lost, or deliberately set aside.

In *Brazil,* Sam, the hero, is able at last to escape the clutches of the state's torturers by escaping into his mind, into his art. "He got away from us," they say at the end.

I think Gilliam will forever be able to continue getting away from them. ◆

ON MARTHA
COOLIDGE

Often I depend on my wife to find my friends, with happy results. Back in the late 1970s, when Cee Cee was trying to work as an actress, she landed a role in an educational film, sponsored by the Bureau of Indian Affairs, a film designed to inform reservation women of their rights. She came home from the shoot energized by the director, a dynamic young woman named Martha Coolidge.

It was only an educational film, a gig, but Martha attacked it with precision and passion. It was *work,* good and important. She had done her preparation, knew her material, had a goal. She rallied the cast and crew and they nailed it, and everyone went home feeling fine.

For days afterward, Cee Cee talked about this diminutive point of power, and how gracefully she managed the men on the set, taciturn Indians, some of them, who brought to the camera a cultural and spiritual distrust.

"If any woman," Cee Cee said, "can break into the Boys' Club," meaning the A-list of directors at the time, "Martha is the one to do it." And so she has.

MARTHA COOLIDGE
Born 1946
New Haven, Connecticut

*Not a Pretty Picture** 1976
The City Girl 1982
Valley Girl 1983
Joy of Sex 1984
Real Genius 1986
Plain Clothes 1988
Rambling Rose 1991
Lost in Yonkers 1993
Angie 1994
Three Wishes 1995
Out to Sea 1997

* also screenwriter

We were living in Ojai then, eighty miles north of what some of our friends in Los Angeles began calling the War Zone. Martha was alone and we invited her to come spend a weekend with us. We sat around the kitchen table and she told us, without self-pity, of struggles bordering on the horrific, starting in New York and continuing to Los Angeles, any one of which might have finished a less determined director.

I didn't know her or her work, didn't realize that she had already done a couple of handmade films, one of them as close an examination of rape as any, and more personal than most because it was her own: *Not a Pretty Picture.* But for all her vulnerability, here was sure resilience. Like the reed, nature's best role model, she would bend before the storm but not break. Is it necessary for a woman to be tough to be a film director? Yes, it is. It is necessary for a woman to be tough to be a woman.

My theory, based on close observation, about those directors with a sweet tooth for fake blood and simulated torture—you know who you are—is that they are weaklings, frail of heart and stomach, with a history of being picked upon, now exorcising their cowardice through film. In a fair fight I'd bet on Martha and give you odds.

Critics like to look for the director's signature, and most directors like to show them one. But the movies I like best are clean, that is, without the

119

DARRYL PONICSAN
Born in Shenandoah,
Pennsylvania

The Last Detail 1970
(novel)
Cinderella Liberty 1973
(novel and screenplay)
Taps 1981
(co-screenwriter)
Vision Quest 1985
(screenplay; based on
the novel by Terry Davis)
Nuts 1987
(co-screenwriter)
The Boost 1988
(screenplay)
School Ties 1992
(co-screenwriter)
The Enemy Within 1994
(co-screenwriter)

graffiti of directors, writers, or set designers, that is, lifelike. The writer's signature is always easy to overcome, but for a director to overcome his own ego is not only selfless, it is smart, and Martha is nothing if not smart.

I've heard her say that she likes actors—I like them myself, but mark, they will betray you, they can't help it—but what she really means is that behavior is what fascinates her. Yes, the lighting must be right, the script must be storylike, the music should be Bernstein-like, but finally it all rests on what goes on between the people on the screen.

Hard work, trial and error, gold is never found without taking a risk, and most times it is never found at all, or when found not seen as the genuine article. Still, she looks, she finds.

Among us she is known as writer-friendly, a quality rare in directors of either gender. She values words, but she knows the silences are worth more. Writers know that, too. A rambling rose ambling down a Texas street says more than words can convey. Come to think of it, so does this picture of Martha. ◆

JOAN JULIET BUCK

ON BERNARDO
BERTOLUCCI

ROMANTICISM AND THE SPIRIT OF THE AGE

There is a bridge in Paris where pedestrians walk under railroad tracks, at the end of which stands an apartment building with turrets at the corners, and over the round rooms nearest to the bridge is a phallic dome, and in one of those rooms was enacted the defining love affair of a generation: the anonymous, unclothed, entirely erotic encounters between a young girl with large, hanging breasts and a desperate American widower who summed up their relationship as "your happiness, my hap-penis."

Even as the very notion of being romantic has become old-fashioned, uncool, Bertolucci has remained a romantic. His first allegiance is to the conclusions drawn from the imperatives of the unconscious.

Last Tango in Paris had a tango in it, but that was not what was remembered. Although in terms of the totality of its creator's work, the dancing was perhaps the most enduring trope, what was remembered had to do with butter and caused Bertolucci to be stripped of his civil rights in Italy for five years.

It was difficult for a man committed to a collective ideal to be unable to vote. That may be what led to *1900*. As a child in the country, just after the war, he had heard a peasant woman say the word "communist" with such intensity and conviction that he decided that was what he would be. His next film after *Last Tango in Paris,* not incidentally, was a retelling of the history of Italy in the twentieth century up until the end of World War II, charting "the end of feudalism and the rise of communism," a rise as organic and inevitable in his eyes and on his celluloid as the succession of the seasons.

A sort of passionate pantheism allowed him to explain that he was shooting in sequence with the seasons, the drama gathering in "the winter that is the dark night of fascism," and spring both bringing and signifying the Liberation. Dialectical materialism was the interpretive tool of choice; this was before irony and quotes, pre–Umberto Eco, pre-semiotics, pre-postmodern.

Bertolucci's constituency had been taught history by Marxist professors, and around that mental architecture hung the gentle collective haze of marijuana. We of that generation all desperately wanted to both understand

121

and belong, and Bertolucci was the first person to join together Marx and Freud, political idealism and sex. And he did it with a romantic sensuality that surfaces again and again in his films, even as he has moved away from Marx and made his more recent subjects power, and Buddha, and virginity. His subject has always been interdependence; whether its nature was political (*Before the Revolution, The Conformist*), sexual (*Last Tango in Paris*), social (*The Sheltering Sky, The Last Emperor*), or religious (*Little Buddha*).

Even as the very notion of being romantic has become old-fashioned, uncool, Bertolucci has remained a romantic. His first allegiance is to the conclusions drawn from the imperatives of the unconscious. His way of processing and expressing the period he lived in became more real than the period itself. He did not live the prewar anguish of the hero in *The Conformist,* but his stylish Art Deco world had a peculiar charge beyond the narrative. The specific stylishness of that film makes me think of a line from Doris Lessing's *The Golden Notebook,* where a character says she could never wear a black shirt, because of the connotations. He might not have lived the desperate sex of *Last Tango,* but in its wake, it was to that kind of anonymous orgasm that a generation aspired.

He proceeds, it seems, by instinct and osmosis. Twenty years ago, an actor who had half-killed himself embodying a fascist for Bertolucci, and who seemed ready and eager to go even further, said, "Bernardo can take everything going on and absorb it and make you participate in it." Years before he thought about making *Little Buddha,* Bertolucci had mastered the art of making experience communal, universal. The terrain for accepting this illusion was well-prepared; I'm talking about a time when the dominating myth was based on a sense of community so extreme as to embrace, beyond other human beings, the cup of coffee on the table, the chairs and the crumbs on the ground, and the sky as well. He could make large numbers of people believe the same thing, without oratory, without coercion. His imagination was so powerful that it inspired people around him to lose themselves in his concrete fictions.

I met him on November 6, 1974. Certain dates you never forget. It was on the set of *1900.* He had black eyes that have become smaller, and black hair that has become shorter, a tall figure that has become broader. He was thirty-three, with two great films already behind him: *The Conformist* and *Last Tango in Paris.* He wore a battered green hat and a cape, because it was cold. He spoke Italian and French and English with the slightly cutting inflections of a Florentine accent, but always in a confidential whisper, sentences coming out as if they were secrets he had only just decided to reveal. The scene he was shooting was the funeral of four men burned to death in a fire set by Fascist militiamen. The setting was the foggy main square of Guastalla, a village near Parma, where Bertolucci was born.

BERNARDO BERTOLUCCI
Born 1941
Parma, Italy

*The Grim Reaper*** 1962
*Before the Revolution***
1964 Cannes Film
Festival Young Critics
Prize
*La Via del Petrlio (Oil
Route)* 1967
Agony 1967
Love and Anger 1967
(segment: Il Fico
infruttuoso)
*Partner*** 1968
*The Spider's Stratagem***
1970
*The Conformist** 1971
*Health Is Sick (The Poor
Die Sooner)* 1971
*Last Tango in Paris***
1972
*1900 (Novecento)***
1976
*Luna*** 1979
*Tragedy of a Ridiculous
Man** 1981
*The Last Emperor***
1987 Academy Awards
for Best Director and
Best Adapted Screenplay;
Golden Globe Awards for
Best Director and Best
Screenplay
*The Sheltering Sky***
1990
Little Buddha 1993
*Stealing Beauty*** 1996
(based on a story by
Bertolucci)
*The Siege (L'Assedio)***
1998

 * also screenwriter
** also co-screenwriter

JOAN JULIET BUCK
Born 1948
Los Angeles, California

The Only Place to Be
1982
Daughter of the Swan
1987
Editor in Chief, *Vogue*,
Paris 1994–

Now the first of the Bertolucci moments happened: I stood under the arches, carefully away from the camera's view, in new red boots and a long black raincoat. I watched the young French actor Gérard Depardieu, his body solid like a tree (playing the peasant character Olmo, which means elm) lead the procession with Stefania Sandrelli, and watched the hundreds of people walking behind them, all in black, each with a little red kerchief or fabric at their necks. "The Internationale" began to play softly. The dramatic idea was that suddenly the peasants had allies, that the battle song had been taken up, that they were no longer alone.

Having grown up dully watchful on movie sets, waiting for the two close-ups to follow the master shot, and waiting most of all for lunch break or the tea trolley with the fat slices of cheddar in the round buns, having watched narrative being broken into discrete pieces of business that needed to be in the can by six o'clock, having seen films made with the overriding impression of people simply getting through the job, I was astonished: everyone here seemed to believe in what they were doing. The cast and crew and strays were all joined, linked in some wildly idealistic and risky adventure. Something huge was at stake—the opportunity to understand, to be part of a coherent definition of the time.

I suddenly found that I had an urgent and inappropriate longing to be in the scene that was being shot. Wildly, impossibly, to be not an actor nor an extra but all of it, the situation and its meaning, the town, the square, the cobblestones, the gray lowering sky. Up in Turin that day, the police had fired on strikers; fifty years of labor relations and the social history had compressed and vanished. But the feeling that overwhelmed me was not political, nor social. It was the swoon of one transformed into a groupie, an acolyte. "I always become seduced by the emotions engendered during filming," Bertolucci said in Parma in 1974. His tool, his ally in bewitching those around him and then audiences, is his own ability to be bewitched, his own vulnerable permeability. It is his own weakness, self-admitted and mined with years of analysis, that allows him to rule.

The place where he was born is suited to the navigation of dissolved boundaries. Parma is misty and dreamy, foggy and dense, romantic and wistful. It is where the Empress Maria Louisa was exiled after the fall of her husband Napoleon, and where she picked violets in the rain and bothered to record that in her diary. Mansions with Palladian pediments rise out of the flat farmlands, poplars line the raised banks of the river Po, the local food is thick, heavy parmesan and prosciutto as pale and fine as rose petals, and in the air, along with the thick fog, floats a slight smell of manure.

Bertolucci's grandmother's family was the model for the rich landowners in 1900; his father Attilio is a poet whose work holds to a narrow, precise focus on domestic felicities. If he wrote a poem about a flower at the bottom of the garden, the child Bernardo could run down to the bottom of the garden and look at that flower. "Poetry was as humble and real as anything else," says Bertolucci. A few years ago, he told me, "My father didn't only teach me poetry; he taught me hypochondria and the fear of death."

The dread was partially exorcised by twenty-two years of analysis, which sometimes went too far, as when a congress of psychiatrists watched *1900* together in Venice. He likes to open himself to immense psychic risks. As a young man he had written poetry; it seemed the only thing to do. He published a little book of poems at twenty-one, *In Search of Mystery,* made his first film, and never wrote another poem. It was another poet, the Bertoluccis' downstairs neighbor in Rome, Pier Paolo Pasolini, who asked him to be his assistant on his first film, *Accattone.* Bertolucci's first film in 1962, *La Commare Secca,* was from a script of Pasolini's. In all his films you find leaves and dancing: *La Commare Secca* showed leaves dancing over the body of a murdered prostitute, and the leaves carry on through every film, blown about, crunching underfoot. The dancing is in *The Conformist*— Stefania Sandrelli and Dominique Sanda together—*Last Tango in Paris, 1900, The Last Emperor,* and *Stealing Beauty*. It serves as the moment of seduction or the moment of evasion from reality; the invocation of another way of being, of another reality.

I have never seen Bertolucci dance, but I have seen him staring at the leaves. If he was political for *1900,* he was Freudian for *Luna,* earthy for *Tragedy of a Ridiculous Man,* operatic for *The Last Emperor,* nomadic for *The Sheltering Sky,* Buddhist for *Little Buddha,* and sensually patriarchal for *Stealing Beauty*. Each time he was his material, and believed it entirely. Twenty years on, he still believes in interdependence, perhaps more than ever. During the GATT dispute, when France wanted to impose quotas on the number of American films distributed in Europe, he sat down at a dinner table with an American director of cynical, devilishly clever thrillers. He put forward the proposal that the great American directors—for he is also a flatterer—refuse to allow their films to be shown in Europe until the GATT problem was resolved, thereby helping European cinema. The American director looked at him and said, "Why would I do anything like that?"

To help everyone. That is what a romantic does. ◆

ON JAMES
CAMERON

When I was a kid, in kindergarten, thirty-seven or so years ago, we had a kiss-your-ass-goodbye drill once a week. We were told that, on signal, we must all run to the walls, crouch down, "duck and cover," put our heads betwixt our legs, and turn our backs on our vulnerability.

I had nightmares about nuclear war. Cameron, he's my generation. I don't know him personally, but I know we both grew up in the shadow of impending nuclear war: before Glasnost, before the SALT treaties. We all knew about "the football," the president's special briefcase, the "button" he would press if pressed.

And we all knew that the world our parents had built was a flimsy construct and that whatever promises life held, an early death was promised with a greater certainty. Maybe we were wrong; there has been some nuclear disarmament, the cold war is over. But now there's more and more talk of nuclear terrorists—as in Cameron's *True Lies.*

Genre devices aside, Cameron's first important film, *The Terminator,* was a demand to know: *Have we turned over our future to mindless assholes? Have we surrendered to machines? Are we going to wake up or are we going to die in a nuclear war?*

The philosopher G.I. Gurdjieff believed we are all machines, all the time; that we are always mechanical. He also believed we possess the capacity to become more than a machine; but that capacity is asleep in us. We are a world of sleepwalkers relying on the machinery of our conditioning to fumble us through our lives. This perception seems to me to underlie the more obvious messages of James Cameron's films.

The Terminator; Terminator 2: Judgment Day (T2 for short*); The Abyss; True Lies; Titanic*: the Cameron canon, all are genre films. And genre films are of only passing interest to critics, or perhaps of no interest, judging by *Chambers' Concise Encyclopedia of Film and Television,* which makes no mention of Cameron or any of his films. (I'll be using that volume to line the cat box.)

But Cameron's films burst with meaning, and, yes, symbolism; his films are asking the bigger questions, usually, which calls for bigger symbols. Despite the rigorous structuring of genre films, there is room for any amount of detailing, for exquisite styling—e.g., Hitchcock—and for the masterful exploitation of the plasticity of cinema so characteristic of Cameron. Even the action shots are artful—Schwarzenegger peeling out on a motorcycle becomes a curving paintbrush stroke in chrome and rubber on the screen; Ed Harris sinking helplessly in *The Abyss,* a human falling star in a far corner of the screen, almost swallowed by the darkness: a striking visual personification of the feeling of helplessness, insignificance.

Let's look at the Cameron cinematic template: *The Terminator,* in which murderous robots roam the ruins of our wrecked future, trying to exterminate the brave human resistance. Machines amidst ruin.

And we all knew that the world our parents had built was a flimsy construct and that whatever promises life held, an early death was promised with a greater certainty.

Cut to the present-day, ongoing ruin of the Los Angeles inner city: the mechanical arm on a garbage truck; a machine in the wreckage. (Again and again in the *Terminator* films Cameron makes his visual point: he cross-references the machines of our time with the machines of the future; one mindless machination leading to another.) Schwarzenegger, the Terminator itself, crackles into view, a time traveler on a mission of death. *Kill Sarah Connor.* The Terminator is a killing machine that looks like a man, but at first, interestingly, Cameron doesn't reveal that he's *literally* a machine. And prior to that revelation we don't question his machinelike behavior—we know, as Cameron knows, that men can easily become dehumanized killing machines.

A second time traveler arrives wanting to protect Sarah. Later he explains to her that he was sent to protect her because she will someday become the mother of his hero, John Connor, the guy who's the hope of future Earth. How did all of this come about? Nuclear holocaust.

In *The Abyss* (director's cut), aquatic aliens create a giant civilization-smashing tidal wave that will sweep over our most populated centers. And they *show* us why, flashing images for our protagonist of the classic human follies, the sort that aliens—blurry glimpses of our own higher selves, perhaps—have been warning us against for decades before Cameron, in films like *The Day the Earth Stood Still.*

Compare *True Lies* and *The Terminator.* In *True Lies* our heroic lovers kiss as a nuclear bomb goes off: the notorious "nuclear kiss" sneered at by some critics; a kiss against the incandescent world-busting backdrop of a nuclear explosion. This is simply affirmation, satirical and serious both, of conscious love against the mindless power of a hostile universe, a hostile civilization.

JAMES CAMERON
Born 1954
Kapuskasing, Canada

Piranha II: The Spawning
1981
*The Terminator*** 1984
*Aliens** 1986
*The Abyss** 1989
*Terminator 2: Judgment Day*** 1991
*True Lies** 1994
*Titanic** 1997
11 Academy Awards including Best Director and Best Picture; Golden Globe Award for Best Director

* also screenwriter
** also co-screenwriter

Where does the Terminator finally locate Sarah Connor? A nightclub called Technoir. A nightclub celebrating the dark side of technology, where patrons dance into the night, oblivious, as Rome burns.

Sarah's roommate is murdered by the Terminator, caught unaware because the Walkman headphones she's wearing make her oblivious to his entry. Technology deafens her to the approaching tread of Death.

In *True Lies* Schwarzenegger's character uses technology to mask his interrogation of his wife; the machinery of the intelligence service he works for comes between them, distorts the camouflaged question that is ultimately: *Do you love me?*

"You're talking to a machine," says the roommate's answering machine in *The Terminator*. "Machines need love too . . ." But the machine's incapacity to feel is effectively dramatized when the Terminator operates on himself with a razor, cutting into his arm to reveal his shiny metallic endoskeleton.

Cameron is one of those masters of telling, whenever he can, by showing. In *The Terminator* a couple of cops worry about the killing spree. Do they display their tension in the obvious ways, in snarling, improbable dialogue? Not in a Cameron film. The black cop asks for a cigarette, takes the pack, then realizes he already has a lit cigarette in his other hand. An incisive detail that tells us how anxious, how distracted he is feeling.

Cameron is prized in the film capital for his capacity to make us see, with a few deft strokes, the relationships between people while they are caught up in action: in *Aliens,* Ripley and Hicks, while talking over strategy and guns, are also obliquely talking about trust and the possibility of intimacy with one another.

All Cameron's heroines are strong, postfeminist women. One woman making a difference, standing up to the implacable, the relentless forces that you cannot bargain with. In *Terminator 2,* Sarah has toughened, become the personification of a woman's will to power, as she escapes the asylum and swims against all the currents of history to save the world.

The Terminator and *Terminator 2* and *Aliens* all climax in factories or factory-like sets: Sarah and her allies use the existing technology to destroy the technology that would otherwise destroy her; Ripley, in *Aliens,* uses an exoskeletal "forklift" device to fight the gigantic Mother alien.

Taking control of technology, mastering technology. Rising above it. Crush it if necessary, melt it down and start over, rethink it, make it your own.

Thus the monster of *The Terminator* becomes a savior in *T2*, this time an ally protecting Sarah against an even more dangerous technology; the enemy from the first *Terminator* film has been controlled, in *T2*, converted by the addition of human feeling, into an ally.

Cameron is no Luddite: he seems to be an advocate of the *intelligent* use of technology. "Make it happen," is his filmmaking motto. He creates new technology just to get his effect, constantly pushing the envelope, insisting that the cinematically impossible become possible. Hence his stunning

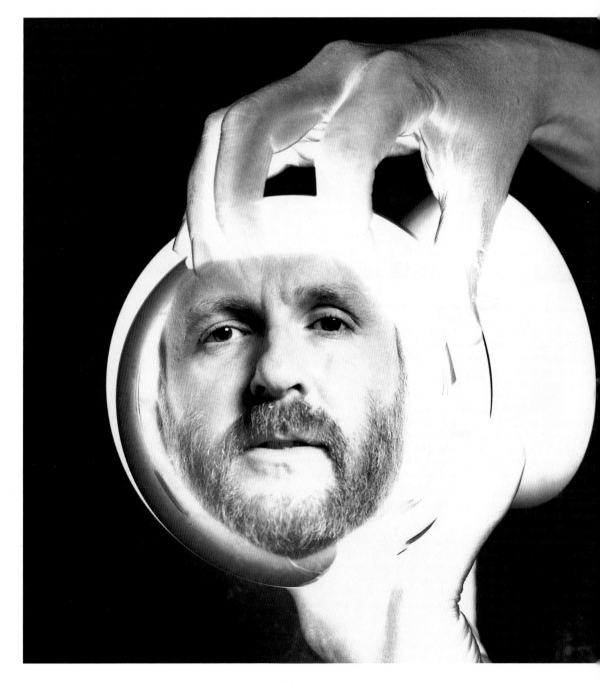

JOHN SHIRLEY
Born 1953
Houston, Texas

Dracula in Love 1976
Transmaniacon 1976
Three Ring Psychus
1977
City Come A-walking
1978
The Brigade 1980
Cellars 1981
The Eclipse Trilogy
1982–1989
Specialist 1985/1988
(novels and screenplay)
In Darkness Waiting
1986
A Splendid Chaos 1987
*The Black Hole of
Carcosa* 1989
Wetbones 1991
Software 1991
(screenplay; based on the
novel by Rudy Rucker)
The Crow 1993
(co-screenwriter with
David J. Schow)
Stinger 1994 (screenplay;
based on the novel by
Robert McCammon)
Silicon Embrace 1997
The New Rose Hotel
1998 (co-screenwriter
with William Gibson)
Black Butterflies 1998

leaps of computer animation capability: the conscious probe of water sent by the aliens in *The Abyss*; the morphing, liquid-metal nanotechnological killer robot in *T2*. Cameron seems obsessed with mastering technology, mastering what will otherwise master him.

The Abyss, Cameron once said, was inspired by his recurrent nightmare of a huge tidal wave. Not until he made a movie about it—and literally stopped the tidal wave in midripple on the screen, in the director's cut—did the nightmares go away. He had used his medium to control the uncontrollable, to stop the unstoppable, death itself.

With *Titanic,* Cameron is filming the ocean itself almost entirely in computer animation, generated by his new company Digital Domain— a name that reiterates control of the environment. This time, he doesn't have to deal with real water or the real ocean: he's created his own. He's stopped the tidal waves, and taken command of them, digitally.

Cameron's billion-dollar-grossing *Titanic* has been widely, oceanically discussed. Some critics complained of the film's overfamiliar, somewhat gimmicky plot: a freethinking young artist (iconically American) from the wrong side of the tracks falls in love with a wealthy, mournful young debutante when they meet by chance on the ship. True love triumphs over a sleek plutocrat and parental agendas, until the unexpected sinking of the great ship forces our heroic freethinker to sacrifice himself for her. I'm tempted to use the old saw "you can't argue with success"—but you can, of course, normally. Except in this case the success you can't argue with isn't financial, it's emotional. It's the film's amazing capacity to move unprecedented numbers of people to see it again and again. It's Cameron's success in taking that clichéd story and making it come alive in the hearts of millions of teenagers, of anyone with a shred of sentiment. The success is in the currency of pure empathy. It wasn't just spectacle; something wonderfully Capraesque connected with audiences worldwide. It was a timeless tale about the sterility of class, the superficiality of wealth, and the mortality inherent in love itself.

Titanic is apocalyptic, like the underrated *True Lies,* like the *Terminator* films, and like *The Abyss.* And like those films, and *Aliens,* it's about the vanity of our civilization, our species. The ship, the *Titanic,* represents the hubris of a civilization that supposes it can build the "unsinkable"; it is vanity made of iron and wood and brass. It is a clear-cut symbol of civilization itself: always headed for an iceberg, as far as Cameron is concerned. It's not enough for Cameron to rage against the dying of the light in a simple tale of tragic love and death. *Romeo and Juliet* doesn't say enough for Cameron. For him, the whole world must share in the tragedy—at least until we wake up, step out of our denial, and look around. Because there are always, always icebergs ahead. ◆

ON JOHN
SCHLESINGER

The myth of the child rescued by art does not hold an especially exalted position in the American pantheon. We generally prefer our children to be rescued by cunning and courageous pets, ferociously devoted parents, wonder drugs flown in through ice storms, masked men, benign aliens, zen masters, cantankerous old coots, lovable ex-cons, living toys, or, in extreme cases, by themselves as adults, returned to the scenes of the childhood crimes via plot contrivances and convenient time warps.

I myself was rescued by art, specifically by John Schlesinger's *Sunday, Bloody Sunday*.

As a gay kid growing up in suburban Los Angeles, I was in particular need of rescue. The suburbs probably come in for more than their fair share of scorn and blame—a big, comfortable house on a half-acre of lawn is hardly a figure of menace in and of itself. Suburbs, however, extend all the way to their own horizons, and beyond those horizons lies little except vague intimations of misfortune and a glamour that only temporarily conceals the misfortune to come. Suburbs seek to reassure. They banish fear in favor of comfort, mystery in favor of peace.

In short, *Sunday, Bloody Sunday* accomplished a trick that could only be turned by great narrative art: it simultaneously illuminated and complicated life.

As a dreamy, unathletic child, I couldn't see any acceptable future with me in it. This was the early sixties, and to whatever extent I imagined gay men at all, I imagined them rouged and desperate, too fond of their pets, carrying home a single chop and a single potato every evening, haunting the men's rooms in bus stations and truck stops.

At about the age of twelve, I started suffering panic attacks, terrifying fits of breathlessness that I managed, somehow, to conceal from everyone. I worried that these fits were just further evidence of my general inability to live happily in the world.

By the time I got to high school, I'd devised an alternate self and became highly adept at portraying him. I invented a swagger, kept my voice steady and my hands at my side. Like an undercover agent, I forced myself to remain in character even when I was alone. I bathed as my alternate self. I slept as him.

**JOHN
SCHLESINGER**
Born 1926
London, England

Terminus 1961
A Kind of Loving 1962
Billy Liar 1963
Darling 1965 Golden
Globe Award for Best
English-Language
Foreign Film
*Far From the Madding
Crowd* 1967
Midnight Cowboy 1969
Academy Awards for Best
Director and Best Picture
Sunday, Bloody Sunday
1971
Visions of Eight 1973
(segment: The Longest)
The Day of the Locust
1975
Marathon Man 1976
Yanks 1979
Honky Tonk Freeway
1981
*The Falcon and the
Snowman* 1984
The Believers 1987
Madame Sousatzka**
1988
Pacific Heights 1990
A Question of Attribution
1992
The Innocent 1993
Cold Comfort Farm 1995
Eye for an Eye 1995

** also co-screenwriter

During my junior year of high school I saw *The Boys in the Band* directed by William Friedkin, and felt all my darkest fears confirmed. The movie just about destroyed me. I don't mean, of course, to imply that it shouldn't have been made, I only mean that its limitations as a work of art were nearly lethal to me at the age of sixteen. I didn't know then what I can clearly see now: *The Boys in the Band* had a hidden agenda, one that was probably as well hidden from its makers as it was from me. While it purported to show an almost impossibily diverse group of gay men who were, somehow, all friends, it in fact brought all these men together to reveal how utterly miserable they were, each in his own way, except for the one straight character who eventually summoned up the courage to call his estranged wife and tell her he loved her and was going to return.

After seeing it, I controlled myself with renewed vigor. I got a girlfriend, drank more, studied less. I'm ashamed to say that I helped persecute an effeminate boy in my class, and if by any remote chance he reads this, I ask his forgiveness. I was acting out of mortal terror.

I saw *Sunday, Bloody Sunday* late in my senior year, and if I'd known anything about it beyond the fact that it was the new film by the director of *Midnight Cowboy,* I'd surely never have agreed to see it at all. *Sunday, Bloody Sunday* is the story of two middle-aged Londoners, a gay man and a straight woman, who both love the same young man and both lose him. I identified, guiltily, narcissistically, with Bob Elkin, the young man played by Murray Head, but I was fascinated—almost mesmerized—by Alix Greville, the older woman played by Glenda Jackson, and Daniel Hirsh, the fiftyish doctor played by Peter Finch. Like most great characters, all three were intricately heroic, foolish, and tragic. Like most great *movie* characters, all three demonstrated, every moment, how thoroughly but uncomfortably the soul inhabits the flesh.

Bob, the object of desire, was not shallow or venal, as the stereotype demanded. He was just young and more in love with the future than he could possibly be with another person. Alix was not grasping or shrill or deluded; she was simply a smart, passionate woman who had once been young and was young no longer.

It was Daniel, however, who affected me most. He, an aging gay man in love with somebody much younger, was the character whose doom was most ardently prescribed by stereotype. To my astonishment, Schlesinger refused to deliver anything as obvious as ordinary doom.

He showed us Daniel's loneliness. We saw Daniel eating a glacéed fruit and staring out the window at Bob's sculpture while Bob himself lay in

Alix's bed. We saw him practicing his Italian for a trip he'd planned with Bob and would end up taking alone.

But we saw, too, that he had resources, friends, work, a full inner life. We saw the pained compassion he felt for Alix when he ran into her by chance after Bob had abandoned them both for a career in New York.

Daniel did not end up much better satisfied than did any of the characters in *The Boys in the Band,* but unlike those men, Daniel was a complex and highly ambiguous amalgam of his circumstances, his choices, his needs, and his plain, rampant humanity. Like most fully realized characters, he came to an end that couldn't easily be labeled good or bad. He didn't get what he wanted, but he was canny enough to feel a certain wry gratitude for the fact that he was still present in the world, had felt a great deal, and might still feel much more, the world being capable of springing vast surprises, even at the last minute.

In short, *Sunday, Bloody Sunday* accomplished a trick that could only be turned by great narrative art: it simultaneously illuminated and

MICHAEL CUNNINGHAM
Born 1952
Cincinnati, Ohio

A Home at the End of the World 1990
Flesh and Blood 1995
The Hours 1998

complicated life. It did some kind of justice to human fate, which is never a clear-cut proposition, and it offered the richness of the world instead of anything as simple and singular as sorrow or happiness.

I did not experience an epiphany as I watched it, at least not consciously. I remember being quiet as we drove to the diner for coffee afterward, and I seem to remember sitting in a booth with my girlfriend and another couple carrying on about how the movie had transcended its sleazy subject matter.

But I can see now, over twenty years later, that the movie created a hairline crack in my own defenses, and that once the damage had been done no excess of will or terror would repair it.

Sunday, Bloody Sunday got under my skin and stayed there because it was a significant work of art, not because it sought to reassure me or any other member of the population that being gay was okay. It simply told the human truth, and after seeing it, I began slowly, over a period of years, to abandon my self-deceptions. After seeing it, I began to know that I would survive my childhood after all. ◆

BRUCE BENDERSON

ON PAUL
VERHOEVEN

THE MAN WHO SHOWED TOO MUCH

America can't understand Dutchman Paul Verhoeven. In this country, his triumphs are mixed with the taste of ashes; his defeats are never honestly judged. Audiences want to love him as a maker of the quintessential action-packed movie. Critics want to condemn him for being sex-obsessed, sleazy, or amoral. Neither image really fits. Paul Verhoeven has never changed.

In 1984 *The Fourth Man*, a sexual horror film, brought him to the attention of the American public. Its not very sympathetic protagonist is a novelist who is traitorously bisexual. He is also tortured, opportunistic, and desperate for sensation. He escapes the prosaic world of literary careerism by pursuing a female hairdresser, then sets his sights upon her young male lover. Images of sexual morbidity plague his daydreams. He drinks to escape his fantasies, but they are really prophecies. Or are they?

How could we have identified with such a character? Did we ever have a choice? Through a labyrinth of color-drenched imagery we entered his nervous breakdown. It was a maddening experience since Americans expect from a protagonist behavior they can condone and want to know the truth about what is really happening. But Verhoeven and his team denied all these easy certainties. Were the main character's premonitions of death just a figment of a sick imagination? Or was he really in touch with some occult power? Was the hairdresser with her sharp scissors really a spider? Or was she just a provincial swinger? Was the Virgin Mary really the special guardian of this deranged alcoholic? Or was she just a cowardly hallucination? Perhaps. Perhaps not. One stopped wondering and was sucked into the world of the film. A spider's web was spun around a crucifix in the opening credits, then it was inescapably spun around us. We became entangled in the shifting narrative, convinced by the totally believable characterizations.

This chastising, inescapable web comes up again and again in Verhoeven's films. It is like a confession repeated and regretted. It is the admission that liberty and sensation do not come without an ultimate price. It is a message that impulses do not remain unpunished. Not by God, but by the social order.

> Still Verhoeven refused to abandon his own particular brand of outsider-hero, that ruthless sensualist who is disdainful of middle-class propriety. The American censors, the box office, and the conventional values of Hollywood never really changed Verhoeven's priorities. He only made it look as if they had.

PAUL VERHOEVEN
Born 1938
Amsterdam,
The Netherlands

Business Is Business
1971
Turkish Delight 1973
Keetje Tippel (Katie's Passion) 1975
Soldier of Orange 1978
Spetters 1980
The Fourth Man 1983
*Flesh & Blood*** 1985
RoboCop 1987
Total Recall 1990
Basic Instinct 1992
Showgirls 1995
Starship Troopers 1997
The Hollow Man 2000

** also co-screenwriter

Or are they curtailed by something even more oppressive that lies beyond society, something linked to nature itself in a way that resembles fate?

Verhoeven has made a conscious decision to flaunt sex and violence in his films. And the decision has had metaphysical parameters. He wants to see what happens to human beings as these impulses flower. Way back in 1973, a handsome blond sculptor (Rutger Hauer) roared through Amsterdam on a motorscooter in the film *Turkish Delight*. He accosted pretty women with an aggressiveness that we would call harassment. He was brazen and irreverent, too—permanently caught in the kindergarten of his id.

Before his viewers had a chance to get used to him, the film suddenly jerked into a permanent flashback. We are with the same rebellious, libidinous character, but it is four years earlier. This time his sexual antics have a youthful, utopian quality. He meets an adolescent girl with the same subversive, bacchanalian spirit. They marry, and for us they are the only real people in the world. Everyone else is a cliché of bourgeois stupidity and pettiness. The antidote to such a world is to flout every convention. The young couple mock the Church, and the sculptor pukes at a bourgeois dinner party; they thumb their noses at the art establishment, and she negligently bares her nipples to the Queen of Holland.

They fuck and fuck and fuck. And as they do, another web is spun. As natural beings, they have become the victims of nature. They can flout the rules of society, but not those of life and death. The girl, who is the representative of all that is spontaneous, succumbs quite spontaneously to a brain tumor. The sculptor, who is the recalcitrant rebel, is left in the prison of his own sensuality, which becomes a rather tired and repetitive quest for kicks.

With American films, the game doesn't really change. On the surface the action has to seem as if it were there for its own sake. The sex has to be more suggestive but less honest. Americans like a semblance of telling all— but they shirk the task of facing the ugliness and vacuity that's revealed. It would be too demoralizing, and that's going too far. They don't like attacks on the Church, either. Critics might counter such moves by accusing them of bigotry.

Still Verhoeven refused to abandon his own particular brand of outsider-hero, that ruthless sensualist who is disdainful of middle-class propriety. The American censors, the box office, and the conventional values of Hollywood never really changed Verhoeven's priorities. He only made it look as if they had.

In America, the disruptive, irreverent Rutger Hauer of *Turkish Delight* became the sneering, entitled, and ruthless Sharon Stone of *Basic Instinct*.

Like most of Verhoeven's protagonists, she's an antihero, an artist who compels us to enter her world. But she is also a sensual snare, a sister to the scissor-wielding hairdresser in *The Fourth Man.*

This time, Verhoeven could not show animal sexuality as blatantly as he did in Holland, but he could show its repercussions. Merely attributing deadpan sexual frankness to a woman character upped the shock value. This time, Verhoeven could not mock the Queen of Holland or the Church,

**BRUCE
BENDERSON**

Pretending to Say No
1990

My Father Is Coming
1990 (co-screenwriter)

User 1994/1995

*Toward the New
Degeneracy* 1997

but he could attack one of America's most sacred institutions: the police department. He had already pointed out the shallow morality of the police in *RoboCop*. In *Basic Instinct*, he and screenwriter Joe Eszterhas ridiculed the institution to the point of castrating it. The Michael Douglas character, like the writer in *The Fourth Man*, is unstable; his mind is corrupted by drink. Like the writer in *The Fourth Man*, he and his colleagues are misled and humiliated by an enchanting woman.

Basic Instinct is another sexual horror film, but the plot ambiguities are simpler and Americans prefer to call it a sexual thriller. Is she or isn't she the murderer? That's about it. Still, the labyrinth of sex and danger is just as compelling as it was in *The Fourth Man*. The Sharon Stone character represents total freedom of appetite. What threatens to decimate everything around her isn't so much capricious nature as it was in *The Fourth Man*, but the unleashed human id.

Americans feel a rapport with the Dutch tendency to show and tell all. Visit a provincial Dutch town and you'll see house after house without curtains in the parlor, baring clean, gleaming interiors to the judgmental world. *"We have nothing to hide!"* is what they are saying. In the Dutch cultural consciousness, what you see must be what you get. All must be spoken and shown. If sex exists, it must be brought into the light and demystified. If violence boils in the heart, it has to bubble to the surface and be analyzed away.

As another people dominated by the plainspoken, soul-baring Protestant ethic, Americans like to think that they, as well, reveal all and practice what they preach. But in comparison to the Dutch, the American predilection for forthrightness seems like cliché. It is a homily created for appearances. Only the Dutch vow to illuminate all appetite and impulse, to trace their repercussions to the very last strand.

What happened to Verhoeven after the release of *Showgirls* was a result of the reluctance on the part of Americans to follow impulses to their logical end. The film was panned and ridiculed, but the negative reviews were defensive, outraged, and self-protective. Americans love sex as long as its engulfing, reductive powers are concealed. Verhoeven and his screenwriter Joe Eszterhas merely reproduced the futility and sensation and competition that is a part of sex and that has built Las Vegas. In this simple way they said what must not be told.

In a sense, all of Verhoeven's films are comedies. The excess or vulgarity in them comes from the social absurdities that we agree to live. Verhoeven shows too much, breaking the unspoken rules that keep these engines of appetite functioning. In his 1980 film *Spetters*, he cast a cold eye upon the fates of a group of young working-class men. One of them robs homosexuals. Later he is graphically raped in vengeance by a homosexual gang. Such a gang is unlikely, but Verhoeven and screenwriter Gerard Soeteman created it to reveal the character's own latent homosexuality. Americans wouldn't go that far. They prattle on about the injustice of gay bashing but don't want to reveal the psychoanalytic truths behind it. It isn't appetizing to show a leather-jacketed tough taking it up the ass. So let's forget about that part. Pushing revelations beyond the point of suggestion is unsightly and absurd. But when Verhoeven does it, excess leads to comedy.

Spetters, Basic Instinct, RoboCop, and even Verhoeven's *Soldier of Orange* are all funny because of the absurdity of their excesses. They show the unsightliness of ambition and the futility of action. Verhoeven undercuts all his striving heroes. In *Basic Instinct,* no underwear on a beautiful woman is enough to reduce a pack of hard-boiled cops to blithering schoolboys. In *RoboCop,* law and order has been reworked as corporate strategy. In *Soldier of Orange,* World War II Dutch resistance fighter Rutger Hauer discovers that the government dignitary for whom he is risking his life may himself be a traitor. Hauer's heroism and the big moment of meeting the Queen of Holland are suddenly cynically deflated.

All of this is funny in a sad, nihilistic kind of way. But Verhoeven's funniest movie to date is *Showgirls.* It tells what happens when the American dream of "making it" is stripped of every other human quality. It shows what results when all the energy of sex is packaged to serve ambition. *Showgirls* is the story of a desperate careerist hoping to lap-dance her way into the big-buck spectacles of Las Vegas. Her ambitions are so excessive, the competition around her so relentless, that we should be laughing. But perhaps the film struck too close to home for some hard-working Americans. The movie failed us not because it is mindless or excessive but because we are. It's not that we don't love ruthless competition for employment, extravagant spectacle, color, music, cynical sex, and aggression. It's that we can only admit that we do when the director attaches a disclaimer to them. This disclaimer must assert that there is something more beyond the glitter and quest for pleasure we prefer watching—even if there is not. ◆

ON MILOS
FORMAN

O n our first day of shooting *Hair,* we ran out of track. Someone forgot to order enough for a crucial dolly shot, the most important setup of the day. It was a major snafu, and I looked round for Milos in case he needed moral support, or some suggestions for revising the sequence. He was halfway down St. Marks Place darting between technicians firing off instructions, an unlit cigar in one side of his mouth, a toothpick in the other (he could manage both at once, *and* direct!) rubbing his palms together in glee, unfazed by the catastrophe. I asked how he could be so cheery, considering the monumental screwup at hand. He gestured expansively around the set—at the camera, the equipment van, the crew, and grinned from ear to ear.

"This is my toy, Welleray! I'm playing now!"

Forman's energy, his gusto, his intensity, both on a set and in life, are as irresistible as they are legendary. His philosophy of filming is simplicity itself. It's not about angles, it's not about camera moves, it's about one thing only—telling the story as it would happen in real life. "It all begins in the script," he told me once. "If what's happening is interesting, it doesn't matter where you shoot from, people will be interested to watch. If you write something boring, you can film from mosquitoes' underpants and it will still be boring."

Though known for being a brilliant actor's director, he in fact says very little to his cast. "You cannot make an actor play a role on film. In theater, yes, but in a movie you must cast the exact person. This way you can use all his mistakes."

With Forman my film education began. In a sense, it ended as well. I knew virtually nothing about movie writing when I started with him, and what of value I've learned since could be comfortably stored in the hole of a Cheerio, with room to wobble.

When we began working together on *Hair,* I took elaborate pains to assure Forman of my ignorance. "Don't worry, Welleray, I teach you everything for film, I just need you to help me make good dialogues in English."

We got down to business at his apartment overlooking Central Park. I sat by a bookshelf with very few books, but an odd assortment of knickknacks, including an unopened bottle of murky-looking French cognac. He lay back on a sofa opposite me with a bottle of Pilsner Urquell in hand, lit a cigar, and made himself comfortable. "So, how we will start the story?" Just like that. So I said something, then *he* said something, and without knowing quite how it evolved, we were writing together.

Forman's energy, his gusto, his intensity, both on a set and in life, are as irresistible as they are legendary. His philosophy of filming is simplicity itself.

There were no rules for the collaboration besides a tacit understanding that all ideas were allowed, the dumber the better. Often Forman would suggest startling ways to jolt us out of an impasse. "What if he says *no* to her instead of yes in this moment?" Well, I would find myself thinking, what if Hamlet is a girl, and she's in love with her uncle—it sort of changes the story, don't you think? But in fact, as often as not, these sudden horseshoe turns would open a hidden door to the best idea imaginable.

Inside the cognac bottle on the bookshelf was a pickled rattlesnake coiled in a corkscrew shape. It might have been an adder. Anyway, it was some snake that can kill with a single bite. Forman explained that the French like how the poison seeps out and gives the intoxicant an extra kick, much admired by people who like that sort of thing.

For the first week I couldn't pull my eyes away from that snake. In midafternoon, the sun made the bottle glow. One day, in the midst of describing a possible scene, I heard a loud snore across the room. It was Forman on the sofa. I had bored him to sleep.

I sat quietly, staring at the pickled snake, listening to Forman's wheezing, and wondered about the proper etiquette for such a situation. Sit, wait, and watch the snake? Wake the boss from his nap? What if he was up late the night before and needed to catch up on his sleep? Perhaps this whole scene was a symbolic warning about my film career ahead— poisonous snake and a bored director? Soon the phone on the floor beside him rang, and after a brief exchange in Czech with someone on the other end, he rolled his head toward me as if nothing had happened, "So where were we?"

Over the following months, and years, through our collaboration on the films for *Hair* and *Ragtime,* true to his word Forman proceeded to teach me tricks of the trade, both small ("When you write this scene, put that there's one hundred people in the checkout line. I only need twenty, but I can trade for something when we make budget") and sublime ("This is too much like radio dialogue, you can close your eyes and understand what's going on. You must write dialogue so we need to see picture before we understand what's happening").

His lessons were concrete and practical. "Always bring the audience into a big scene *through* someone. Follow the waiter's tray into the banquet, don't just point the camera and show the banquet. You must

MILOS FORMAN
Born 1932
Cáslav, Czechoslovakia

Konkurs** 1963
If There Were No Music
1963
Black Peter** 1963
Loves of a Blonde**
1965
The Firemen's Ball**
1967
Taking Off **1971
Cannes Film Festival
Grand Prize of the
Jury (tie)
Visions of Eight 1973
(segment: Decathlon)
*One Flew Over the
Cuckoo's Nest* 1975
(screenplay co-written by
Bo Goldman) Academy
Award for Best Director;
Golden Globe Award for
Best Director
Hair 1979 (screenplay by
Michael Weller)
Ragtime 1981 (screenplay
by Michael Weller)
Amadeus 1984 Academy
Award for Best Director;
Golden Globe Award for
Best Director
Valmont 1988
*The People vs. Larry
Flynt* 1996 Golden Globe
Award for Best Director
Man on the Moon 1999

** also co-screenwriter

always tell the story from the point of view of someone *in* the story."
It drove him crazy when a camera would start to move in a film simply
because a director deemed it stylish. "Are there Indians creeping around
behind the chair in this scene, who's eyes are *seeing* this?" Nothing, in
his view, should call attention to the storyteller. In this regard, Forman
is a classicist.

Perhaps because he began his career as a screenwriter in Czechoslovakia,
he has an exceptionally high regard for writers. He likes us on the set with
him. Welcomes us, even! He—God help us—asks our opinion from time
to time. "Is this convincing yet? Do you believe it?" I once described a way
that we could clarify a sequence and finished thus: "It will make the audience
understand why the character is acting this way." Forman thought for a
moment, shook his head, and told me, "I don't care to understand, I want
only to *believe.*"

Though the comment was offhand, I have thought of it a great deal
since. At bottom, what Forman is after in his work is a sense of truth, of
things that appear to happen as they would in life, so that an audience
recognizes every moment as real, and develops total faith in the storyteller's
honesty.

Coming of age under a repressive government, he developed an
early distrust of the elitist mentality in politics and in art. What he loves
most is a truly popular film. As an American snob, I was in the habit
of looking down my nose at all sorts of crude popular entertainment.
To me, Forman was a maker of "art" films. But this was not at all how
he saw himself. His audience was *everyone,* and if something in a script
wouldn't be immediately clear to the least educated human on earth,
he'd reject it.

In the beginning this attitude baffled me, but as he told stories of
his early struggles to get films past the censors in Prague, it became clear
that the act of pleasing a specific segment of the audience, pandering to
a select group or a certain rarified taste was for him a reminder of the
days when he had to please party officials in order to get his films made
and distributed. For Forman, the truly radical act was making a film that
appealed to the public so deeply that no censor could stand in the way
of its success.

What an idea! Popular success as a radical aesthetic! And this, finally,
is what best describes Milos's peculiar genius as a filmmaker. His work is
always personal, even at times eerily private, but his aim is to communicate

MICHAEL WELLER
Born 1942

Moonchildren 1970 (play)
Fishing 1975 (play)
Loose Ends 1979 (play)
Hair 1979 (screenplay; film directed by Milos Forman)
Split 1981
Ragtime 1981 (screenplay; film directed by Milos Forman; based on the novel by E. L. Doctorow)
Ghost on Fire 1985 (play)
Spoils of War 1988 (play)
Lost Angels 1989 (screenplay)
Lake No Bottom 1990 (play)
Jellybean 1998 (screenplay for John Coles and Liz Oliver)
The Ballad of Soapy Smith 1998 (film musical of his play with Milos Forman and Elton John)
In the Blue Light of African Dreams (screenplay; based on the novel by Paul Watkins)

with the world. A Westerner with his sensibility, raised in the luxurious embrace of democracy, would in all likelihood gravitate to the "independent" or art film.

But to Forman, to leap past the deadening reach of censorship directly into the public's heart, to achieve the freedom and power of popular success, and to assume the responsibility it demands, this is the highest artistic challenge. Only this outlook, I believe, could have given us such a memorable list of successful and idiosyncratic films as his. ◆

ON ROBERT
ALTMAN

If it doesn't crack the heavens for a director/writer to quote a critic in support of another director, let me quote Pauline Kael: "If Robert Altman succeeds aesthetically, audiences may not respond, because the light prodigal way in which he succeeds is alien to them." I was lucky to meet Altman when he'd been out of favor for a few years, because the test of an artist isn't how well he responds to the applause, but how closely he stays to his essential vision. When *The Player* came out everyone said that Altman was back, but the truth may be that Altman hadn't gone anywhere, it was the audience who moved away.

> **When *The Player* came out everyone said that Altman was back, but the truth may be that Altman hadn't gone anywhere, it was the audience who moved away.**

There's no sense in saying what it was like to work with him. Writers are seldom happy with their directors while the films are being made. I've never met a writer who ever really had a kind word to say about any of his directors after the second drink, and when a writer praises a director to other writers there's reason to suspect emotional trauma. This is a matter of professional pride. I imagine that Eastwood's writers like him, but in my fantasy of how he works, I also imagine that his writers never meet him, that he buys a script and shoots it. Of course that's not likely. This is what every screenplay needs from the director, someone who can take all the intentions and make sense of them for the reality of a production. All scripts are too long, all written scenes are too long, all dialogue is too wordy; this is the inevitable dividend of being written in a room, usually alone.

Altman's movies have a unique relationship to dialogue; it's there, but it doesn't serve the usual function of dialogue, or if it does, the relationship may be incidental. Am I making it up that I heard Altman tell me that *Short Cuts* was going to be white jazz, or did I read that somewhere? I know what he means, the voice is just another instrument in the band, the singer is not the reason for the band, and in Altman's films the dialogue is not the reason for the band, and in Altman's films the dialogue is not the reason for the acting. I'm thinking of *The Long Goodbye*, where the plot rolls along beneath the log of Elliott Gould's incessant mumbling and it seems that all of the meandering and ranting and chatter isn't going anywhere, until the last seconds of the film, by a creek in Mexico,

ROBERT ALTMAN
Born 1925
Kansas City, Missouri

*The Delinquents** 1957

The James Dean Story
1957 (co-director)

Countdown 1968

That Cold Day in the Park
1969

*M*A*S*H* 1970 Golden
Globe Award for Best
Director; Cannes Film
Festival Palme d'Or

Brewster McCloud 1970

*McCabe & Mrs. Miller***
1971

*Images** 1972

The Long Goodbye 1973

*Thieves Like Us*** 1974

California Split 1974

Nashville 1975

*Buffalo Bill and the
Indians, or Sitting
Bull's History Lesson***
1976 (co-screenwriter
Alan Rudolph)

*3 Women** 1977

*A Wedding*** 1978

*Quintet*** 1979

*A Perfect Couple*** 1979

*HEALTH*** 1979

Popeye 1980

*Come Back to the Five &
Dime, Jimmy Dean, Jimmy
Dean* 1982

Streamers 1983

Secret Honor 1984

O.C. and Stiggs 1985

Fool for Love 1985

*Beyond Therapy*** 1987

*Aria*** 1987 (segment:
Les Boréades)

*Vincent & Theo** 1990

The Player 1992 Cannes
Film Festival Award for
Best Director

*Short Cuts*** 1993

*Prêt-à-Porter*** 1994

*Kansas City*** 1996

*Robert Altman's Jazz '34:
Remembrances of Kansas
City Swing* 1996

*The Gingerbread Man**
1998

* also screenwriter
** also co-screenwriter

MICHAEL TOLKIN
Born 1950
New York, New York

The Player 1988/1992
(novel and screenplay;
film directed by Robert
Altman)

The Rapture 1991
(screenwriter and
director)

Deep Cover 1992
(co-screenwriter)

Among the Dead 1993

The New Age 1994
(screenwriter and
director)

The Burning Season
1995 (co-screenwriter)

*The Player, The Rapture,
The New Age: Three
Screenplays* 1995

Deep Impact 1998
(co-screenwriter)

when Gould shoots Jim Bouton. What's good about the scene is the way it suddenly redeems every seemingly random moment in the movie, because for the one time in the film, Gould shows that he's not the shambling fool he's been pretending to be all along. I don't know if that movie made any money or not, I don't think Altman's body of work has been especially profitable, but of course you can always watch his movies, and two frames in, you know you're in the hands of someone who knows what he's doing, even when he doesn't; in Altman's best films the gratuitous gestures are the reason the movies work. ◆

ON SIDNEY
LUMET

In the summer of 1975, I was an angry and confused fifteen-year-old. My parents had gotten divorced a few years before and our family's place in the world was no longer certain. Money was scarce and even the normal teenage distractions of sports and music weren't working. The Mets had become a sluggish, boring team, the last two Stones records frankly sucked, and punk rock was mostly just a rumor. It was gorilla-suit hot and I was too alienated to even settle into a normal adolescent drug habit. I felt like I didn't belong anywhere, including my own skin.

Lumet's great theme is the human heart under extraordinary pressure.

I got a job selling Good Humor ice cream to the sweatshop workers and transvestite hookers on Delancey Street, but that wasn't working out terribly well either. A Carvel truck down the block was killing me with Flying Saucers and Cookie Pusses.

One afternoon, I took off early and sought refuge in a cool movie theater on the Upper East Side showing Sidney Lumet's *Dog Day Afternoon*. And after that, everything changed.

Here was a world I knew recast in dramatic terms. Al Pacino and John Cazale hunkered down in the bank, surrounded by hundreds of cops, feds, media people, freaks, and hecklers. Facing down the world with a mixture of smart-ass defiance and insane desperation. "Attica!! Attica!!" All right, so I wasn't robbing a bank to pay for my lover's sex-change operation. But there was something that touched me in Pacino's determination to make a last stand: leaning against a wall, sweating and bleeding, facing his own mortality after getting disowned by his father and ragged out by his mother in front of half the city.

"I'm a fuck-up and an outcast and that's it. You come near me and you're gonna get fucked."

Somehow, Lumet, who was fifty-one at the time, had crystallized that exquisite teenage moment of isolation and outrage. And when I left the theater that day, I knew I wasn't alone anymore.

So why is Sidney Lumet not widely acknowledged as one of the great directors of our time? What the hell is the matter with everyone?

The rap on Lumet is more or less as follows: He has no distinctive visual style and no overriding thematic concerns; his films are photographed plays, they're hectoring and insistent; he's shrill and earnest. Andrew Sarris consigned him to the "Strained Seriousness" category in *American Cinema*, the bible of auteurist critics. In a brilliantly malignant essay about the making of the movie *The Group*, Pauline Kael indicted him for first-degree hackdom, accusing him of having a slovenly technique and a head full of trashy ideas derived from other films.

Will the defendant rise.

SIDNEY LUMET
Born 1924
Philadelphia,
Pennsylvania

12 Angry Men 1957
Stage Struck 1958
That Kind of Woman 1959
The Fugitive Kind 1960
A View from the Bridge 1961
Long Day's Journey into Night 1962
Fail Safe 1964
The Pawnbroker 1965
The Hill 1965
The Group 1966
The Deadly Affair 1967
The Sea Gull 1968
Bye Bye Braverman 1968
The Appointment 1969
Last of the Mobile Hot Shots 1970
The Anderson Tapes 1971
Child's Play 1972
The Offence 1973
Murder on the Orient Express 1974
Serpico 1974
Lovin' Molly 1974
Dog Day Afternoon 1975
Network 1976
Equus 1977
The Wiz 1978
Just Tell Me What You Want 1980
*Prince of the City*** 1981
Deathtrap 1982
The Verdict 1982
Daniel 1983
Garbo Talks 1984
Power 1986
The Morning After 1986
Running on Empty 1988
Family Business 1989
*Q & A** 1990
A Stranger Among Us 1992
Guilty as Sin 1993
*Night Falls on Manhattan** 1997
Critical Care 1997
Gloria 1999

* also screenwriter
** also co-screenwriter

Sidney Lumet was born on June 25, 1924, the son of a Yiddish theater actor. As a child, he did some acting himself, playing the infant Jesus and understudying to one of the *Dead End Kids* on Broadway, but he decided against pursuing acting as a career. "I had asked him during one of our first talks why he had given up acting and he had begun a long explanation about how acting was a faggot's career and how he knew that if he was ever going to give a woman a real human relationship, etc.," Kael writes in her essay. "I had simply jotted down 'too short for acting career.'"

After a military stint, he did some directing for theater and television before getting his shot at directing the feature film *12 Angry Men* with Henry Fonda in 1957. Early critics praised the film, but revisionists condemned it as slightly elevated television. He went on to do *The Fugitive Kind, Fail Safe, Long Day's Journey into Night,* among many others, earning a reputation in the industry as a director who worked fast, cheap, and without any particular style.

In 1966, when *The Group* appeared, Kael hurled the reviewer's equivalent of a gypsy's curse at him, saying he would never improve as a director, because of his fundamental lack of taste and rigor.

So, how does the defendant plead?

As his advocate, I'd not only enter a plea of not guilty, I'd say rebuild the courthouse. Yes, Lumet has made some obnoxious dreadful movies. *Equus* was a dog. *The Group* was Mary McCarthy without wit. And *The Wiz* was, well, *The Wiz,* and let's just leave it at that. But the best of his films—including *12 Angry Men, The Pawnbroker, Serpico, The Offence, Dog Day Afternoon, Network, Prince of the City, The Verdict,* and *Q & A*—have as much stylistic and thematic consistency as the best of Scorsese and John Ford.

Lumet's great theme is the human heart under extraordinary pressure. Paul Newman struggling under the weight of alcoholism in *The Verdict.* Rod Steiger having the humanity crushed out of him by the legacy of the Holocaust in *The Pawnbroker.* Sean Connery as a soul-sickened cop poisoned by the images in his mind in *The Offence.*

The charge that his films are loud and strident doesn't hold water, either. His best moments are often the quietest ones. Paul Newman staring into a glass of scotch in *The Verdict.* Steiger slipping into the mental vortex of the past in *The Pawnbroker,* which introduced the now widely imitated technique of using subliminal cuts to suggest repressed memory. The term that's often used to praise and denigrate Lumet is "gritty," but in truth, his best movies are richer and more complex than that.

PETER BLAUNER
Born 1959
New York, New York

Slow Motion Riot 1991
Casino Moon 1994
The Intruder 1996
Man of the Hour 1999

So what's the problem? Why is it that Lumet still hasn't gotten his due?

Perhaps part of the beef is the kind of artist he is. Great American artists are supposed to burst forth like supernovas and then quickly flame out like Orson Welles and F. Scott Fitzgerald. Or they're supposed to be magisterial and remote, like Stanley Kubrick, spending ten years between projects pondering. With his some forty films in forty years, Lumet inspires a kind of suspicion. Instead of sitting around, he dives from one film into another, scrabbling for the emotional heart of each one, doing whatever it takes to make an impact, technique be damned.

"It obviously, too obviously, wants to be moving," Kael grumbled about his directing. "But damn it, it is."

All right. So enough already with the carping. Do the films hold up or don't they?

Well, *Dog Day Afternoon* is still a hilarious and poignant study in urban entropy and the inevitability of things falling apart in Brooklyn. The crowd scenes, in particular, are memorable, giving lie to Kael's claim that Lumet would never learn to photograph more than two people at a time. *The Pawnbroker* is heartbreaking. *Network* seems much sharper and more prescient than ever before, thanks to the rise of the Fox Network and cable T.V. *The Offence* is so intense that I had to go into a room and get drunk after watching the video. But then I watched *The Verdict* and I had to lock the liquor cabinet.

Sidney Lumet a hack? Yeah, right. Sure. The guy just happened to be standing there when some of the best movies of the last forty years got made. ◆

ON NEIL
JORDAN

THE DREAM OF A DIRECTOR

"For three years, out of key with his time,
He strove to resuscitate the dead art
Of poetry.

"The chopped seas held him, therefore, that year."

Ezra Pound: Hugh Selwyn Mauberley.

I dreamed a director in a place I knew but did not know; in long shot he stood, eyes fixed on the firmament as wisps of dune-sand blew about his feet, the sea close by with the movement of cloth and the texture of glass trying to hold him with a story of melancholy but it did not matter for he'd known it many years. Because it was a dream-place, a phantom zone where amorphous beasts might pass in anguish searching for the flesh that had once been theirs, a peace that once they'd known, miles in seconds with ease were travelled, and as he turned it was then I saw it, the shining Uzi, with a Joycean click clack clunk in the wink of an eye assembled, wolfishly his features and the weapon changing, as folding me in those angel's wings that rose up virgin white behind him in the misty morning, he leaned in close, conspiratorial, whispering of death's intimacy, of how it can be so close, a warm embrace, a sweet and tender kiss, the final, desperate expression of the need to have a chat. Of how men, starting out as angels, must in the end brutes become or so it in that moment seemed until across the empty strand which seemed forever early morning, I heard them drifting from the boathouse, plangent as ever, the first notes of *The Crying Game* played on a broken piano, taking us to a place we both knew we were in yet somehow trying to reach. Towards which we could walk but never get there because all along it was there beside us. And which was why in mute amazement I watched as that fluid movement began, like dripping liquorice the synthetic gunflesh mutating as it might for Cronenberg, the weapon with which Danny wreaked havoc in a world that had become impure and let him down, curving sinuously into shape until it was no longer made for murder but for pursuits of no less passion as the director fixed the reed in the

NEIL JORDAN
Born 1950
Sligo, Ireland

*Angel** 1982
The Company of Wolves* 1984
Mona Lisa* 1986
High Spirits 1988
We're No Angels 1989
The Miracle 1991
The Crying Game 1992
Academy Award for Best Original Screenplay
Interview with the Vampire 1994
Michael Collins 1996
The Butcher Boy* 1998
(based on novel by Patrick McCabe, who also co-wrote the screenplay)
In Dreams* 1999
The End of the Affair 1999 (in production)

* also screenwriter
** also co-screenwriter

mouthpiece,settled his fingers and spun a web of sound,the grey-green gaberdine billowing out behind him,until the music he made became like unto speech itself;a speech that his mouth was the vehicle for but that sprang from the knot of his stomach,the crook of his legs.Out across the silver sea of Bettystown and into the heart of the universe that euphonious manifesto was dispatched,operatic,magical,as if from the golden bowl of the weathered Selmer there had mysteriously but mischievously emerged a pink-eared white rabbit,the purest symbol of that world he wanted,bringing tears to my eyes as I fell to my knees and in the aftermath of that humbled silence,exulted.Who,I wondered would one day call back in answer from the distant places—Sligo,New Orleans,King's Cross,Tunisia—to which those psychic reports now sailed—might put their lips together and blow for the citizens of one country alone,that which it was possible would never be reached,where perhaps dwelt Nobodaddy,the faceless one,tall-hatted Nothingness who would hug you lovingly,whisper to you intimately until you were gone,a curl of smoke into the cosmos,but towards which nevertheless you'd always wind your way,until that day the seas dried up,the fish stopped whistling,and wild strawberries once so sweet now withered in your hand—there to find them,a showband of spirits,a bunch of crazy skatmen who behind the clouds would play their hearts out,entertaining angels very much awares until St.Peter served more drink;a celestial combo who'd blow a hole in heaven every chance they got;who went by the names of Louis Prima;Stan Getz;Charlie Parker;Nat King Cole.All of whom one day would see their songs take triumphant shape upon a screen,in colours painted by the man in the flowing gaberdine,who would through haunting melody,moving image,make the world a place where miracles could happen,but who now once more past bleached dogfish,ragged wrack,across the sands was gone.As he must,for he is always searching,and this time knows it will be found;that lost paradise just beyond the end of his journey,from which he has long been exiled,as have Danny and George and Lucifer and Lestat,a revolutionary called Michael Collins who too once watched his trees of golden apples rot when at last the pearly gates were swinging open.Where he will,like Danny,chosen for a purpose,before him find a soft-lit ballroom which this time does not go up in flames,a Laughing Boy who does not die.Where another dream,which one time came in a Californian motel,will end the way it always ought to have;the black-clad palmist coffin salesmen,smiling as they read his hand,nodding as they say:"This director's credit's good and somehow I reckon that's the way it's gonna stay." Where stands old Charlie Parker in his staff-notated wings,fingers trying out the silver keys,waiting patiently for the Clontarf-Sligo man as still towards Eden he makes his solitary way.Along a road where beasts there will surely be,and whole cities which change shape even as you look upon them,and ghosts who wildcat-tumble centuries to make love with the living,and white horses who speak with brogues and any amount of cherubims and seraphims on hand to work whatever miracle it is you might require

PATRICK McCABE
Born 1955
Clones, County
Monaghan, Ireland

Carn 1989
The Butcher Boy 1992
(co-screenwriter with
director Neil Jordan;
based on his novel)
The Dead School 1995
Breakfast on Pluto 1998
Mundo Desperado 1999

(A weeping Virgin! A praying elephant! An Immortal vampire!),but more important than all of it will be,as well he knows,the pen and paper that awaits him upon a magicked rolltop desk beneath a vast and sweeping Madonna-blue sky;placed there,a marbled ledger in a neat hand marked:*DREAMS-N.JORDAN*,arrayed all about it,postcards,photos,fragments,semaphoring from a time that was—*white metal bandstand,old black Ford*—and a gentle Jesuit upon an esplanade alone.Nearby,a camera whose lens is tilted towards yet another undiscovered country,where soon once more no doubt will gather all manner of wraiths and revenants,streaming from that fevered,scratching nib,rising from that once-bare page,who,in the company of wolves and demons and demi-gods,will strain to listen as it comes across the sky,hard to name as its pattern changes like water,a tune which may shift and never settle,but you'll always know is there;a music with no one source,which comes from many places:the west of Ireland;the generations before him and maybe those that have yet to be;from the poetry of Yeats and the othersongs of Joyce,the night-dreams of Chandler,of Aristotle,Jung and Hammett,fellow travellers of the shadow place who always walk beside him,as once more the quest begins and poetry stirs inside its grave,behind him the chopped sea snapping at his heels,furious that he has again confounded it,slipped its grasp once more,("*I was supposed to hold you!*",is its pathetic cry),Bird watching over all as instinctively he feels the heavens tremble,realising at last that this soul is one so singular and rare they just might not be able to deal with it.And to which,from a fellow jazzman and kindred spirit,there can be only one response,as he lifts the instrument once more,beloved talisman,mother-of-pearl on gold,the twinkle in his eye lighting up the skies as he smiles:"A dream of a director and let you never doubt it!",and with a nod to the soul-sleuth's father who stands waiting proudly on a cloud close by,fiddle at the ready,like a lifeguard from a story in the long ago,just puts them old lips to the mouthpiece and blows. ◆

ON DAVID CRONENBERG

DAVID CRONENBERG FROM HEAD TO TOE

1 Start with the eyes. An extreme light blue, microscopically aware. Set in a thin face, they are neutral, dispassionate, the eyes of a surgeon or scientist, dissecting cell life under laboratory conditions. Think of the artist as technocrat, as an apostle of the machine, not its enemy. There is something Nordic about these eyes, speaking of clear winter skies and empty, snowy landscapes. Nonetheless, they contain a mystery. David Cronenberg's closest friends and colleagues can say, in all truthfulness, that they don't really know him.

As our leading cinematic existentialist, David Cronenberg believes firmly in the principle that existence precedes essence. In other words, he has invented a life and a style of filmmaking that is unique to himself.

2 Consider the "Idea of North" and all its implications. David Cronenberg has more in common with a Scandinavian like Ingmar Bergman or Canadian artists and thinkers like Glenn Gould and Marshall McLuhan than with his Hollywood contemporaries. While he likes and appreciates America, it is a foreign place. Things are different down there. His films, like this country, have taken up a position somewhere between America and Europe. The technological enthusiasms, while naturally come by, are in harmony with McLuhan's ideas. Where David Cronenberg differs from those notably puritanical Canadians, Gould and McLuhan, is in his concern with the human body in its relation to technology. The most important machine is always the soft machine.

3 Like Glenn Gould, like Bergman on his island, David Cronenberg is something of a recluse, albeit a reluctant, affable one. One might consider that the house where he has lived for two decades now is only a few blocks from the late Gould's apartment. His is not a visceral, passionate rejection of the world. It's just the way things seem to have worked themselves out. Communication is most often a function of the telephone. His new film, *Crash,* based on the novel by J. G. Ballard, takes place in an ambience of isolation, its protagonists inhabiting the rarified atmosphere in which the director lives in his own life. Bergman seldom strayed, for filmmaking purposes, too far from home ground. The same is true of David Cronenberg. In *Naked Lunch,* Tangiers was created in a studio not too far from his house in Toronto.

4 Very few of us live according to a philosophical principle. While other directors look to exotic religion as a guide to their perplexities, David Cronenberg studies technical volumes of difficult European thought. As our leading cinematic existentialist, David Cronenberg believes firmly in the principle that existence precedes essence. In other words, he has invented a life and a style of filmmaking that is unique to himself. Both take

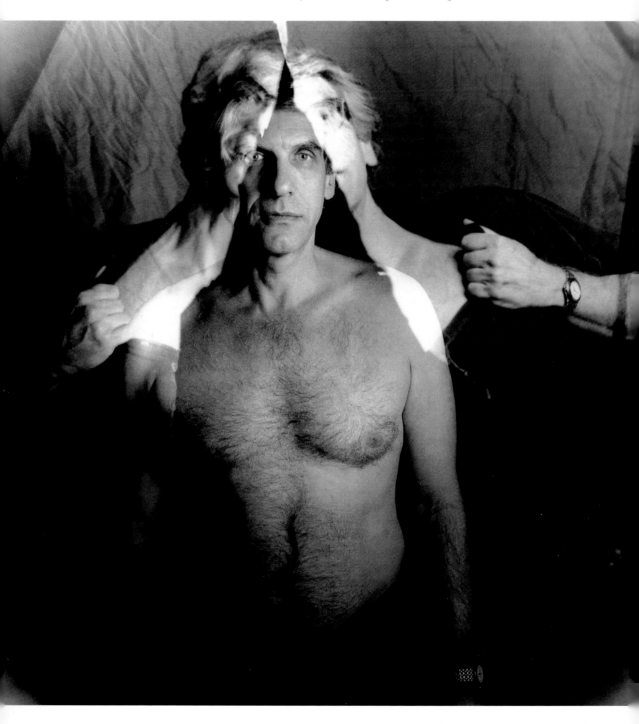

**DAVID
CRONENBERG**
Born 1943
Toronto, Canada

*Stereo** 1969
*Crimes of the Future**
1970
*Shivers** 1975
*Rabid** 1977
*The Brood** 1979
*Fast Company*** 1979
*Scanners** 1981
*Videodrome** 1983
The Dead Zone 1984
*The Fly*** 1986
*Dead Ringers*** 1988
(screenplay by Norman
Snider)
*Naked Lunch** 1992
M. Butterfly 1993
Crash 1997 Cannes
Film Festival Jury
Special Prize
*eXistenZ** 1999

* also screenwriter
** also co-screenwriter

place in a laboratory-style environment, completely controlled. There are few rogue elements that could conceivably create chaos. David Cronenberg seldom steps out of this climate-controlled milieu if he can avoid it. How does one devise such an atmosphere? First, there is a process of self-examination. Put one's own psyche under the microscope, as if it were just another organism. What causes this organism pleasure? Invite it in. What causes the organism pain. Keep it out.

5 All this might sound somewhat bloodless if it weren't for a crucial ingredient, namely, obsession. Think of a chapter in *Understanding Media,* "The Gadget Lover: Narcissus as Narcosis." This passage in McLuhan could be written as description of David Cronenberg. The Internet, computers, motorcycles, automobiles, cell phones, pocket organizers, electronic devices of all kinds are subject to prolonged absorbed investigation, for many solitary hours. Night is turned around and converted into day. Again, there is more freedom in the dark. Those who might interrupt or intrude are all asleep. The machines are not inanimate for David Cronenberg, but living. They have sex appeal. He lusts after them.

6 Then, there is the passage of time. Consider what fame, accomplishment, have wrought in the case of David Cronenberg. If the conventional path is toward compromise and diminution of self as the years take their toll, David Cronenberg has moved resolutely in the opposite direction. He has become more uncompromising, ever more himself, staying true to the ideals of his youth. Like his films, he has become more austere, even more cerebral, less willing to yield to the commonplace. Rather than affirm the mainstream, he has deliberately chosen the singular path.

7 Then, there is David Cronenberg, cameo role specialist. If Alfred Hitchcock's signature was the fleeting appearance in his own films, David Cronenberg's is the guest appearance in the movies of other directors. To date, he has played, among others, a Beverly Hills gynecologist, a mob hit man, an evil psychoanalyst, a movie director, and a lawyer. Among his friends, there are varying estimations of his thespian talents. David Cronenberg, I suspect, believes himself to be one cameo away from stardom. An egoist, certainly. But a refined, subtle one.

8 An intellectual, certainly. But also an intellectual in show business. David Cronenberg does not disdain limousines or first-class accommodation or the other perquisites of celebrity. Yet he remains the loyal family man, never the star covered in women. Attribute this last to a certain mistrust, a leeriness, considering the female species as a whole and its power to wreak disorder. Feminist critics have noticed this quality in his movies.

NORMAN SNIDER
Born 1945
Toronto, Canada

The Changing of the Guard 1985
Dead Ringers 1988
(co-screenwriter; film
directed by David
Cronenberg)
Body Parts 1991
(screenplay)
Valentine's Day 1998
(screenplay)

9 Consider the politics of David Cronenberg. There one encounters a vacuum. A confirmed nonreader of newspapers, events in the great world reach him late, as from a great distance, or not at all. That world, too, is to be kept at bay. For David Cronenberg, the artist remains an outlaw. He expects that one day, inevitably, the police will come knocking at the door. Accordingly, there is one issue, however, on which he remains passionate: freedom of expression.

10 There is a kind of journalistic perplexity considering David Cronenberg. The journalist views films as dark and perverse as *Dead Ringers or M. Butterfly.* Then he meets a charming, apparently normal guy leading an apparently normal life. What do they expect? Capes and oversized incisors? But then, most journalists labor under preconceived and naive notions about authenticity and the imagination. They fail to appreciate the distinction between the criminologist and the criminal. One can make films about the dark side without living one's life with the Marquis de Sade as role model. This is not to say that David Cronenberg is without his dark side.

11 There is, for instance, the passion for speed. Anybody who's sat in the passenger seat while David Cronenberg drives knows the meaning of terror—outside his films. Freeways and city streets are transformed into his own private Grand Prix course as the higher reaches of the speedometers are explored. If there is in fact a dark, psychopathic side to his character, most of it is therapeutically channeled into his films and onto the raceway where it is nicely controlled. The devoted family man well understands that the wild man must have his say, too. Audacity is one of the chief characteristics of the art of David Cronenberg. Underneath a deceptively mild exterior, boldness too has a place in his life.

12 One doesn't readily speak of genius. But these are the terms of reference that must be considered here. It has been defined as the ability to explore areas of experience where mere talent cannot go. Gynecology in *Dead Ringers,* sex and the automobile in *Crash,* the rarified reaches of gender confusion in *M. Butterfly:* these are subject matters no other director has chosen to illuminate. Long may he thrive.

13 Finally, consider the toes of David Cronenberg. They are webbed. ◆

ON WILLIAM
FRIEDKIN

Most Hollywood directors want to push the envelope as much as they want to commit hari-kari. William Friedkin, then, has *committed* hari-kari not once, but over and over again. The man seems to crave the big knife.

French Connection and *The Exorcist* are obvious big knives, but they look at *Sorcerer* and *Cruising* and *To Live and Die in L.A.* and *Jade*—movies all ahead of their time, daring, moody, visceral, explosive, and always jagged with a thrusting, pounding, swirling visual magic. His love of opera is obvious on screen, but it is his own inner psychic opera that he puts up there: shadowed, existential, dusky, and sometimes dark, its notes often jazzy and blue.

If a director is the god of his creative universe, then he has dared to create even stars, even pushing the envelope there, daring to cast unknowns who then become household words: Gene Hackman, Roy Scheider, Ellen Burstyn, Jason Miller, and Willem Dafoe are Friedkin creations, created in the face of sometimes vehement studio opposition. Vehement opposition, of course, doesn't intimidate him: if you are drawn to the big knife, using it to nick some studio head now and then isn't exactly going to overwhelm you with angst.

He began doing documentaries, and you can still see that in the street sizzle and sometimes jarring, eye-blinking reality that he puts on screen. It is that sense of reality that gives a special jolt to his work. The people in his movies don't act—they *are*. They are, for better or worse, human beings.

When I began writing screenplays in the mid-seventies, the very first piece of advice my very first agent, Kitty Hawks, gave me was: "Work with Billy Friedkin." Nearly twenty years later, I wrote a screenplay called *Jade* and asked him to direct it. When my son Joseph Jeremiah was born in 1993, I did an interview with Army Archerd in which I talked about how happy I was that Joey was born and how happy I was that Billy Friedkin was going to direct *Jade*. Re-reading the interview recently, I was struck by how equally happy I seemed to be—about Joey and about Billy.

I didn't know William Friedkin personally when I asked that he direct my script, I only knew his work. The people I spoke to about him said that he was brilliant, mercurial, hot-tempered, and that he just might drive me crazy.

WILLIAM FRIEDKIN
Born 1939
Chicago, Illinois

Good Times 1968

The Night They Raided Minsky's 1968

The Birthday Party 1969

The Boys in the Band 1970

The French Connection 1971 Academy Award for Best Director; Golden Globe Award for Best Director

The Exorcist 1973 Golden Globe Award for Best Director

Sorcerer 1977

The Brink's Job 1979

*Cruising** 1981

Deal of the Century 1983

*To Live and Die in L.A.*** 1985

*Rampage** 1987

*The Guardian*** 1990

Blue Chips 1993 (screenplay by Ron Shelton)

Jade 1995 (screenplay by Joe Eszterhas)

Rules of Engagement 1999

* also screenwriter
** also co-screenwriter

I wasn't worried about it: Sly Stallone hadn't driven me crazy, Debra Winger hadn't driven me crazy, Paul Verhoeven hadn't driven me crazy, Costa-Gavras hadn't driven me crazy. I believed in Casey Stengel's wisdom: "I don't get ulcers, I *give* ulcers."

Well, I can say now, two years after we began working together, that Billy Friedkin didn't drive me crazy—and I didn't give him ulcers—but, boy, for a while there, it was *close*. He is, may God help us all, the perfectionist's perfectionist. He chews on a script and then he chews on it some more and

> **The people in his movies don't act—they *are*. They are, for better or worse, human beings.**

JOE ESZTERHAS

Thirteen Seconds: Confrontation at Kent State 1970 (co-author Michael D. Roberts)

Charlie Simpson's Apocalypse 1973

The Jagged Edge 1985 (screenplay)

Big Shots 1987 (screenplay)

Hearts of Fire 1987 (screenplay)

Betrayed 1988 (screenplay)

Checking Out 1989 (screenplay)

Music Box 1989 (screenplay)

Basic Instinct 1992 (screenplay; film directed by Paul Verhoeven)

Nowhere to Run 1993 (co-screenwriter)

Sliver 1993 (screenplay; based on the novel by Ira Levin; film directed by Phillip Noyce)

Jade 1995 (screenplay; film directed by William Friedkin)

Showgirls 1995 (screenplay; film directed by Paul Verhoeven)

some more. We'd agree on something and then, in the process of chewing, he'd discover that he didn't like the taste of it after all. He'd disagree with our *agreement*. At times, I'd agree with our *disagreement*. And we'd go around and around. One afternoon we discussed one word—*one word*—for four hours. I realized, finally, that he simply couldn't help his damn chewing. It was some kind of artistic reflex action. His inner voice was saying to him, *Billy, keep chewing, you can't ever chew on it enough!*

I can say now, two years later, that he is all of those other things, too: brilliant, mercurial, and hot-tempered, but he is also one other thing that most people don't talk about when they talk about William Friedkin. He is a kind man and a good one. He is sensitive and compassionate. His intensity, his *eruptibility,* is tied only to his craving for the big knife, his sense of artistic perfection.

I'll give you the best example that I know. Our movie, *Jade,* had the lamentable misfortune of being released two weeks after another of my scripts, *Showgirls,* which got one of the bloodiest critical hammerings in film history. It wasn't just a hammering, it was a forensic dismemberment. What was mostly dismembered was my screenplay.

Well, here comes *Jade* right on top of it and it was like the critics needed even more blood, needed to be absolutely sated, with clots dribbling down their cheeks. *Jade,* too, was forensically dismembered and, once again, what was mostly dismembered was my screenplay.

I was depressed, convinced that had I not written the screenplay, had our movie not come out right after *Showgirls, Jade* would have lived and prospered instead of being cannibalized. I felt, on a very personal level, that I had let Billy down. I knew that he, too, was depressed. I knew, too, and had painfully learned from past experience, that in most cases in Hollywood, when a movie fails, the director and writer stay as far away as possible from each other to avoid creative reinfection.

Billy called me at the worst moment of our mutual depression. He started talking about Mahler. Perfect, I thought, vintage Billy Friedkin. Our movie was down in flames, the hills out there were still swathed in smoke, and here he was, talking about Mahler.

Mahler, Billy Friedkin said, had never gotten a good review in his life. Fuck them, he said, what do they know?

I'll say this about him, and it's the most any screenwriter can say about a director: I'd love Billy Friedkin to direct anything I ever write. ◆

ON SYDNEY POLLACK

THOMAS CAPLAN

Once upon a time, before sensation had become a goal in itself, before characters had metamorphosed into types, when the American man, woman, boy, and girl were not generic, but individuals, we went to the movies to learn things: how to dance and dress and drive a car, how to hold a cigarette or wear a six-shooter, how to mix a martini, how to seduce or yield to seduction. Lives then were defined by concrete details, many obvious, others subtle, and among these details the most important and revealing—and, inevitably, the most provocative of suspense—were the decisions human beings made, sometimes casually, but especially under pressure.

The world then was unashamedly stratified according to innumerable, overlapping criteria. Class and income, for example, were not, in every case, congruent. Nor were style—that peculiar ability to beguile through originality—and income, or, for that matter, style and class. Race and ethnicity and religion all mattered—and mattered terribly—as one navigated life in post-World War II America. And one had little hope of success if one could not efficiently decode the thousands of signals—accents and attitudes, the cut of tennis clothes, the shapes of handbags—that assaulted the senses without ever announcing that they were, in actual fact, signals.

When the young, hopeful actor Sydney Pollack "ran away as fast as I could" from Indiana for New York and, eventually, Stanford Meisner's Neighborhood Playhouse in the mid-1950s, the art of storytelling still reigned supreme among theatrical and literary values and the newly ascendant nation and city were rich in those who were attempting to employ its ancient principles in service to new realities. Elia Kazan, whose cinematic artistry would inspire Pollack, was the preeminent stage director of the day. Tennessee Williams, Arthur Miller, and William Inge were at their most prolific, dissecting, with abrupt candor, the psychosexual, urban, and faux-innocent Midwestern landscapes of an America frantically re-imagining itself as it reconciled dreams to actualities. Words, in and of themselves, were critical, for characters were meant to possess intelligence as well as physicality, to reflect upon and debate, if not merely to represent, ideas; and, inevitably, for the subtext they implied.

SYDNEY POLLACK
Born 1934
Lafayette, Indiana

The Slender Thread 1965
This Property Is Condemned 1966
The Scalphunters 1968
Castle Keep 1969
They Shoot Horses, Don't They? 1969
Jeremiah Johnson 1972
The Way We Were 1973
The Yakuza 1975
Three Days of the Condor 1975
Bobby Deerfield 1977
The Electric Horseman 1979
Absence of Malice 1981
Tootsie 1982
Out of Africa 1985
Academy Awards for Best Director and Best Picture
Havana 1990
The Firm 1993
Sabrina 1995
Random Hearts 1999

Having arrived with a passion to tell stories already full blown in his heart, Pollack learned his craft, then, after being drafted and serving two years in the army, taught it, developing his directorial aptitude "by years of teaching actors." By the time he reached Hollywood in the mid-1960s, he was an accomplished director of television drama, one of the "second wave," along with Robert Altman, Mark Rydell, Arthur Hiller, and Stuart Rosenberg, who came to features from *filmed* T.V.; the "first wave," which included

Sidney Lumet and John Frankenheimer, having made the transition to the big screen immediately from *live* broadcasting.

Art prospers from constraint. Rigors of form, even the simple imperative of having to make do (in the physical world, for example, without orchidaceous special effects) forces the imagination to concentrate upon character and upon the story that proceeds from the intrinsic nature of that character, as it is catalyzed, over time, by events. "What draws me to any story is an argument at its center," Sydney Pollack explains, "something I don't know and let the characters argue out." While, at first, this may seem merely an aphoristic restatement of the primary dramatic dictum "to conflict and resolve," in the context of Pollack's oeuvre it assumes telling accuracy. Beginning with *The Slender Thread,* his first feature, Pollack's films have all recognized that individuals exist within more or less elaborate social structures and the "argument" at their cores has inevitably been between the limits of these structures and some inextinguishable yearning of his characters' souls. His is a world in which physical (*Castle Keep* and *Jeremiah Johnson*), economic (*This Property Is Condemned* and *They Shoot Horses, Don't They?*), legal (*Absence of Malice* and *The Firm*), political (*Three Days of the Condor* and *Havana*), professional (*Tootsie* and *Bobby Deerfield*), and social (*The Way We Were* and *Out of Africa*) realities not only exist, but frequently layer one another, simultaneously enabling and constraining human will and fantasy. The larger canvas of cinema having afforded more room for the accretion and observation of detail, Pollack, by adhering to his theatrical roots, defining his stories in particular settings, his characters' lives against particular structures (themselves, of course, all finally manifestations of human nature), and resisting the auteur's temptation to derive and wander, gained without losing. He has given us some of our very best cinematic looks at the world of work, locating profound, inherent drama where others have professed to find only routine and tedium.

"Specificity," suggests Sydney Pollack, "is the foundation of any character." This is true, but descriptively incomplete, for the ambiguity of Pollack's people shadows their résumés. This can be easy to miss beneath such Hollywood A-picture veneers as those of *The Way We Were* and *Out of Africa*. The professional tightness of such stories, however, cannot, on reflection, obscure the fact that the characters have come *onto* the screen with histories and, even more crucial to their durability in our memories, that they will at least seem to *go forward* into the same unknowable future we will. "Sometimes, in poker, it's smarter to lose with a winning hand, so you can win later with a losing one," says Jack Weil, the hero of *Havana* played by Robert Redford. Thus, through a simple, perfectly pitched, offhand remark, not only a man's work, style, and irony, but his past and hypothetical future snap alive.

Eschewing both the pyrotechnics that technology began to make available to Hollywood about a decade after his arrival and the self-aware hipness to film that has characterized many independent movies of the same period, Sydney Pollack has seemed to enjoy taking the world as it is—following his characters through the complicated maze of life, where paths of work and love, glory and humiliation, intersect often and unpredictably.

THOMAS CAPLAN
Born 1946
Baltimore, Maryland

Line of Chance 1979
Parallelogram 1987
Grace and Favor 1997

Eschewing both the pyrotechnics that technology began to make available to Hollywood about a decade after his arrival and the self-aware hipness to film that characterized many independent movies of the same period, Sydney Pollack has seemed to enjoy taking the world as it is—following his characters through the complicated maze of life, where paths of work and love, glory and humiliation, intersect often and unpredictably. The glamour with which we overlay life where and when we can is, he understands, at once another way of making it bearable and a cry from our hearts, a virtually religious impulse to uncover some temporal beauty, as well as order (which may be the same thing) on our way from and toward mystery.

In his novella *We're Friends Again,* John O'Hara, a novelist of the generation before Pollack's who shared (and perhaps partly inspired) the filmmaker's fascination with the manners and speech and structure of society wrote: "What really can any of us know about any of us, and why must we make such a thing of loneliness when it is the final condition of us all? And where would love be without it?" O'Hara, too, instinctively comprehended the inextricability of human comedy and nightmare, of success and futility, beauty and frailty—and O'Hara, too, examined the people of a great country exactly as it was coming into its moment of greatness. If there are occasionally more questions—shallower wells of certainty and confidence—beneath the surface of Pollack's characters' lives, it is probably due to the displacement in time from which they are observed. Nothing, after all, is quite so sure as it once seemed. But, years into the next millennium, when those who may be curious seek to understand what precisely life was like in the last half of the "American Century," they will have few more arresting and spot-on informants than O'Hara and Pollack. All the shades of gray will be there—trademarks of those stories and films because they are the very stuff of those characters' experiences and consciousness.

No doubt, we shall seem quaint, perhaps gulled, plainly no more than superficially informed to those who follow us. But be that as it may. For, thanks to Sydney Pollack among a handful of others, there will also be flashes of dialogue, sudden skyscraper smiles, transfixed and wondrous gazes at prizes won or lost or contemplated—even wistful glances at the simple artifacts, the daring and disappointments of our lives. Surely, beholding them, the young will once more shudder with their unique, spine-tingling knowledge of human possibility and the old will cock half-smiles at the paradox that it should be both so fleeting and so immutable. ◆

ON ROGER CORMAN

ROGER CORMAN
Born 1926
Los Angeles, California

Five Guns West 1955
The Apache Woman 1955
The Day the World Ended 1956
Swamp Woman 1956
The Oklahoma Woman 1956
The Gunslinger 1956
It Conquered the World 1956
Not of This Earth 1957
The Undead 1957
Naked Paradise 1957
Attack of the Crab Monsters 1957
Rock All Night 1957
Teenage Doll 1957
Carnival Rock 1957
Sorority Girl 1957
The Viking Women and the Sea Serpent 1957
War of the Satellites 1958
The She Gods of Shark Reef 1958
Machine Gun Kelly 1958
Teenage Caveman 1958
I, Mobster 1959
A Bucket of Blood 1959
The Wasp Woman 1959
Ski Troop Attack 1960
The House of Usher 1960

I n 1974 I got my first paying gig in the film business courtesy of Roger Corman. Nothing too glamorous, just driving a truck on one of Roger's New World films, Monte Hellman's *Cockfighter,* down in Georgia. But it had perks. I was straight out of Fontana, California, birthplace of the Hell's Angels and damn little else, and I instantly became friends with the film's cinematographer, the late Nestor Almendros, one of the most inspiring film artists I've ever met. I got to kick around with Warren Oates and Harry Dean Stanton. I got to help Monte fine-tune moments in the script. I got to hang out with Charles Willeford, who wrote the picture and took a small role as a cockfight judge.

But most importantly, I joined "The Club," which includes Martin Scorsese, Francis Coppola, Jonathan Demme, James Cameron, Joe Dante, Peter Bogdanovich, Monte Hellman, Ron Howard, Robert Towne, John Sayles, et al. All started their careers toiling on low- to guerilla-budget projects for Corman via either American International Pictures or Corman's 1970s-era film company, New World Pictures. It's worth noting that there was an indie film scene before Soderbergh and Tarantino, most of it centering around Corman. Were most of these films genre toss-away projects you wouldn't necessarily want to bring home to Mother or the National Society of Film Critics? Sure, but I'm not so enamored of the countless navel-gazing, edge, and irony-addicted solipsisms that constitute the bulk of today's indie offerings. Little down and dirties such as *Student Nurses, Caged Heat, Battle Beyond the Stars,* and *Alligator* stack up quite nicely next to the glut of "why I hate my family" pictures currently making their way onto screens. Besides, Corman was to the crop of 1970s talent what N.Y.U. was to the 1980s and Manhattan Beach video store jobs were to the 1990s.

Twenty-two years later, as a member of the Los Angeles Film Critics Association, I was on hand as Corman was presented with the Career Achievement Award, a fairly controversial choice given that his output does skew more to *Carnosaur* than Carné. I was touched by tributes delivered that day, courtesy of Corman school vets like actor Dick Miller and directors such as Hellman, Dante, and Bogdanovich. Hellman was especially illuminating, noting that he learned from Corman the valuable

The Little Shop of Horrors 1960

The Last Woman on Earth 1960

Creature from the Haunted Sea 1961

Atlas 1961

The Pit and the Pendulum 1961

The Intruder 1962

The Premature Burial 1962

Tales of Terror 1962

Tower of London 1962

The Raven 1963

The Terror 1963

The Man with X-Ray Eyes 1963

The Haunted Palace 1963

The Young Racers 1963

The Secret Invasion 1964

The Masque of the Red Death 1964

Tomb of Ligeia 1965

Wild Angels 1966

St. Valentine's Day Massacre 1967

Target: Harry 1968

Bloody Mama 1970

Gas-s-s! 1970

Von Richtofen and Brown 1971

Frankenstein Unbound 1990

lesson of trimming a movie deftly by removing a frame at the beginning and end of every scene, losing no continuity but carving down the running time and speeding up the action.

Though I was wearing my journalist cap that day, I related because I also spent the years between 1974 and 1996 chipping away at the indie and foreign-financed film worlds, co-writing several pictures with Hellman, including two in the late 1980s that were worthy of the grand days of New World; *Iguana,* a sadomasochistic pirate picture shot in the Canary Islands and *Better Watch Out,* a horror thriller involving a blind girl and a crazed killer in a Santa Claus suit. I wear my kinship to Roger proudly, since I always loved the idea that you could make low-budget genre pictures that were smart, funny, maybe even subversive. In that kinship, however, there's also an uneasy confusion that has troubled and clouded my esteem and appraisal of Corman's justifiably lauded career.

Though he's run two companies, the aforementioned New World and later Concorde, and directed dozens of cult films, from *Little Shop of Horrors* to the Poe pictures of the 1960s, Corman has always seemed wholly mysterious to me. I've never understood why the man who directed *The Masque of the Red Death, The Wild Angels,* and *Von Richthofen and Brown* and distributed *Cries and Whispers* and *Amarcord* would choose to spend the last two and a half decades overseeing the manufacture and sale of grind-'em-out exploitation pictures. Sure, he was following his career path, but he'd abandoned directing, which he did with wit, intelligence, and economy. If you've been disappointed at the multiplex lately, you'll appreciate those qualities in a director as much as I do. Back in 1974, I assumed that Corman was only taking a breather from directing. I had shown *The Masque of the Red Death,* starring Jane Asher and photographed by Nicolas Roeg, back in my Cal Arts film series I programmed just prior to the *Cockfighter* shoot. *Von Richthofen and Brown* was a solid World War I aerial war picture that was released only three years earlier. I never imagined that Corman would only direct one picture in the next twenty-four years. I've spent the time in between trying to piece together the answers to Corman's almost complete compartmentalization of film artist and film businessman. And in 1970 compartmentalization became bifurcation, with Roger leaving behind the half of him that was directorial.

Back in 1975 I asked Monte Hellman who was the smartest person he ever met in the movie business. "Roger Corman" he answered. Monte also surmised that Roger was deeply conflicted over his role in the moviemaking scheme of things. He guessed that the commercial failure of *The Intruder,* Roger's ambitious movie about race relations, somehow had scarred him or scared him into a retreat from his ambitions as a film artist.

STEVEN GAYDOS
Born 1954
Fontana, California

One Month Later 1987
(co-screenwriter)

Iguana 1988
(co-screenwriter)

Better Watch Out 1989
(co-screenwriter)

*Movie Talk from the
Front Lines* 1995
(co-author)

All Men Are Mortal 1996
(co-screenwriter)

*Cannes: 50 Years of Sun,
Sex and Celluloid* 1997
(co-editor)

*The Variety Guide to Film
Festivals* 1998 (editor
and co-author)

But I don't buy Roger's retreat. There must be something else, something deeper, darker, more compulsive, less controlled than the man in the producer's seat. Money is an obvious suspect in this mystery, but it's too simple an explanation.

In my almost thirty years in Hollywood, I've learned that producers live in big houses and writers live in little houses. I've learned that film artists have to compromise or kiss away private schools, first-class air tickets, and invitations to the golden inner sanctum of everything from pricey watering holes to top-drawer material. Roger is legendarily cheap, but cheap doesn't explain retreat. I'm sure he and his wife Julie, an accomplished professional in her own right, enjoy the finer things in life. But I wouldn't take an extra weekend at Two Bunch Palms if it meant I could never swing the bat creatively.

I've watched Corman in tasty little cameo roles in films like *Apollo 13, Godfather II,* and *Philadelphia,* and I think the answer lies in the eyes of a wonderfully creative mind buried several layers underneath an armor only he knows why he donned back in the early 1970s. Yes, he's been the godfather and film school for countless filmmakers, including quite a few bona fide American directing giants. And he's made piles and piles of money, mostly from selling New World and building Concorde into a nifty money-making outfit. Now, in his post-Concorde phase, he's ambitiously making movies overseas, taking advantage of tax schemes and subsidies and a cheap labor force. But my fascination with Corman as Garbo of B-movie auteurship is unabated. For me, he's as mysterious as Welles' *Citizen Kane,* but the supporting characters in Corman's story are a lot more fun. Maybe there is no mystery. Maybe it's just my own nostalgia for the Hollywood of the early 1970s, when a kid from Fontana could go to work in Georgia on a movie written by a pulp detective master craftsman like Charles Willeford, shot by Truffaut's cinematographer starring a Peckinpah stable player and directed by the man who did *The Shooting* and *Two Lane Blacktop.* What a time! The same Roger Corman that cranks out an endless stream of indistinguishable video fodder brought New Orleans novelist John William Corrington to Hollywood for the script of *Von Richthofen and Brown* around the same time. And cast Robert De Niro in *Bloody Mama* the year before. And devised an entirely new genre of camp horror with the Vincent Price, Peter Lorre, Edgar Allen Poe pictures a few years earlier. And practically invented the 1960s outlaw biker genre that led to *Easy Rider* and the creation of an iconography that still endures. And was feted by the National Film Theatre in London for his fifty directorial efforts.

I still have a dog-eared copy of *Take One* magazine from 1970 that celebrated Corman and cinematographer Laszlo Kovacs. Corman spoke at length about his fascination with the World War I setting of *Von*

Richthofen, calling the aerial ace the "last of the knights . . . replaced as the commander of the squadron by Hermann Goering."

He also described his 1970 picture, *Gas-s-s-s! Or It Became Necessary to Destroy the World in Order to Save It* as "a picture in which middle class American society is represented by the Hell's Angels driving golf carts and a fascist society is represented by a football team travelling across the country in dune buggies, complete with their own marching bands, and where Edgar Allen Poe rides in on a Harley-Davidson chopper from time to time commenting on the morality of what takes place."

I miss that Roger, that time, that place, that spirit. I hope he finds it again in Ireland. And if he needs someone to drive trucks for $100 a week, I'm ready to rock. ◆

ON MICHAEL
MANN

Michael Mann has a modus operandi as distinctive as any master criminal's. He's a hard-boiled sensualist: half muckraker and half fabulist. If he had been born a hundred years ago, he'd have followed Jack London's path, not just into bare-knuckled journalism but also into transcendent evocations of the beautiful and the wild.

Talking to Mann is as surprising as it is stimulating. His unfettered intuition and exquisite awareness compel your rapt attention. It's as if you're tuning your radio dial to a brainy, original talk-show host on a faint college-town station—you strain not to miss his special code words and hard-won observations. You feel Mann gets extraordinary commitments from actors like James Caan in *Thief* or Tom Noonan and Brian Cox in *Manhunter* or Daniel Day-Lewis in *The Last of the Mohicans* because he catches them up in his enthrallment with his material.

When I listen to tapes of the marathon interview sessions I held with him five years apart, one before the release of *Thief* in 1981 and the other before the release of *Manhunter* in 1986, they sound as if they're halves of an ongoing conversation, whether he's discussing his past or the projects then at hand. He grew up near, if not in, "the Patch," one of the roughest areas of Chicago. ("It was very aggressive, it was very masculine, and it was very heterosexual.") He still has a flat-A accent. It was at the University of Wisconsin in Madison, where he majored in English, that movies first got their hooks into him. The film that clinched the obsession was (appropriately enough) G.W. Pabst's coruscating study of urban vice, *The Joyless Street.* By the time he graduated from college, Mann knew he wanted to make movies. But he didn't like the curricula of most American film schools: "It was like vocational training. You're not supposed to do 'student' films; you're supposed to do a show reel." So, in 1965, Mann entered the London Film School, where he got an M.A. in film and did what he thought he "should" do: "make two-and-a-half-minute, fully symbolic statements on the nature of reality that'll shame you ten years later." Mann stayed on in London for about six years, filming documentaries and T.V. commercials and working as an assistant production supervisor for Twentieth Century Fox. Having been part of the Madison campus's radical days, he began to feel the contradictions of his position: "I would make money on commercials and try to put it to use on my own projects. Some material I filmed on the Paris student riots wound up on NBC's *First Tuesday* because NBC's own people couldn't get close to the radical leaders. You never resolve these contradictions."

Missing the "intensity" of life in the United States—"the patterns and the rhythms, the color tones and the frequencies"—Mann returned in the early seventies, eventually settling in Los Angeles. He learned how to write by toiling on *Starsky and Hutch:* "For structure, nothing beats the melodrama of episodic T.V." He graduated to what he calls "the Rolls-Royce of T.V. shows," *Police Story,* and created the hit series *Vega$,* before embarking on his 1979 movie-directing debut, *The Jericho Mile*—a prison film unlike any other.

It was made for television, but on *The Jericho Mile* Mann crystallized all his trademark techniques. First he absorbed whatever "soft" information he could find about prison subcultures. He tapped into the essence of Big House pride in the sports pages of the prison newspapers: "Everyone *seemed* to be doing great, probably because if you criticized anyone in an article your ass would be grass." Then he put that data at the service of his artifice. The story centered on a convict (Peter Strauss) who based his integrity on becoming a world-class runner. Mann was able to get around the claustrophobia built into jailhouse movies by placing the bulk of the action (filmed at Folsom State Prison in California) in the exercise yard. Each racial and ethnic group had its own turf—blacks dominating the weight-lifting area, Hispanics the handball court. Add a music track that spun off from "Sympathy for the Devil" and "No Expectations" and you had a movie that externalized the prisoners' state of mind and conjured up what Mann called "social Technicolor."

Mann likes to talk about a movie's "genetic coding": a swirling double helix of image and sound, character and story, fantasy and fact. His first theatrical feature, *Thief,* floats on a neon-lit Styx into the heart of the underworld. The camera descends in a downpour to nighttime Chicago, where, operating with a precision that suggests telepathy, the thief (James Caan) guides a drill that seems to liquefy as it chews into a vault containing diamonds. In this asphalt Hades the heist technology is out of *Star Wars* and the underworld bureaucracy is Byzantine. When a don persuades Caan to work full time on mob-sponsored heists, the thief hopes to make some big scores and ease off. Instead, the don, in his own icy phrase, ends up "owning the paper" on the thief's life. What better metaphor could there be for the constrictions of modern America than having an organization—the government, a credit card company, or the mob—"own the paper" on you?

Mann's perennial attempt to infuse elemental tales like *Thief* with allegory and atmosphere led him far astray in *The Keep,* a vampire movie set in Nazi-occupied Romania. But again and again, he's broken through to the mass audience in the medium that masters of moviemaking usually abjure: the weekly T.V. series. In the mid-1980s, when asked to produce an MTV-style cop show, Mann exploited the breakthroughs he'd achieved in *The Jericho Mile* and *Thief* and came up with the phenomenon of *Miami Vice.* With avant-garde vehicles and clothing, pastel backdrops to bloodletting, and guest appearances by hard-news celebrities like G. Gordon Liddy as

MICHAEL MANN
Born 1943
Chicago, Illinois

Thief* 1981
The Keep* 1983
Manhunter* 1986
The Last of the Mohicans** 1992
Heat* 1995
Man of the People** 1999

* also screenwriter
** also co-screenwriter

well as rock icons like Glenn Frey, Mann turned the urban schizophrenia of the 1980s into an influential style. (To Mann, of course, this style was primarily "an expression of place and content, the milieu the guys are moving through.") The series used its sound track the way urbanites use Walkmans and car radios—either to articulate surrounding chaos or provide a defiant counterpoint.

Returning to the movies, Mann audaciously adapted Thomas Harris's first Hannibal Lecter novel, *Red Dragon:* in *Manhunter* he soldered an FBI search for a serial killer to an eerie exploration of the murderer's mind and awkward elements of family melodrama. When Mann follows the point of view of the killer as he moves from a van to a bedroom, where he shines a light in the face of a sleeping wife and mother, the director (who also served as a camera operator) puts fear and loathing in your belly. He twists the knot further when the FBI manhunter retraces the killer's steps and analyzes the bloodstains on the walls and floor. Mann conveys all the horror of a serial killer using murder as a means of aesthetic expression. And Brian Cox is a sardonic, chilling Lecter—he talks with terrifying blandness and looks like a bleached Bela Lugosi.

Simultaneously, Mann set up another groundbreaking T.V. series, *Crime Story* (1986)—a show about cars with fins and cops with teeth. Dennis Farina played the crusading detective in charge of the Major Crimes Unit of the Chicago Police Department. In Mann's words, he's a guy with a "personalized" sense of justice: "he has his own cosmic sense of right and wrong. And that makes him a hell of a cop in 1963. It doesn't make him one hell of a cop in '69 or '70." In the pilot (the series' high point), the trail of a dangerous new criminal crew leads Farina to a cocky Irish kid (David Caruso), who happens to be the son of the hero's surrogate parents. It's a headlong story of neighborhood connections and betrayals done in an explosive mix of styles: the serious guys wear fedoras and the punks go out in ducktail haircuts; Del Shannon melds with Johnny Mathis on the sound track; age-old Sicilian traditions unravel in a suburban estate fitted out with space-age décor. The show's V-8 engine pickup powered a vision of a hyper-masculine culture— the virile pop Zeitgeist of Mann's adolescence—on its eve of destruction.

Nothing Mann has done has lacked intrigue, even when he returned to familiar territory in the ultra-contemporary *Heat*. This cops-versus-crooks epic pitted an untouchable target—master thief Robert De Niro—against an irresistible force—police lieutenant Al Pacino. It suggested new arenas of stressed-out yuppie fantasy. De Niro is prudent and code-abiding, Pacino manic and instinctive. They play out a *macho* version of sense and sensibility in a vicious, morally booby-trapped universe. Ultimately, these *doppel-heroes* are too limited to propel a near three-hour saga, and their domestic scenes are as stilted as the ones in *Manhunter*. Still, the movie

MICHAEL SRAGOW
Born 1952
Roosevelt, New York

Currently a staff writer for the *New Times* chain of weekly newspapers. He has been a movie critic for *Rolling Stone* and *The New Yorker* as well as a frequent contributor to *The Atlantic Monthly*.

Produced and Abandoned: The Best Films You've Never Seen 1990 (editor)

Victor Fleming: A Biography 2001

does capture a fresh urban fatalism. In *Heat,* exhilaration is out. The freedom that high-stakes crime can buy has little to do with esprit; it's about practicing an illicit craft and living according to your own rules, which can be even more restrictive than society's. For the characters, excitement comes from seeing a calculation work or an educated guess pay off. For the spectators, it comes from catastrophe.

In 1992, Mann's voluptuous wide-screen retelling of that fictional warhorse of the French and Indian War, *The Last of the Mohicans,* proved the breadth of his vitality and talent. Once again, Mann immersed himself in data, drawing not just on James Fenimore Cooper's original 1826 novel, and on Philip Dunne's script for the 1936 Randolph Scott version, but also on the diaries of the comte de Bougainville and histories and essays by Francis Parkman and Simon Schama. Most important, he enlisted Daniel Day-Lewis to play Nathaniel Poe (a.k.a. Hawkeye), the Indian-raised white scout who tries to save the English maiden he loves from the Huron massacre of the British retreating from Fort William Henry. Day-Lewis's "white Indian" hero, with his frontier-Samson locks and prehensile alertness, rebels against bogus English authority and bridges gaps among all those who live honestly (and sensually) in the woods. Using virtuoso guerilla and survival skills for his own ethical purposes, he's the noblest expression yet of the Michael Mann hero. *The Last of the Mohicans* reinvents the legend of the honest, all-capable frontiersman in a way that honors whites and Indians alike. It's no more "accurate" yet no less moving than, say, *Young Mr. Lincoln,* and it leaves you guessing at what wonderment the filmmaker will create for us next. This writer-director is an unpredictable individualist. For him (as for Nathaniel), a Mann's gotta do what a Mann's gotta do. ◆

CREDITS

SUSAN GRAY

Susan Gray is a New York-based photographer whose work has appeared in the following books: *A Life on the Road* by Charles Kuralt; *Three Generations of Wyeth Art* by James H. Duff *et al.*; *Shooting Stars: Contemporary Glamour Photography* by Ricky Spears; *Great African Americans*; and *Denzel Washington: His Films and Career* by Douglas Brode.

Her photographs have been used by many magazines and corporations and have been exhibited at the Brandywine River Museum, Chadds Ford, Pennsylvania. Her photo stock agency is RETNA Ltd. (telephone: 212-255-0622, Lori Reese/Julie Graham).

Writers on Directors is her first book.

LEONARD MALTIN

(Commentator and interviewer on television's *Entertainment Tonight*; film critic for *Playboy* magazine; weekly column for Microsoft's Cinemania Online; hosts daily syndicated radio feature; regular on the Encore and Starz cable T.V. channels; member of National Film Preservation Board; teaches at the University of Southern California; and actually has a life with wife, Alice, and children.)

Movie Comedy Teams (NAL) 1970/1985 rev. ed.

The Great Movie Comedians (Crown) 1978

The Art of the Cinematographer (Dover) 1978 (originally published as *Behind the Camera* in 1971)

Of Mice and Magic: A History of American Animated Cartoons (NAL and McGraw-Hill) 1980

Selected Short Subjects (DaCapo) 1983 (originally published as *The Great Movie Shorts* in 1971)

The Little Rascals: The Life and Times of Our Gang (Crown) 1992 (co-authored with Richard M. Bann) (originally published as *Our Gang: The Life and Times of the Little Rascals* in 1977)

Leonard Maltin's Movie Encyclopedia (Dutton) 1994

The Disney Films (Hyperion) 1995 (originally published by Crown in 1973)

The Great American Broadcast: A Celebration of Radio's Golden Age (Dutton) 1997

Leonard Maltin's Movie and Video Guide (Penguin) 1969–1998

Leonard Maltin's Family Film Guide (Penguin) 1999

RUSSELL BANKS

b. 1940, Newton, Massachusetts; raised in New Hampshire and eastern Massachusetts.

(Member of the American Academy of Arts and Letters. Married to poet Chase Twichell.)

Continental Drift (HarperCollins) 1985 Finalist for Pulitzer Prize

Success Stories (HarperCollins) 1987

Affliction (HarperCollins) 1989 Finalist for Pulitzer Prize; Shortlisted for the *Irish Times* International Literary Prize

The Sweet Hereafter (HarperCollins) 1991

Rule of the Bone (HarperCollins) 1995 (film directed by Carl Franklin)

Cloudsplitter (HarperCollins) 1998

BRUCE BENDERSON

(Lives in New York City. Manuel Puig, author of *Kiss of the Spider Women*, called Benderson "the new poet of the underworld.")

Pretending to Say No (Plume) 1990

My Father Is Coming 1990 (co-screenwriter)

User (Dutton/Plume) 1994/1995

Toward the New Degeneracy (Edgewise) 1997

PETER BLAUNER

b. 1959, New York City.

(Former journalist and Good Humor man.)

Slow Motion Riot (William Morrow) 1991 Edgar Allan Poe Award for Best First Novel of the Year

Casino Moon (Simon & Schuster) 1994 *Time Out* (London) Best Books of the Year

The Intruder (Simon & Schuster) 1996 *The New York Times* and *Sunday Times* of London Best-seller

Man of the Hour (Little Brown) 1999

ADAM BROOKS

b. 1956, Toronto, Canada.

Almost You 1985 (director) Special Jury Prize Sundance Film Festival

Red Riding Hood 1987 (director)

Heads 1993 (screenwriter)

French Kiss 1995 (screenwriter; film directed by Lawrence Kasdan)

Duke of Groove 1995 (screenwriter) AAN Best Short

Beloved 1998 (co-screenwriter; based on the novel by Toni Morrison; film directed by Jonathan Demme)

Practical Magic 1998 (co-screenwriter; based on the novel by Alice Hoffman; film directed by Griffin Dunne)

JOAN JULIET BUCK

b. 1948, Los Angeles, California; raised in Paris and London.

(New York Film Festival selection committee 1993–1994; member of the PEN newsletter committee; book reviewer and assistant fashion editor *Glamour* 1968–1969; features editor *Vogue* (London) 1972 and 1976–1977; London editor *Interview* 1972; London correspondent *Women's Wear Daily* 1973; Italian correspondent *Women's Wear Daily* 1973–1975; contributor *Plays and Players* (UK) 1970s; contributor *Telegraph* (UK) 1970s; associate editor *Observer* (London) 1977–1978; columns *Vogue* (USA)

1976–1980; contributing editor *Vogue* (USA) 1980–1994; contributing editor *Vanity Fair* 1988–1994; contributing editor *Conde Nast Traveler* 1988–1994; *Vogue* (USA) film critic 1991–1994; contributor *The New Yorker* 1992–1994; *Vogue* (Paris) editor in chief 1996–present.)

The Only Place to Be (Random House) 1982

Daughter of the Swan (Weidenfeld & Nicolson) 1987

THOMAS CAPLAN

(Lives in Maryland. Travels frequently to England. Director of the Pen/Faulkner Award for Fiction.)

Line of Chance (William Morrow) 1979

Parallelogram (Viking) 1987

Grace and Favor (Thomas Dunne Books/St. Martin's Press) 1997

SEYMOUR CHATMAN

b. 1928, Detroit, Michigan.

(Professor Emeritus of Rhetoric and Film.)

A Theory of Meter 1965

Essays on the Language of Literature 1967 (co-editor, Samuel R. Levin)

Literary Style: A Symposium 1971

The Later Style of Henry James 1972

Approaches to Poetics: Selected English Institute Essays 1973

Story and Discourse 1978

Proceedings of the First International Congress on Semiotics 1979 (co-editor Umberto Eco)

Michelangelo Antonioni: Identificazione di un Autore 1985

Antonioni, or the Surface of the World 1985

Michelangelo Antonioni's L'Avventura: A Screenplay 1989 (co-editor Guido Fink)

Coming to Terms: The Rhetoric of Narrative in Fiction and Film 1990

Reading Narrative Fiction 1992

"2¹/₂ Film Versions of Heart of Darkness" in *Conrad on Film* 1998 (edited by Gene Moore)

MICHAEL CRISTOFER

(Resides in New York.)

The Shadow Box 1975 (play and screenplay) Pulitzer Prize; Tony Award

Ice 1976 (play)

Black Angel 1978 (play)

Falling in Love 1984 (screenplay)

The Lady and the Clarinet (Drama Play Service) 1985

Witches of Eastwick 1987 (screenplay; based on the novel by John Updike)

The Bonfire of the Vanities 1990 (screenplay; based on the novel by Tom Wolfe)

The Blues are Running 1994 (play)

Amazing Grace 1995 (play)

Breaking Up 1995 (play and screenplay)

Gia 1998 (director and screenwriter)

Jello Shots 1998 (director and screenwriter)

MICHAEL CUNNINGHAM

(Resides in New York City. Fellowships from the National Endowment for the Arts, the Guggenheim Foundation, and the Mrs. Giles Whiting Foundation.)

Flesh and Blood (Farrar, Straus and Giroux) 1990

A Home at the End of the World (Farrar, Straus and Giroux) 1995

The Hours (Farrar, Straus and Giroux) 1998

EDWIDGE DANTICAT

b. 1969, Port-au-Prince, Haiti.

Breath, Eyes, Memory (Vintage Contemporaries) 1995

Krik? Krak! (Vintage Contemporaries) 1996

Island on Fire (Kaliko Press)1997 (co-author with Jonathan Demme)

The Farming of Bones (Soho Press) 1998

Odilon Pierre: Artist of Haiti (Kaliko Press) 1999 (co-author with Jonathan Demme)

ARIEL DORFMAN

b. 1942, Buenos Aires, Argentina; Chilean citizen.

How to Read Donald Duck (International General) 1974 (with Armand Mattelart)

Missing (Amnesty International) 1982

The Empire's Old Clothes (Pantheon) 1983

Widows (Pantheon) 1984 (play based on novel 1997)

The Last Song of Manuel Sendero (Viking) 1987

Last Waltz in Santiago (Viking-Penguin) 1988

Mascara (Viking-Penguin) 1988

My House Is on Fire (Viking-Penguin) 1990 (short film based on novel 1997; co-writer and co-director)

Some Write to the Future (Duke University Press) 1991

Hard Rain (Reader's International) 1991

Death and the Maiden (Penguin) 1992 (play; co-screenwriter with Rafael Yglesias; film directed by Roman Polanski)

Prisoners in Time (co-screenwriter; BBC film) 1995 British Screenwriters Guild Award for Best Screenplay

Reader (Nick Hern Books) 1995

Konfidenz (Farrar, Straus and Giroux) 1996

Heading South, Looking North: A Bilingual Journey (Farrar, Straus and Giroux) 1998

The Resistance Trilogy (Nick Hern Books) 1998

The Nanny and the Iceberg (Farrar, Straus and Giroux/Hodder) 1999

KATHERINE DUNN

b.1945, Garden City, Kansas.

(Resides in Oregon. Neighbor of Gus Van Sant Jr. and cartoonist John Callahan. Long-time reporter on the sport of boxing.)

Attic (Warner Books) 1970

Truck (Warner Books) 1971

Geek Love (Knopf) 1989 Finalist for the National Book Award; Finalist for the Bram Stroker Award

Why Do Men Have Nipples? (Warner Books) 1992

Mystery Girls' . . . Circus (M. Kimberly Press) 1991 (commissioned by the National Museum of Women in the Arts, Washington, D.C.)

Death Scenes (Feral House Press) 1996 Winner of 1997 Firecracker Award

JOE ESZTERHAS

(Resides in Malibu, California.)

Thirteen Seconds: Confrontation at Kent State (Dodd Mead) 1970 (co-writer Michael D. Roberts)

Charlie Simpson's Apocalypse (Random House) 1973

Flashdance 1983 (co-screenwriter)

The Jagged Edge 1985 (screenplay)

Big Shots 1987 (screenplay)

Hearts of Fire 1987 (screenplay)

Betrayed 1988 (screenplay)

Checking Out 1989 (screenplay)

Music Box 1989 (screenplay)

Basic Instinct 1992 (screenplay; film directed by Paul Verhoeven)

Nowhere to Run 1993 (co-screenwriter)

Sliver 1993 (screenplay; based on the novel by Ira Levin; film directed by Phillip Noyce)

Jade 1995 (screenplay; film directed by William Friedkin)

Showgirls 1995 (screenplay)

SCOTT FRANK

b. 1960, Fort Walton Beach, Florida.

Dead Again 1991(screenplay; film directed by Kenneth Branagh)

Little Man Tate 1991 (screenplay)

Malice 1993 (screenplay)

Get Shorty 1995 (screenplay; based on the novel by Elmore Leonard)

Heaven's Prisoners 1996 (screenplay; based on the novel by James Lee Burke)

Out of Sight 1998 (screenplay; based on the novel by Elmore Leonard)

STEVEN GAYDOS

b. 1954, Fontana, California.

One Month Later 1987 (co-screenwriter)

Iguana 1988 (co-screenwriter)

Better Watch Out 1989 (co-screenwriter)

Movie Talk from the Front Lines (McFarland & Co.) 1995

All Men Are Mortal 1996 (co-screenwriter; based on the novel by Simone de Beauvior)

Cannes: 50 Years of Sun, Sex and Celluloid (Hyperion) 1997 (co-editor)

The Variety Guide to Film Festivals (Perigee) 1998 (editor and co-author)

BO GOLDMAN

b. 1932, New York City.

(Started as script editor and film producer for Playhouse 90 and Public Television; Writers Guild of America Screen Laurel Award for Life Achievement 1998.)

One Flew Over the Cuckoo's Nest 1975 (co-screenwriter; based on the novel by Ken Kesey; film directed by Milos Forman) Academy Awards for Best Director and Best Adapted Screenplay; BAFTA Award for Best Director; Golden Globe Awards for Best Director and Best Screenplay; Writers Guild Award for Best Adapted Screenplay

The Rose 1979 (co-screenwriter)

Melvin and Howard 1980 (screenplay; film directed by Jonathan Demme) Academy Award for Best Original Screenplay; New York Film Critics Award for Best Screenplay; Writers Guild Award for Best Original Screenplay

Shoot the Moon 1982 (screenplay)

Scent of a Woman 1992 (screenplay; film directed by Martin Brest) Academy Award Nominations for Best Director and Best Adapted Screenplay; BAFTA Award for Best Adapted Screenplay; Golden Globe Awards for Best Drama and Best Screenplay

City Hall 1996 (co-screenwriter)

Meet Joe Black 1998 (co-screenwriter; film directed by Martin Brest)

WILLIAM GOLDMAN

b. 1931 Chicago, Illinois.

(Resides in New York City. Writers Guild of America Laurel Award; Writers Guild of Great Britain Lifetime Achievement Award.)

The Temple of Gold 1956

Soldier in the Rain 1963

Boys and Girls Together 1964

Harper 1966 (screenplay; based on the novel *The Moving Target* by Ross MacDonald)

No Way to Treat a Lady 1968

Butch Cassidy and the Sundance Kid 1969 (screenplay) Academy Award for Best Writing, Story, and Screenplay Based on Material Not Previously Published or Produced; Writers Guild of America Award for Best Adapted Screenplay

The Great Waldo Pepper 1975 (screenplay)

All the President's Men 1976 (screenplay; based on the book by Bob Woodward and Carl Bernstein) Academy Award for Best Adapted Screenplay; Writers Guild of America Award for Best Adapted Screenplay

Marathon Man 1976 (novel and screenplay; film directed by John Schlesinger)

A Bridge Too Far 1977 (screenplay)

Magic 1978 (novel and screenplay)

Tinsel (Delacorte) 1979

Control (Delacorte) 1982

The Season: A Candid Look at Broadway (Proscenium) 1984

Heat 1987 (novel and screenplay)

The Princess Bride 1987 (novel and screenplay; film directed by Rob Reiner)

Wait Till Next Year 1988 (co-author Mike Lupica)

Adventures in the Screen Trade: A Personal View of Hollywood and Screenwriting (Warner Books) 1989

Misery 1990 (screenplay; based on the novel by Stephen King; film directed by Rob Reiner)

Hype and Glory 1991

Year of the Comet 1992 (screenplay)

Chaplin 1992 (co-screenwriter)

Maverick 1994 (screenplay; film directed by Richard Donner)

The Ghost and the Darkness 1996 (screenplay)

Absolute Power 1997 (screenplay)

BRIAN HELGELAND

b. 1961, Providence, Rhode Island.

Assassins 1995 (co-screenwriter; film directed by Richard Donner)

Conspiracy Theory 1997 (screenplay; film directed by Richard Donner)

L. A. Confidential 1997 (co-screenwriter) Academy Award for Best Adapted Screenplay

RICHARD LOURIE

b. 1940, Cambridge, Massachusetts.

(Resides in New York City. Author of nine books. Translated more than forty books into English from Russian and Polish.)

Sagittarius in Warsaw (Vanguard) 1973

Dreamland 1980 (feature-length documentary; producer and writer)

Everything is Lovely 1980 (documentary; producer and writer)

First Loyalty (Harcourt Brace) 1985 Nominated for Pulitzer Prize

Zero Gravity (Harcourt Brace) 1987

Predicting Russia's Future (Whittle) 1991

Russia Speaks: An Oral History from the Revolution to the Present (HarperCollins) 1991

Bread and Salt 1992 (feature-length documentary; producer and writer)

Hunting the Devil (HarperCollins) 1993

Andrei Sakharov: A Biography (New England Univ. Press) 1999

The Autobiography of Joseph Stalin (Counterpoint) 1999

PATRICK McCABE

b. 1955, Clones, County Monaghan, Ireland.

Carn (Dell) 1989

The Butcher Boy (Fromm International) 1992 (novel and co-screenwriter with director Neil Jordan) *Irish Times'* Aer Lingus Prize; Shortlisted for the Booker Prize

The Dead School (Dial Press) 1995

Breakfast on Pluto (HarperCollins) 1998 Shortlisted for the Booker Prize

Mundo Desperado (HarperCollins) 1999

WALTER MOSLEY

(Resides in New York City. Poet. Potter. Former president of the Mystery Writers of America. Member of the executive board of the PEN American Center.)

Devil in a Blue Dress (Norton) 1990 (film directed by Carl Franklin) Mystery Writers of America Award Nomination

A Red Death (Norton) 1992 Edgar Award Nomination

White Butterfly (Norton) 1993 Edgar Award Nomination

Black Betty (Norton) 1994 Edgar Award Nomination

RL's Dream (Norton) 1995 Book of the Month Club

A Little Yellow Dog (Norton) 1996 *The New York Times* Book Review Best-seller

"The Watts Lion" 1994 (short story) Nominated Best PI Short Story

"The Thief" 1996 (short story) O. Henry Prize

Gone Fishin' (Black Classic Press) 1997 *Publishers Weekly* Best-seller

Always Outnumbered, Always Outgunned (Norton) 1997 (co-screenwriter of HBO movie, *Always Outnumbered*, 1998, based on the novel)

Blue Light (Little Brown) 1998

RICARDO PIGLIA

b. 1940, Buenos Aires, Argentina.

Nombre Falso (Assumed Name) 1975

Respiración Artificial (Artificial Respiration) 1980

Crítica y Ficción (Criticism and Fiction) 1986

Prisión Perpetua (Life in Prison) 1988

La Ciudad Ausente (The Absent City) 1992

Foolish Heart 1995 (co-screenwriter with director Hector Babenco)

La Sonámbula (Sleepwalker) 1996 (screenwriter)

Plata Quemada (Burnt Money) 1997

DARRYL PONICSAN

(Born in Shenandoah, Pennsylvania, prior to the baby boomers, prior to the war that made them. Educated at Muhlenberg College and Cornell University. Served in the U.S. Navy during the Vietnam war. Experienced as a teacher, social worker, and circus clown—season of 1976. Resides in Seattle.)

The Last Detail 1970

Cinderella Liberty (novel and screenplay) 1973

Taps 1981 (co-screenwriter)

Vision Quest 1985 (screenplay; based on the novel by Terry Davis)

Nuts 1987 (co-screenwriter)

The Boost 1988 (screenplay)

School Ties 1992 (co-screenwriter)

The Enemy Within 1994 (co-screenwriter)

JOHN RIDLEY

b. 1965, Milwaukee, Wisconsin.

Cold Around the Heart 1996 (director and screenwriter)

Stray Dogs (Ballantine) 1997 (also screenplay for *U Turn* was based on this novel; film directed by Oliver Stone)

Love Is a Racket (Knopf) 1998

Everybody Smokes in Hell (Knopf) 1999

Standing on Dead Game 1999 (screenplay; film directed by David Russell)

Three Kings 1999 (director and screenwriter)

TOM ROBBINS

(Born 1936 in the Bible Belt, where the public library and the moving-picture show quickly became his preferred places of worship. Honor graduate of Virginia Commonwealth University, studied Asian philosophies at University of Washington. Resides near Seattle.)

Another Roadside Attraction (Doubleday, Ballantine) 1971

Even Cowgirls Get the Blues (Bantam) 1976 (film directed by Gus Van Sant Jr.)

Still Life with Woodpecker (Bantam) 1980

Jitterbug Perfume (Bantam) 1985

Skinny Legs and All (Bantam) 1990

Half Asleep in Frog Pajamas (Bantam) 1994

DAMIAN SHARP

When a Monkey Speaks: And Other Stories from Australia (HarperCollins) 1994

JOHN SHIRLEY

b. 1953, Houston, Texas.

(Resides in California. A writer's writer.)

Dracula in Love (Zebra Books) 1976

Transmaniacon (Zebra Books) 1976

Three Ring Psychus (Zebra Books) 1977

City Come A-walking (Dell) 1978

The Brigade (Avon) 1980

Cellars (Avon) 1981

The Eclipse Trilogy (Warner Books) 1982–1989

Specialist 1985/1988 (novels and screenplay)

In Darkness Waiting (Signet) 1986

A Splendid Chaos (Franklin Watts) 1987

The Black Hole of Carcosa (St. Martins) 1989

Wetbones (Mark V. Ziesing Books) 1991

Software 1991 (screenplay; based on the novel by Rudy Rucker)

The Crow 1993 (co-screenwriter with David J. Schow)

Stinger 1994 (screenplay; based on the novel by Robert McCammon)

Silicon Embrace (Mark V. Ziesing Books) 1997

The New Rose Hotel 1998 (co-screenwriter with William Gibson)

Black Butterflies (Mark V. Ziesing Books) 1998 *Publishers Weekly* Best Books List

NORMAN SNIDER

(Resides in Toronto. Former journalist. Has ten toes.)

The Changing of the Guard (Lester & Orpen Dennys) 1985 Book of the Month Club

Dead Ringers 1988 (co-screenwriter; film directed by David Cronenberg) Genie Award for Best Motion Picture

Body Parts 1991 (screenplay)

Valentine's Day 1998 (screenplay)

MICHAEL SRAGOW

b. 1952, Roosevelt, New York.

(Currently a staff writer for the *New Times* chain of weekly newspapers. He has been a movie critic for *Rolling Stone* and *The New Yorker* as well as a frequent contributor to the *Atlantic Monthly*.)

Produced and Abandoned: The Best Films You've Never Seen (Mercury House) 1990 (editor)

Victor Fleming: A Biography (Pantheon) 2001

CATHERINE TEXIER

(Born in France. Resides in New York City. Recipient of New York Foundation for the Arts Fellowship and the National Endowment for the Arts Award.)

Chloe L'Atlantique (Editions Ramsay) 1983

Love Me Tender (Penguin) 1987

Panic Blood (Penguin) 1990

Love Is Strange (W.W. Norton) 1993 (co-editor)

Breakup: The End of a Love Story (Doubleday) 1998

MICHAEL TOLKIN

("An L.A. Antonioni with a sense of humor," *The New Yorker*. ArtForum, "Tolkin is the only American filmmaker working near the level of Pasolini and Kiezlowski.")

The Player (Atlantic Monthly Press) 1988/1992 (novel and screenplay; film directed by Robert Altman) Academy Award Nomination for Best Writing, Screenplay Based on Material from Another Medium; Writers Guild Award for Best Screenplay Based on Material Previously Produced or Published; BAFTA for Best Screenplay; The Chicago Film Critics Award for Best Screenplay; PEN Center USA West Literary Award; Edgar Allan Poe Award for Best Crime Screenplay. As producer, Golden Globe Award for Best Motion Picture—Comedy/Musical;

New York Film Critics Circle Award for Best Film, Independent Spirit Award for Best Feature.

The Rapture 1991 (screenwriter and director)

Deep Cover 1992 (co-screenwriter)

Among the Dead (William Morrow) 1993

The New Age 1994 (director and screenwriter)

The Burning Season 1995 (co-screenwriter) Humanitas Prize and Emmy Nomination

The Player, The Rapture, The New Age: Three Screenplays (Grove Press) 1995

Deep Impact 1998 (co-screenwriter)

BRUCE WAGNER

(Lives in Los Angeles. Creator/executive producer of Oliver Stone's widely acclaimed mini-series for television, *Wild Palms*.)

Scenes from the Class Struggle in Beverly Hills 1989 (screenplay)

Force Majeure (Random House) 1991

I'm Losing You (Villard) 1996 (film based on novel 1998; screenwriter and director)

A Nightmare on Elm Street 3: Dream Warriors 1987 (co-screenwriter with Chuck Russell, Wes Craven, and Frank Darabont)

Tensegrity 1993 (director of volumes one, two, three; based on Carlos Castaneda's works)

WENDY WASSERSTEIN

b. 1950, Brooklyn, New York.

(Lives in New York City.)

Uncommon Women and Others (Dramatists Play Service and Avon) 1978

The Sorrows of Gin 1979 (WNET Great Performances; based on a short story by John Cheever)

Isn't It Romantic (Harcourt Brace) 1985

The Sisters Rosensweig (Harcourt Brace) 1993 (play) Outer Critics Circle Award and Tony Nomination

The Heidi Chronicles 1989 (play) Pulitzer Prize and Tony Award

Bachelor Girls (Knopf) 1990

Pamela's First Musical 1996 (Hyperion)

An American Daughter 1997 (Harcourt Brace)

The Object of My Affection 1998 (screenplay; based on the novel by Stephen MacCauley)

DAVID WEDDLE

b. 1956, Irvington, New York.

(Resides in Los Angeles.)

Memoirs of an Awkward Lover 1980 (play)

Under the Nutcracker 1982 (play)

"If They Move . . . Kill 'em!": The Life and Times of Sam Peckinpah (Grove Press) 1994

Star Trek: Deep Space Nine 1997–1999 (executive story editor)

MICHAEL WELLER

(Resides in New York City. More than forty plays and films. Established a program for apprentice playwrights to work one-on-one with mentor playwrights at Cherry Lane Theater.)

Moonchildren (Delacorte Press) 1970

Fishing: A Drama in Two Acts (Samuel French) 1975

Hair 1979 (screenplay; film directed by Milos Forman)

Loose Ends (Samuel French) 1979

Ragtime 1981 (screenplay; film directed by Milos Forman; based on the novel by E.L. Doctorow)

Split (Samuel French) 1981

Ghost on Fire (Grove Press) 1985

Spoils of War 1988

Lost Angels 1989 (screenplay)

Lake No Bottom 1990

Jellybean 1998 (screenplay for John Coles and Liz Oliver)

In the Blue Light of African Dreams (screenplay; based on the novel by Paul Watkins)

The Ballad of Soapy Smith 1998 (film musical of his play with Milos Forman and Elton John)

MIKE WERB

b. 1960, Hollywood, California.

(Lack of musical ability and intolerance to heavy drugs led to his exile from the North Hollywood–based punk band, Girl on Top. He fled three miles to Hollywood and the community of screenwriting, where he currently resides.)

The Mask 1994 (screenplay; based on the Dark Horse comic book series)

Face/Off 1997 (co-producer; co-screenwriter with Michael Colleary)

DONALD E. WESTLAKE

(Resides somewhere in New York. Three Edgar Awards: Best Novel, Best Short Story, Best Screenplay; 1994 Grand Master of the Mystery Writers of America; 1996 President of the Mystery Writers of America; more than sixty novels. Twelve movies based on his novels. His long-ago pen name, Richard Stark, wrote twenty novels between 1962 and 1974 including the source of the movie *Point Blank*. Richard Stark returned with *Comeback* and *Backflash* in 1998.)

The Mercenaries (Random House) 1960

The Fugitive Pigeon (Random House) 1965

God Save the Mark (Popular Library) 1967 Edgar Allan Poe Award

The Hot Rock (Simon & Schuster) 1970

Cops and Robbers 1973 (screenplay)

Jimmy the Kid (M. Evans) 1974

Dancing Aztecs (M. Evans) 1976

Hot Stuff 1976 (screenplay)

Nobody's Perfect (Warner Books) 1977

Kahawa (Viking) 1981

Why Me (Warner Books) 1983/1990 (novel and screenplay)

A Likely Story (Penzler Books) 1984

The Stepfather 1987 (screenplay)

Sacred Monster (M. Evans) 1989

The Grifters 1990 (screenplay; based on the novel by Jim Thompson; film directed by Stephen Frears) Academy Award Nomination for Best Adapted Screenplay; Writers Guild Nomination for Best Screenplay

Drowned Hopes (Warner Books) 1991

Humans (Warner Books) 1992

Don't Ask (Warner Books) 1993

What's the Worst that Could Happen? (Mysterious Press) 1996

The Ax (Mysterious Press) 1997

Backflash (Little Brown) 1998

Comeback (Mysterious Press) 1998

TOBIAS WOLFF

(Resides in Palo Alto, California.)

In the Garden of the North American Martyrs (Ecco Press) 1981 St. Lawrence Award

The Barracks Thief (Ecco Press) 1984 PEN/Faulkner Award

Back in the World: Stories (Houghton Mifflin) 1985 Rea Award for the Short Story

This Boy's Life: A Memoir (Atlantic Monthly Press) 1989 *Los Angeles Times* Book Award

In Pharaoh's Army: Memories of the Lost War (Knopf) 1994 Esquire/Volvo-Waterstone's Award

The Night in Question (Knopf) 1996

JACK WOMACK

b. 1956, Lexington, Kentucky.

Ambient (Grove Press) 1987

Terraplane (Grove Press) 1988

Heathern (Grove Press) 1990

Elvissey (Grove Press) 1993

Random Acts of Senseless Violence (Atlantic Monthly Press) 1994

Let's Put the Future Behind Us (Atlantic Monthly Press) 1996

Going, Going Gone (Atlantic Monthly Press) 1999

Absence of Malice, 164
The Abyss, 127, 128, 130
Accatone, 125
The Accidental Tourist, 105, 106
Adventures in the Screen Trade, 25, 52
The Adventures of Baron Munchausen, 116
Affliction, 48
Afterglow, 26
Agnes of God, 24
Agony, 124
Alice in Hollywood, 57
Aliens, 128
All Men Are Mortal, 170
All the President's Men, 25, 52
Almendros, Nestor, 168
Almost You, 107
Altman, Robert, 145–148, 165
Always Outnumbered, Always Outgunned, 110
Amadeus, 143
Amazing Grace, 80
Ambient, 116
An American Daughter, 55
The American President, 50
Among the Dead, 148
. . . And Justice for All, 24
The Anderson Tapes, 151
André the Giant, 52
Andrei Sakharov: A Biography, 100
Angel, 154
Angie, 118
Angry Harvest, 98, 100
Annaud, Jean-Jacques, 71–75
Another Roadside Attraction, 28
Antonioni, Michelangelo, 101–104
Antonioni, or the Surface of the World, 101, 104
The Apache Woman, 168
Apocalypse Now, 67
Apollo 13, 108
The Appointment, 151
Approaches to Poetics: Selected English Institute Essays, 104
Aria, 146
The Art of Love, 24
Assassins (movie), 111
Assassins (screenplay), 113
At Play in the Fields of the Lord, 67, 68, 70
Atlas, 169
Attack of the Crab Monsters, 168
Attic, 60
Austen, Jane, 55
The Autobiography of Joseph Stalin, 100
The Ax, 88

Babenco, Hector, 67–70
Bachelor Girls, 55
Back in the World, 40
Backdraft, 108
Backflash, 88
Backroads, 94, 95
The Ballad of Soapy Smith, 144
Banks, Christina, 36

Banks, Russell, 12, 45, 48
The Barracks Thief, 40
Bartel, Paul, 43
Basic Instinct (movie), 136, 138, 139
Basic Instinct (screenplay), 163
Bates, Kathy, 50
Beach, Michael, 46
The Bear, 71, 72, 75
Beetlejuice, 43
Before the Revolution, 124
Being There, 14
The Believers, 132
Beloved (movie), 34, 37
Beloved (screenplay), 107
Benderson, Bruce, 135, 138
Bergman, Ingmar, 157
Bertolucci, Bernardo, 121–125
Besieged (L'Assedio), 124
Best Friends, 24
Betrayed, 163
A Better Tomorrow, 64
A Better Tomorrow II, 64
Better Watch Out, 169, 170
The Beverly Hillbillies, 90
Beverly Hills Cop, 82
Beyond the Clouds, 102, 103, 104
Beyond Therapy, 146
The Big Chill, 105
Big Shots, 163
Billy Liar, 132
The Birthday Party, 161
Bitter Moon, 18
Black and White in Color, 71, 72, 73–74
Black Angel, 80
Black Betty, 110
Black Butterflies, 130
The Black Hole of Carcosa, 130
Black Peter, 143
Black Sheep, 90, 92
Blade Runner, 102
Blast Off, 94
Blauner, Peter, 15, 149, 152
Blaze, 30
Blind Fury, 94
Bliss, Michael, 36
Bloody Kids, 86
Bloody Mama, 169
Blow-Up, 102
Blue Chips, 161
Blue Light, 110
The Blues Are Running, 80
Bobby Deerfield, 164
Body Heat, 105, 106
Bogus, 24
The Bone Collector, 94
The Bonfire of the Vanities, 80
The Boost, 120
Born on the Fourth of July, 38
Bosch, Hieronymus, 115
Boys and Girls Together, 25, 52
The Boys in the Band, 132, 161
The Boys Next Door, 89, 90
Boys on the Side, 78, 80
Branagh, Kenneth, 13, 61–63
Brazil, 115, 116, 117

Bread and Salt, 100
Breakfast of Champions, 26
Breakfast on Pluto, 156
Breaking Up, 80
Breakup: The End of a Love Story, 74
Breath, Eyes, Memory, 37
Brest, Martin, 82–84
Brewster McCloud, 146
A Bridge Too Far, 25, 52
The Brigade, 130
The Brink's Job, 161
Broken Arrow, 64
The Brood, 159
Brooks, Adam, 105, 107
Buck, Joan Juliet, 121, 124
A Bucket of Blood, 168
Buffalo Bill and the Indians, or Sitting Bull's History Lesson, 146
Bull Durham, 30
A Bullet in the Head, 64
Burgess, Anthony, 71
The Burning Season, 148
Burns, George, 82
Business Is Business, 136
Butch Cassidy and the Sundance Kid, 25, 52
The Butcher Boy (movie), 12, 154
The Butcher Boy (screenplay), 156
Bye Bye Braverman, 151

Caged Heat, 34
California Split, 146
California Suite, 78
Cam, 156
Cameron, James, 126–130
Cannes: 50 Years of Sun, Sex and Celluloid, 170
Caplan, Thomas, 164, 167
Capra, Frank, 11
Carnival Rock, 168
Casino Moon, 152
Castle Keep, 164
The Changing of the Guard, 160
Chaplin, 25, 52
Charlie Simpson's Apocalypse, 163
Chatman, Seymour, 101, 104
Cheadle, Don, 46
Checking Out, 163
Child's Play, 151
Chinatown, 18, 20
Chloe L'Atlantique, 74
Choose Me, 26
Chung Kuo, 102
The Cincinnati Kid, 24
Cinderella Liberty, 120
City Come A-walking, 130
The City Girl, 118
City Hall, 84
Claire's Knee, 38
Clancy, Tom, 94
Clear and Present Danger, 94
Cloudsplitter, 48
Clueless, 53, 54, 55
Cobb, 30, 31–32
Cobb, Ty, 31–33
Cobb, William, 32
Cockfighter, 168
Cocoon, 108
Cold Comfort Farm, 132

Colleary, Michael, 90
Come Back to the Five & Dime, Jimmy Dean, Jimmy Dean, 146
Coming to Terms: The Rhetoric of Narrative in Fiction and Film, 104
The Company of Wolves, 154
The Complex Sessions, 34
The Conformist, 123, 124, 125
Conspiracy Theory (movie), 111
Conspiracy Theory (screenplay), 113
Continental Drift, 48
Control, 25, 52
Cook, Barbara, 78
Coolidge, Martha, 118–120
Cops and Robbers, 88
Corman, Roger, 168–171
Corrington, John William, 170
Countdown, 146
Countdown in Kung Fu, 64
Cousin Bobby, 34, 36
Crash, 157, 159, 160
Craven, Wes, 41–44
Crazy Mama, 34
Creature from the Haunted Sea, 169
Crimes of the Future, 159
Cristofer, Michael, 76, 80
Crítica y Ficción (Criticism and Fiction), 70
Critical Care, 151
Cronaca di un Amore (Story of a Love Affair), 102
Cronenberg, David, 157–160
The Crow, 130
Cruising, 161
Crumquist, Kyle, 10
The Crying Game, 153, 154
Cul-de-Sac, 18, 20
Cunningham, Michael, 15, 131, 134
Curtis, Walt, 57

Dancers, 78
Dancing Aztecs, 88
Dangerous Liaisons, 86
Daniel, 151
Danticat, Edwidge, 34, 37
Darabont, Frank, 43
Darling, 132
Daughter of the Swan, 124
Davis, Miles, 46
The Day of the Locust, 132
The Day the Earth Stood Still, 127
The Day the World Ended, 168
Dead Again (movie), 61
Dead Again (screenplay), 63
Dead Calm, 93, 94
Dead Ringers (movie), 159, 160
Dead Ringers (screenplay), 160
The Dead School, 156
The Dead Zone, 159
The Deadly Affair, 151
Deadly Blessing, 41

Deadly Friend, 41
Deal of the Century, 161
Death and the Maiden (movie), 16, 18, 20, 21
Death and the Maiden (play), 20
Deathtrap, 151
The Decline of Western Civilization, 89, 90
The Decline of Western Civilization II: The Metal Years, 90
The Decline of Western Civilization III, 90
Deep Cover, 148
Deep Impact, 148
The Delinquents, 146
Demme, Jonathan, 12, 34–37
Depardieu, Gérard, 124
Devil in a Blue Dress (movie), 45, 46, 48
Devil in a Blue Dress (screenplay), 110
di Carlo, Carlo, 101
Die Zeit mit Antonioni (The Time with Antonioni), 104
The Discipline of D.E., 57
Dog Day Afternoon, 149, 151, 152
Dominique, Jean, 36
Donner, Richard, 12, 111–113
Don't Ask, 88
The Doors, 38
Dorfman, Ariel, 15, 16, 20
Dracula in Love, 130
The Dragon Tamers, 64
Dreamland, 100
Drowned Hopes, 88
Drugstore Cowboy, 56, 58, 60
Dudes, 90
Duke of Groove, 107
Dunn, Katherine, 56, 60
Duras, Marguerite, 71

Eastwood, Clint, 145
Easy Rider, 170
Echoes of Paradise, 94
The Eclipse Trilogy, 130
Eco, Umberto, 71–72
EDtv, 108
Egoyan, Atom, 12
The Electric Horseman, 164
Elvissey, 116
The Empire Strikes Back (screenplay), 105
The Empire's Old Clothes, 20
The End of the Affair, 154
Endangered Species, 26
The Enemy Within, 120
Equinox, 26
Equus, 151
Essays on the Language of Literature, 104
Eszterhas, Joe, 12, 15, 138, 161, 163
Europa, Europa, 97, 98
Even Cowgirls Get the Blues (movie), 58
Even Cowgirls Get the Blues (screenplay), 28
An Evening with Abdon, 98
Everybody Smokes in Hell, 66

Everything Is Lovely, 100
eXistenZ, 159
The Exorcist, 161
Eye for an Eye, 132

Face/Off (movie), 64
Face/Off (screenplay), 92
Fail Safe, 151
The Falcon and the Snowman, 132
The Falconer, 98
Falling in Love, 80
Family Business, 151
Far and Away, 108
Far From the Madding Crowd, 132
Fast Company, 159
Fast Times at Ridgemont High, 53
Fear and Loathing in Las Vegas, 116
The Fearless Vampire Killers, 18
Fever, 98
A Few Good Men, 50
Fiddler on the Roof, 22, 24
50 Violins, 41
Fighting Mad, 34
The Firemen's Ball, 143
The Firm, 164
First Loyalty, 100
The Fisher King, 116
Fishing, 144
F.I.S.T., 24
Five Guns West, 168
Flesh & Blood (movie), 136
Flesh and Blood (screenplay), 134
The Fly, 159
Follow the Star, 64
Fool for Love, 146
Foolish Heart (movie), 68
Foolish Heart (screenplay), 70
Footloose, 78
Force Majeure, 44
Ford, John, 11
Forman, Milos, 140–144
40 Pounds of Trouble, 24
The Fourth Man, 135, 136, 137, 138
Frank, Scott, 12, 61, 63
Frankenheimer, John, 166
Frankenstein Unbound, 169
Franklin, Carl, 12, 45–48
Frantic, 18
Frears, Stephen, 85–88
The French Connection, 161
French Kiss (movie), 105
French Kiss (screenplay), 105, 107
Friedkin, William, 15, 132, 161–163
From Riches to Rags, 64
The Fugitive Kind, 151
The Fugitive Pigeon, 88
Full Fathom Five, 45
Funny Lady, 78

Gaily, Gaily, 24
Garbo Talks, 151
Gas-s-s!, 169, 171
Gaydos, Steven, 168, 170
Geek Love, 60
Get Shorty, 63
Ghost on Fire, 144
Ghosts of Mississippi, 50
Gia, 80

Gilliam, Terry, 114–117
The Gingerbread Man, 146
Gli Angeli, 18
Gloria, 151
God Save the Mark, 88
Going, Going Gone, 116
Going in Style, 82
Goldman, Bo, 82, 84
Goldman, William, 12, 22, 25, 49, 52, 112, 113
Gone Fishin', 110
Good Times, 161
Good Will Hunting, 58, 60
Goodbye, Mr. Chips, 78
The Goodbye Girl, 78, 80
Goodfellas, 97
The Goonies, 111
Gould, Glenn, 157
Grace and Favor, 167
Grand Canyon, 105, 106, 107
Grand Theft Auto, 108
Gray, Spalding, 34
Gray, Susan, 13, 14
The Great Waldo Pepper, 25, 52
The Grifters (movie), 85, 86, 88
The Grifters (screenplay), 85, 88
The Grim Reaper, 124
Gris, Juan, 15
The Group, 150, 151
The Guardian, 161
Guffroy, Pierre, 16
Guilty as Sin, 151
Gumshoe, 86
Gung Ho, 108
The Gunslinger, 168
Gurdjieff, G. I., 126

Hair (movie), 140, 141, 143
Hair (screenplay), 144
Half Asleep in Frog Pajamas, 28
Hamlet, 61
The Hand, 38
Handle with Care, 34
Hard-Boiled, 64, 66
Hard Rain, 20
Hard Target, 64
Harper, 25, 52
Harris, Barbara, 78
The Haunted Palace, 169
Havana, 164, 166
Hawks, Howard, 106
Hawks, Kitty, 161
Heading South, Looking North: A Bilingual Journey, 20
Heads, 107
HEALTH, 146
Health Is Sick (The Poor Die Sooner), 124
Hearts of Fire, 163
Heat, 25, 52, 175, 176
Heathern, 116
Heatwave, 94
Heaven and Earth, 38
Heaven's Prisoners, 63
Heckerling, Amy, 53–55
The Heidi Chronicles, 55
Helgeland, Brian, 12, 111, 112, 113
Hellman, Monte, 168, 169
Hello, Late Homecomers, 64
Henry V, 61
Hero, 86

The Hi-Lo Country, 86
High Fidelity, 86
High Spirits, 154
The Hill, 151
Hiller, Arthur, 165
The Hills Have Eyes, 41, 44
The Hills Have Eyes Part II, 41
The Hit, 86
Hitchcock, Alfred, 159
Holland, Agnieszka, 97–100
The Hollow Man, 136
Hollywood Vice Squad, 90
A Home at the End of the World, 134
Honky Tonk Freeway, 132
Hot Dogs for Gauguin, 83
Hot Stuff, 88
Hot Tomorrows, 82
Hothead, 72
The Hours, 134
The House of Usher, 168
How the Grinch Stole Christmas, 108
How to Read Donald Duck, 20
Howard, Ron, 13, 108–110
Humans, 88
Hunting the Devil, 100
Hype and Glory, 25, 52

I, Mobster, 168
I Love You to Death, 105
I Ought to Be in Pictures, 78
I Tre Volti (The Three Faces), 102
I Vinti (The Vanquished), 102
Ice, 80
Identification of a Woman, 102
If There Were No Music, 143
If They Move . . . Kill 'em: The Life and Times of Sam Peckinpah, 32
Iguana, 169, 170
Il Grido (The Outcry), 102
I'm Losing You, 44
Images, 146
In Country, 24
In Darkness Waiting, 130
In Dreams, 154
In Pharaoh's Army: Memories of the Lost War, 40
In Search of Mystery, 125
In the Blue Light of African Dreams, 144
In the Garden of the North American Martyrs, 40
In the Heat of the Night, 24
Inge, William, 164
The Innocent, 132
Inside Moves, 111
Interview with the Vampire, 154
The Intruder (movie), 169
The Intruder (screenplay), 152
Ironweed, 68
Isn't It Romantic, 55
It Conquered the World, 168

Jabberwocky, 116
Jade (movie), 161, 163

Jade (screenplay), 161, 163
The Jagged Edge, 163
The James Dean Story, 146
Jello Shots, 80
Jellybean, 144
Jeremiah Johnson, 164
The Jericho Mile, 173, 174, 175
Jesus Christ Superstar, 24
Jewison, Norman, 10, 22–25
JFK, 38
Jimmy the Kid, 88
Jitterbug Perfume, 28
Johnny Dangerously, 53
Jordan, Neil, 12, 153–156
Joy of Sex, 118
Just Heroes, 64
Just Tell Me What You Want, 151
Just to Be Together, 102

Kael, Pauline, 148, 150, 151, 152
Kahawa, 88
Kansas City, 146
Kasdan, Lawrence, 105–107
Kaye, Nora, 78
Kazan, Elia, 164
The Keep, 175
Keetje Tippel (Katie's Passion), 136
Kennedy, Jack, 40
The Killer, 64, 66
A Kind of Loving, 132
King of the Night, 68
Kiss of the Spider Woman, 68, 70
Kissinger, Henry, 39–40
Knife in the Water, 18, 20
Konfidenz, 20
Konkurs, 143
Kovacs, Laszlo, 170
Krik? Krak!, 37
Kubrick, Stanley, 152
Kurosawa, Akira, 105
Kurtzman, Harvey, 115, 116

L. A. Confidential, 113
La Ciudad Ausente (The Absent City), 70
La Commare Secca, 125
La Notte (The Night), 102
La Signora Senza Camelie (The Lady Without Camellias), 102
La Sonámbula (Sleepwalker), 70
La Via del Petrolio (Oil Route), 124
The Lady and the Clarinet, 80
Ladyhawke, 111
Lake No Bottom, 144
L'Amore in Città (Love in the City), 102
The Last Detail, 120
Last Embrace, 34
The Last Emperor, 124
Last House on the Left, 41
Last Hurrah for Chivalry, 64
The Last of Sheila, 78
Last of the Mobile Hot Shots, 151
The Last of the Mohicans, 172, 175, 176

182

The Last Song of Manuel Sendero, 20
Last Tango in Paris, 121, 123, 124
Last Waltz in Santiago, 20
The Last Woman on Earth, 169
The Later Style of Henry James, 104
Laughing Times, 64
Laurel Avenue, 46, 48
L'Avventura, 101, 102
Lazarus and the Hurricane, 24
Le Amiche (The Girl Friends), 102
The League, 38
Lean, David, 105
L'Eclisse (The Eclipse), 102
Leigh, Vivian, 78
Lessing, Doris, 123
Lethal Weapon, 111
Lethal Weapon 2, 111
Lethal Weapon 3, 111
Lethal Weapon 4, 111
Let's Put the Future Behind Us, 116
A Likely Story, 88
Line of Chance, 167
Literary Style: A Symposium, 104
Little Buddha, 123, 124
Little Man Tate, 63
The Little Rascals, 90
The Little Shop of Horrors, 168, 169
A Little Yellow Dog, 110
Lola, 111
Long Day's Journey into Night, 151
The Long Goodbye, 145, 146, 148
Look Who's Talking, 53, 54
Look Who's Talking Too, 53
Loose Ends, 144
Lost Angels, 144
Lost in Yonkers, 118
Lourie, Richard, 97, 100
Love and Anger, 124
Love at Large, 26, 28
Love Is a Racket, 66
Love Is Strange, 74
Love Me Tender, 74
The Lover, 71, 72, 73, 74–75
Loves of a Blonde, 143
Lovin' Molly, 151
Lúcio Flávio, o Passageiro da Agonia, 68
Lumet, Sidney, 149–152, 166
Luna, 124
Lynch, David, 26

M. Butterfly, 159, 160
Macbeth, 18
Machine Gun Kelly, 168
Madame Sousatzka, 132
Made in Heaven, 26
Madonna, 89
Magic, 22, 25, 52
Magic Town, 11
Mahler, Gustav, 163
Mala Noche, 57, 58
Malice, 63
Maltin, Leonard, 13
Man of the Hour, 152
Man of the People, 175
Man on the Moon, 143

The Man with X-Ray Eyes, 169
Mann, Michael, 172–176
Mann, Thomas, 14
Marathon Man (movie), 132
Marathon Man (screenplay), 25, 52
Married to the Mob, 34, 37
Mary Reilly, 86
Mary Shelley's Frankenstein, 61
Mascara, 20
The Mask, 92
The Masque of the Red Death, 169
Maverick (movie), 111
Maverick (screenplay), 25, 52
Max Dugan Returns, 78
McCabe & Mrs. Miller, 146
McCabe, Patrick, 12, 153, 156
McLuhan, Marshall, 157, 159
Meet Joe Black (movie), 82, 169
Meet Joe Black (screenplay), 84
Melvin and Howard (movie), 34
Melvin and Howard (screenplay), 84
Memoirs of an Awkward Lover, 32
The Mercenaries, 88
Michael Collins, 154
Michelangelo Antonioni: Identificazione di un Autore, 104
Michelangelo Antonioni's L'Avventura: A Screenplay, 104
Midnight Cowboy, 132
Midnight Run, 82
A Midwinter's Tale, 61
Miller, Arthur, 164
Mingus, Charles, 46
The Miracle, 154
Misery (movie), 50
Misery (screenplay), 25, 52
Missing, 20
The Moderns, 26
Mona Lisa, 154
Money Crazy, 64
Monty Python and the Holy Grail, 114, 116
Moonchildren, 144
Moonstruck, 24
Moreau, Jeanne, 72
The Morning After, 151
Mortal Thoughts, 26
Mosley, Walter, 108, 110
Movie Talk from the Front Lines, 170
Mrs. Parker and the Vicious Circle, 26
Much Ado About Nothing, 61, 63
Mumford, 105
Mundo Desperado, 156
Murder on the Orient Express, 151
Music Box, 63
My Beautiful Laundrette, 86
My Blue Heaven, 78
My Father Is Coming, 138
My House Is on Fire, 20

My Own Private Idaho, 58, 60
Mystery Girls' . . . Circus, 60
The Mystery of Oberwald, 102

Naked Lunch, 157, 159
Naked Paradise, 168
The Name of the Rose, 71, 72, 74, 75
Nashville, 146
National Lampoon's European Vacation, 53
Natural Born Killers, 38
Network, 151, 152
The New Age, 148
New Degeneracy, 138
The New Rose Hotel, 130
Newsfront, 94, 95–96
The Next Best Thing, 132
Night Falls on Manhattan, 151
The Night in Question, 40
Night Shift, 108
The Night They Raided Minsky's, 161
A Nightmare on Elm Street, 41
A Nightmare on Elm Street 3: Dream Warriors, 43, 44
A Nightmare on Elm Street 4: Dream Master, 113
Nijinsky, 78
1900 (Novecento), 123, 124
Nixon, 38
Nixon, Richard, 38–40
No Way to Treat a Lady, 25, 52
Nobody's Perfect, 88
Nombre Falso (Assumed Name), 70
North, 50
Not a Pretty Picture, 118
Not of This Earth, 168
Notto, Mandorli, Vulcano, Stromboli, Carnevale, 102
Nowhere to Run (movie), 45
Nowhere to Run (screenplay), 163
Noyce, Phillip, 93–96
Nuts, 120

The Object of My Affection, 55
O.C. and Stiggs, 146
O'Connor, Flannery, 38
The Offence, 151, 152
O'Hara, John, 167
The Oklahoma Woman, 168
Olivier, Olivier, 98
The Omen, 111
Once a Thief, 64
One False Move, 12, 45, 46, 48
One Flew Over the Cuckoo's Nest (movie), 143
One Flew Over the Cuckoo's Nest (screenplay), 84
One Month Later, 170
One True Thing, 45
The Only Place to Be, 124
Only You, 24
Other People's Money, 24

Out of Africa, 164, 166
Out of Sight, 63
Out to Sea, 118
The Owl and the Pussycat, 78

Pacific Heights, 132
Pandish, Eddie, 14
Panic Blood, 74
The Paper, 108
Parallelogram, 167
Parenthood, 108
Partner, 124
Pasolini, Pier Paolo, 125
The Passenger, 101, 102
Patriot Games, 94
The Pawnbroker, 151, 152
Peckinpah, Sam, 33
Pennies from Heaven, 78, 80
The People under the Stairs, 41
The People vs. Larry Flynt, 143
Perel, Solomon, 97
A Perfect Couple, 146
Perlman, Ron, 72
Peter's Friends, 61, 63
Philadelphia, 34, 36
Piglia, Ricardo, 67, 70
Piranha II: The Spawning, 128
Pirates, 18
The Pit and the Pendulum, 169
Pixote, 68, 70
Plain Clothes, 118
Plain Jane to the Rescue, 64
Plato Quemado (Burnt Money), 70
Platoon, 38
Play It Again, Sam, 78
The Player (movie), 145, 146
The Player (screenplay), 148
The Player, The Rapture, The New Age: Three Screenplays, 148
Polanski, Roman, 15, 16–21
Pollack, Sydney, 164–167
Ponicsan, Darryl, 118, 120
Popeye, 146
Pound, Ezra, 153
Power, 151
Predicting Russia's Future, 100
The Premature Burial, 169
Prêt-à-Porter, 146
Pretending to Say No, 138
Prick Up Your Ears, 86
Prince of the City, 151
The Princess Bride (movie), 50, 52
The Princess Bride (screenplay), 25, 49, 52
Princess Chang Ping, 64
Prisión Perpetua (Life in Prison), 67, 70
Proceedings of the First International Congress on Semiotics, 104
Produced and Abandoned, 176
Protocol, 78
Provincial Actors, 98

Psycho, 58
PT 109, 40

Q & A, 151
Quest for Fire, 71, 72, 74
A Question of Attribution, 132
Quintet, 146

Rabid, 159
Radio Flyer, 111
Radziwill, Lee, 80
Rafferty, Terrence, 94
The Raft, 18
Raging Bull, 97
Ragtime (movie), 143
Ragtime (screenplay), 144
Raiders of the Lost Ark (screenplay), 105
Rambling Rose, 118
Rampage, 161
Random Acts of Senseless Violence, 116
Random Hearts, 164
Ransom, 108
The Rapture, 148
The Raven, 169
Reading Narrative Fiction, 104
Real Genius, 118
A Red Death, 110
Red Desert, 101, 102
Red Riding Hood, 107
Redd, Gypsy, 90
Reiner, Rob, 49–52
Remember My Name, 26
Remembrances of Kansas City Swing, 146
Repulsion, 18, 20
Respiración Artificial (Artificial Respiration), 70
Return Engagement, 26
Return of the Jedi (screenplay), 105
Ridley, John, 64, 66
RL's Dream, 110
Riskin, Robert, 11
The Ritual, 74
Roadie, 26
Robbins, Tom, 26, 28
Robert Altman's Jazz '34, 146
RoboCop, 136, 139
Rock All Night, 168
Rollerball, 24
The Rose, 84
Rosemary's Baby, 18, 20
Rosenberg, Stuart, 165
Ross, Herbert, 76–81
Roth, Joe, 169–170
Rudolph, Alan, 26–28
Rule of the Bone (movie), 45
Rule of the Bone (screenplay), 48
Rules of Engagement, 161
Run Tiger Run, 64
Running on Empty, 151
Runyon, Damon, 85
Russell, Chuck, 43
Russia Speaks: An Oral History from the Revolution to the Present, 100
The Russians Are Coming! The Russians Are Coming!, 24
Rydell, Mark, 165

Sabrina, 164
Sacred Monster, 88

Sagittarius in Warsaw, 100
The Saint, 94
Salt and Pepper, 111
Salvador, 38
Sammy and Rosie Get Laid, 86
Sarris, Andrew, 150
The Scalphunters, 164
Scanners, 159
Scenes from the Class Struggle in Beverly Hills, 44
Scent of a Woman (movie), 82
Scent of a Woman (screenplay), 84
Scheinman, Andy, 49
Schlesinger, John, 131–134
School Ties, 120
Scream, 41
Scream 2, 41
Scream 3, 41
Screen Tests, 98
Scrooged, 111
The Sea Gull, 151
The Season: A Candid Look at Broadway, 25, 52
The Secret Garden, 98
Secret Honor, 146
The Secret Invasion, 169
The Secret Life of Walter Mitty, 108
The Secret of My Success, 78, 80
Seizure, 38
Sellers, 152
Send Me No Flowers, 24
Senseless, 90
The Serpent and the Rainbow, 41
Serpico, 151
The Seven-Per-Cent Solution, 78
Seven Years in Tibet, 72
The Shadow Box, 80
Sharp, Damian, 93, 96
Shaye, Bob, 43
The She Gods of Shark Reef, 168
The Sheltering Sky, 124
Shelton, Margaret, 30–31
Shelton, Ron, 29–33
Shirley, John, 15, 126, 130
Shivers, 159
Shocker, 41
Shoot the Moon, 84
Short Cuts, 145, 146
Showgirls (movie), 136, 138, 139
Showgirls (script), 163
Shuler, Lauren, 111
The Silence of the Lambs, 34, 35, 37
Silicon Embrace, 130
Silverado, 105
Silverstone, Alicia, 55
Sirk, Douglas, 10

The Sisters Rosensweig, 55
Ski Troop Attack, 168
Skinny Legs and All, 28
The Slender Thread, 164, 166
Sliver (movie), 94
Sliver (screenplay), 163
Slow Motion Riot, 152
The Snapper, 86
Snider, Norman, 157, 160
Soeteman, Gerard, 139
Software, 130
Soldier in the Rain, 25, 52
Soldier of Orange, 136, 139
A Soldier's Story, 24
Some Write to the Future, 20
Something Wild, 34
Songwriter, 26, 27
Sorcerer, 161
Sorority Girl, 168
The Sorrows of Gin, 55
Specialist, 130
Spetters, 136, 138–139
Spheeris, Andrew, 90, 91
Spheeris, Penelope, 89–92
The Spider's Strategem, 124
Splash, 108
A Splendid Chaos, 130
Split, 144
Spoils of War, 144
Sragow, Michael, 172, 176
St. Valenţine's Day Massacre, 169
Stage Struck, 151
Stahl, Anna, 67
Stand by Me, 50
Star Trek: Deep Space Nine, 32
Starship Troopers, 136
Stealing Beauty, 124
Steel Magnolias, 78
The Stepfather, 88
Stereo, 159
Still Life with Woodpecker, 28
Stinger, 130
Stone, Oliver, 38–40
Stop Making Sense, 34, 37
Storefront Hitchcock, 34
Story and Discourse, 104
Stowe, Madeline, 117
A Stranger Among Us, 151
Stray Dogs, 66
Streamers, 146
Streisand, Barbra, 78
Sturges, John, 105
Sturges, Preston, 89
Success Stories, 48
Sullivan's Travels, 89
Sunday, Bloody Sunday, 131, 132, 133–134
Sunday Children, 98

The Sunset Warrior (Heroes Shed No Tears), 64, 66
The Sunshine Boys, 78
Superman, 111
The Sure Thing, 49, 50
Swamp Thing, 41
Swamp Woman, 168
The Sweet Hereafter (book), 48
The Sweet Hereafter (movie), 12
Swimming to Cambodia, 34, 36
Swing Shift, 34

T. R. Baskin, 78
Taking Off, 143
Tales of Terror, 169
Talk Radio, 38
Taps, 120
Target: Harry, 169
Teenage Caveman, 168
Teenage Doll, 168
The Temple of Gold, 25, 52
The Tenant, 18, 20
Tensegrity, 44
The Terminator, 126, 127, 128, 129
Terminator 2: Judgment Day, 128, 129, 130
Terminus, 132
Terraplane, 116
The Terror, 169
Tess, 16, 18, 20
Texier, Catherine, 71, 74
That Cold Day in the Park, 146
That Kind of Woman, 151
A Theory of Meter, 104
They Shoot Horses, Don't They?, 164
They Sleep by Night, 43
Thief, 172, 173, 174, 175
"The Thief," 110
Thieves Like Us, 146
The Third Miracle, 98
Thirteen Seconds: Confrontation at Kent State, 163
This Boy's Life: A Memoir, 40
This Is Spinal Tap, 49, 50
This Property Is Condemned, 164
The Thomas Crown Affair, 24
Thompson, Jim, 85
Three Days of the Condor, 164
Three Ring Psychus, 130
Three Wishes, 118
3 Women, 146
The Thrill of It All, 24
Time Bandits, 116
The Time You Need a Friend, 64
Tin Cup, 29, 30, 31
Tinsel, 25, 52

Titanic, 128, 130
To Die For, 58, 60
To Kill a Priest, 98
To Live and Die in L.A., 161
Tolkin, Michael, 12, 145, 148
Tomb of Ligeia, 169
Tootsie, 164
Total Eclipse, 98, 100
Total Recall, 136
Tower of London, 169
The Toy, 111
Tragedy of a Ridiculous Man, 124
Transmaniacon, 130
Trixie, 26
Trouble in Mind, 26
Truck, 60
True Colors, 78
True Lies, 126, 127, 128
Truth or Dare, 89
Turkish Delight, 136
The Turning Point, 78, 80
12 Angry Men, 151
12 Monkeys, 116, 117
"2¹/₂ Film Versions of Heart of Darkness," 104
Two Men and a Wardrobe, 20

U Turn (movie), 38
U Turn (screenplay), 66
Uncommon Women and Others, 55
The Undead, 168
Under the Nutcracker, 32
Undercover Blues, 78
User, 138
Utt, Kenny, 34

Valley Girl, 118
Valmont, 143
Vampire in Brooklyn, 41
The Van, 86
Van Sant, Gus, 56–60
The Variety Guide to Film Festivals, 170
The Verdict, 151, 152
Verhoeven, Paul, 135–139
Victor Fleming: A Biography, 176
Videodrome, 159
A View from the Bridge, 151
The Viking Women and the Sea Serpent, 168
Vincent & Theo, 146
Vision Quest, 120
Visions of Eight, 132, 143
Von Richtofen and Brown (The Red Baron), 169

Wagner, Bruce, 41, 44
Wait Till Next Year, 25, 52
Wall Street, 38
Walter and June, 86
War of the Satellites, 168
Warhol, Andy, 57

Washington, Denzel, 46
Washington Square, 98
The Wasp Woman, 168
Wasserstein, Wendy, 53, 55
"The Watts Lion," 110
The Way We Were, 164, 166
Wayne's World, 89, 90
A Wedding, 146
Weddle, David, 29, 32
Welcome to L.A., 26
Weller, Michael, 140, 144
Wenders, Wim, 103
Werb, Mike, 89, 92
We're No Angels, 154
Wes Craven's New Nightmare, 41
Westlake, Donald E., 12, 85, 88
Wetbones, 130
Wharton, Edith, 55
What?, 18
What's the Worst that Could Happen?, 88
When a Monkey Speaks: And Other Stories from Australia, 96
When Harry Met Sally . . . , 50
White Butterfly, 110
White Men Can't Jump, 30
Who Am I This Time?, 36
Why Do Men Have Nipples?, 60
Why Me, 88
Widows, 20
Wild Angels, 169
The Wild Bunch, 33
The Wild Side (Suburbia), 90
Willeford, Charles, 168, 170
Williams, Cynda, 46
Williams, Robin, 60
Williams, Tennessee, 164
Willis, Bruce, 55, 117
Willow, 108
Wings of Courage, 72
Witches of Eastwick, 80
The Wiz, 151
Wolff, Tobias, 38, 40
Womack, Jack, 114, 116
Woman On Her Own, 98
Woo, John, 64–66
Writers on Directors, 14–15
Wyatt Earp, 105

X-15, 111

The Yakuza, 164
Yanks, 132
Year of the Comet, 25, 52
The Young Dragons, 64
The Young Racers, 169

Zabriskie Point, 101, 102
Zero Gravity, 100
Ziegler, Evarts, 49